SCHOLASTIC

4–5

Readability
1.0–4.5

Hi-Lo
Nonfiction Passages
for *Struggling Readers*

80 High-Interest/Low-Readability Passages With Comprehension Questions and Mini-Lessons for Teaching Key Reading Strategies

New York ○ Toronto ○ London ○ Auckland ○ Sydney
New Delhi ○ Mexico City ○ Hong Kong ○ Buenos Aires

Teaching *Resources*

Cover design by Jason Robinson
Interior design by Grafica, Inc.
ISBN-10: 0-439-69497-3
ISBN-13: 978-0-439-69497-1
Copyright © 2006 by Scholastic Inc. All rights reserved.
Printed in the U.S.A.

8 9 10   40   15 14 13 12

Table of Contents

Table of Contents

Table of Contents

Introduction

Welcome to *Hi-Lo Nonfiction Passages for Struggling Readers*, your one-stop resource for leveled, high-interest articles complete with comprehension and vocabulary questions. This collection of nonfiction passages, leveled from 1.0 to 4.5, covers a wide range of topics in science, history, and geography, as well as sports, art, entertainment, and more—a perfect motivator for even your most reluctant readers.

Why Use Nonfiction?

As students move up in grade level they encounter more nonfiction when they tackle content-area textbooks, reference materials, newspapers, and Internet articles. What's more, about half of the passages students will find on standardized tests are nonfiction. Reading nonfiction, however, presents a different set of challenges from fiction. Whereas fiction tells a story, nonfiction conveys facts and information—and students need to learn how to comprehend that information in order to succeed in school and in the real world.

The vocabulary contained in nonfiction texts can be tricky for struggling readers. Not only does each content area have its own special set of words, but some of these are familiar words that have specialized or alternate meanings, which can be confusing for students. In addition, identifying main ideas and details, recognizing cause and effect, distinguishing fact from opinion, and synthesizing information can all pose difficulties for students as they read nonfiction texts. *Hi-Lo Nonfiction Passages for Struggling Readers* can help your students navigate these challenging texts.

What's Inside

This book is divided into ten sections, with each section focusing on a specific reading strategy: making inferences, identifying main ideas and details, recognizing cause and effect, identifying problem and solution, categorizing, sequencing, comparing and contrasting, summarizing, drawing conclusions, and distinguishing fact and opinion.

Each section opens with an introduction to a key reading strategy, and offers simple, bulleted suggestions to help students read effectively. A sample passage models the strategy in a meaningful way, and a graphic organizer helps students visualize the strategy and record important points from the passage. Students can then practice this key strategy as they read a second nonfiction passage.

Following each reading strategy are several reproducible nonfiction passages with test-formatted questions so that students can apply their understanding. The high-interest passages are written below grade level to help motivate struggling readers and build their confidence. You'll find the readability range for each passage in the table of contents.

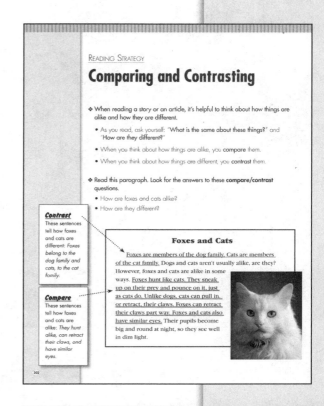

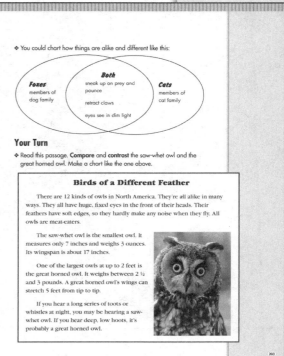

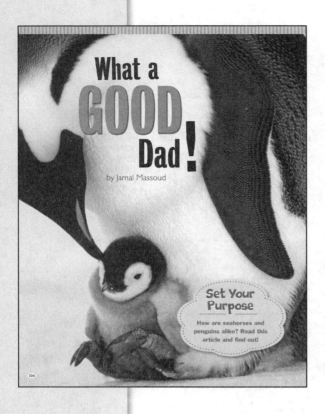

What a GOOD Dad!

by Jamal Massoud

Set Your Purpose

How are seahorses and penguins alike? Read this article and find out!

Here's a **riddle**. What animal father takes very good care of its **young**? If your answer is the male seahorse, you are right. If your answer is the male emperor penguin, you are right, too.

The male seahorse has a pouch on its belly. The female lays her eggs in this pocket. Then she swims away. The male seahorse swims around with the eggs in his pouch. When the eggs hatch, hundreds of babies emerge from the pouch.

A similar story describes the birth of emperor penguins. In the Antarctic, where emperor penguins live, the female climbs onto the ice. She lays one egg on the ice. Then, like the female seahorse, she has done her job, and she swims away.

Like the male seahorse, the male emperor penguin **protects** his unborn young. He does this by rolling the egg onto his feet. He uses the lower part of his fat, warm belly to cover the egg. Then, with the egg on his feet, he joins a group of other males. For two months, they crowd together to keep their eggs and themselves warm. During this time, they don't eat.

After two months, a baby penguin, or chick, hatches. The male penguin feeds the chick with a milky **liquid** that comes from his throat. Soon, the female penguin **appears**. She takes over the care of the baby while the male returns to the sea to hunt for food for his family. After six months, the chick is ready to live on its own.

Think About It

How are penguins and seahorses alike?

The book includes 80 reading passages in all. Each starts with a "Set Your Purpose" question that helps focus students before they begin reading. A critical-thinking question at the end of the passage helps readers reflect on what they've read. In addition, after each passage, you'll find mini-quizzes that assess students' comprehension, vocabulary, and word-attack skills in a bubble-format test. The comprehension questions reinforce the particular reading strategy, while context clues help students develop their vocabulary. In "Word Work," students review or develop word-attack skills, including phonics and structural analysis. Finally, a "Write Now" section invites students to write an open-ended summary or response to the passage. Graphic organizers help them organize their thoughts about the selection they read. The writing activities—ranging in format from business letters to posters, journal entries, articles, and more—provide excellent practice for the short-answer essays students will encounter on standardized tests and writing assessments. An answer key is at the back of the book.

How to Use This Book

Hi-Lo Nonfiction Passages for Struggling Readers is a great supplement to your current reading/language arts program or curriculum. It includes direct instruction and demonstrations of key reading strategies to help students better decode and comprehend nonfiction text. You can use this book in a number of ways:

- Introduce a reading strategy to the whole class. Copy the reading strategy pages onto transparencies and display them on an overhead projector. You may also want to distribute photocopies of the strategy pages to students. Work with students to help them understand how to use the particular strategy—for example, summarizing or making inferences. Together review the model passage before letting students practice on the additional passage provided.

- Work with a small group (preferably at the same reading level). Give each student a copy of a passage, making sure it is appropriate to the group's level. Guide students through the process and strategies for reading the passage. Model how to refer back to the article to find the answers to the mini-quizzes.

- For homework, assign individual students passages based on their interest, reading level, or the skills they need to work on. You may also want to provide a copy of the relevant reading strategy pages for students who need extra help or reinforcement.

- Select reading passages that focus on science or social studies topics, to teach students strategies for reading in the content areas.

However you decide to use this book, you'll find great satisfaction in watching your students become more confident readers as their literacy soars. Enjoy!

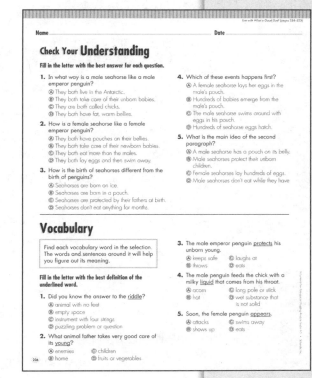

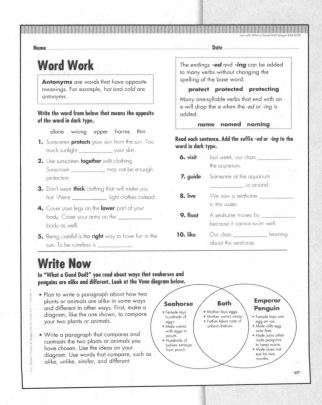

Making Inferences

❖ When reading a story, you can use story clues, along with what you already know, to help you figure out what the author doesn't tell you.

- As you read, look for clues in the text and in the pictures.

- Ask yourself: "What do I already know about this topic?"

- Use the clues to figure out what the author means or does not tell you.

❖ Read this passage. Use clues and what you already know to **make inferences** to figure out where the tour is taking place.

Story Clues

These words and phrases are clues to where the tour is taking place.

A Special Tour

Welcome! The tour is about to begin. First stop is the cornfield. It must be time to pick the corn crop. The cow pasture is near the cornfield. The cows eat grass and drink water. This helps them produce milk. A flock of sheep grazes in their pasture. The sheep have coats of soft wool. At the barn, the pigs are squealing at a dog that's bothering them. The henhouse is the last stop on the tour. The farmer is collecting the eggs. It's time to say good-bye.

How would you like to buy your very own airplane?

Amelia Earhart did!

When she was 22, she used money she **earned** as a truck driver to pay for flying **lessons**. It took her only one year to become a pilot. She also worked for the phone company and saved her money. She used it to buy her first airplane. It was bright yellow.

How would you like to set a record?

Amelia did!

She was the first person to fly up to 14,000 feet. Then, in 1932, she was the first woman to fly across the Atlantic Ocean alone.

How would you like to take the President's wife for a plane ride?

Amelia did!

One night, she took First Lady Eleanor Roosevelt on a **flight**.

Amelia Earhart hoped that one day people would use planes like cars to visit friends and go to work. No one guessed how popular airplane travel would become.

But Amelia did!

During Amelia's around-the-world flight in July of 1937, her plane disappeared. More than 60 planes and ten ships were sent to look for her. They searched for 19 days, but they didn't find a **trace** of her or her plane. Today, people still wonder what happened to her.

Think About It

How would you describe Amelia Earhart?

Name _____   Date _____

Check Your Understanding

Fill in the letter with the best answer for each question.

1. How do you know that even as a girl Amelia liked the idea of flying?
   - Ⓐ She rode on roller coasters all over the world.
   - Ⓑ She would fly into the air on her homemade skateboard.
   - Ⓒ She built an airplane.
   - Ⓓ She drove a truck for an airline company.

2. Which words best describe Amelia as a young woman of 22?
   - Ⓐ lazy and bored
   - Ⓑ foolish, but kind and gentle
   - Ⓒ greedy and selfish
   - Ⓓ bright, dedicated, and hardworking

3. What do Amelia's experiences as a pilot tell you about her?
   - Ⓐ She was brave and daring.
   - Ⓑ She was afraid to try anything new.
   - Ⓒ She was shy.
   - Ⓓ She cared only about breaking records.

4. Eleanor Roosevelt was
   - Ⓐ Amelia's grandmother.
   - Ⓑ the President's wife.
   - Ⓒ Amelia's first flying teacher.
   - Ⓓ a woman who worked at the phone company.

5. If Amelia were alive, she would probably be pleased that
   - Ⓐ people can buy real skateboards.
   - Ⓑ people wonder what happened to her.
   - Ⓒ airplane travel has become so popular.
   - Ⓓ airplanes come in many different colors.

Vocabulary

Find each vocabulary word in the selection. The words and sentences around it will help you figure out its meaning.

Fill in the letter with the best definition of the underlined word.

1. Amelia rode a skateboard down the <u>ramp</u> and high into the air.
   - Ⓐ farm
   - Ⓑ pond or a lake
   - Ⓒ track that slopes down
   - Ⓓ flat piece of metal

2. She <u>earned</u> money as a truck driver.
   - Ⓐ drove a car
   - Ⓑ got by working
   - Ⓒ bought with money
   - Ⓓ couldn't find

3. She used the money to pay for flying <u>lessons</u>.
   - Ⓐ pieces of airplanes
   - Ⓑ airline companies
   - Ⓒ machine repair
   - Ⓓ directions for how to do something

4. One night, on an around-the-world <u>flight</u>, her plane disappeared.
   - Ⓐ battle or a fight
   - Ⓑ ride in a car
   - Ⓒ trip in an aircraft
   - Ⓓ sailing ship

5. They didn't find a <u>trace</u> of her or her plane.
   - Ⓐ something left behind as proof
   - Ⓑ a mystery or a puzzle
   - Ⓒ someone looking for something
   - Ⓓ a photograph

Name _____   **Date** _____

Word Work

The sound /**ûr**/ can be spelled in several ways:

ir as in *first*

ear as in *learn*

The sound /**ou**/ can be spelled in several ways:

ow as in *down*

ou as in *around*

Read the definitions. Complete the word by adding the letters *ir, ear, ow,* or *ou.*

1. looked for   s____ched

2. the sound made by a bird   ch____p

3. a building to live in   h____se

4. a large group of people   cr____d

5. the opposite of late   ____ly

Each sentence below has an incomplete word. Add *ir, ear, ow,* or *ou* to complete the word.

6. I don't know h____ anyone could fly alone in a plane.

7. Amelia was interested in many things when she was a g____l.

8. My m____th dropped open when I saw her fly the yellow plane.

9. They would not all____ me to fly to New York alone.

10. If I can ____n enough money, I'm going to buy a plane!

Write Now

In the selection "Amelia Did!" you read about the famous aviator Amelia Earhart. Look at the web.

• Plan to create a cartoon about Amelia Earhart's life. Copy the web shown. Add more details from the story.

• Draw and write your cartoon about Amelia. Use the details from your web.

invented her own "rolly-coaster" — **Amelia Earhart** — learned to fly in a year — bought a yellow airplane

Hi-Lo Nonfiction Passages for Struggling Readers: Grades 4-5 • Scholastic Inc.

WELCOME TO THE GRAND OLE OPRY

by Claire Franzen

The theater is dark, and the crowd is **noisy**.

All of a sudden, the lights go on. The red velvet **curtain** rises. At the back of the stage is a large red and white barn with a sign that says "Grand Ole Opry." A tall man wearing a colorful suit with sparkles on it announces:

"Ladies and gentlemen, welcome to the Grand Ole Opry!"

Set Your Purpose

What is the Grand Ole Opry? Why do people go there? Read this article to find out.

The stage at the Grand Ole Opry

The Grand Ole Opry is part of the **musical** history of the United States. It is a live country-music radio show that is broadcast from Opryland in Nashville, Tennessee. There are performances each Friday, Saturday, and Sunday night. People come from all over the world to hear the lively music and to see the Opry stars.

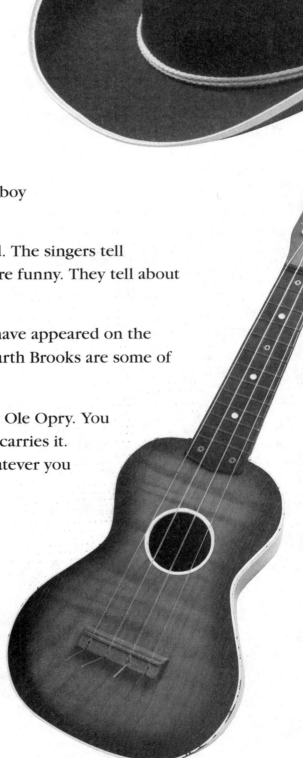

The show is two hours long, and is divided into four half-hour sections. Each section has a different **host**. The host introduces the performers. Each performer or group comes onto the stage, sings or plays one song, and then leaves. The stars usually wear bright clothes with glitter and sparkles. Many of them wear cowboy boots, too. A lot of them are guitarists.

Some of the songs are melancholy, or very sad. The singers tell about friends who have gone away. Other songs are funny. They tell about hound dogs and other pets.

Many famous country singers and musicians have appeared on the Grand Ole Opry. Dolly Parton, Clint Black, and Garth Brooks are some of the stars who have performed at the Opry.

If you go to Nashville, you can visit the Grand Ole Opry. You can also listen to the show on a radio station that carries it. Another option is to watch it on **television**. Whatever you do, it will be a night you'll never forget.

Think About It

Why do people visit the Grand Ole Opry?

Name _____   Date _____

Check Your **Understanding**

Fill in the letter with the best answer for each question.

1. Because people from all over the world go to the Grand Ole Opry, you can infer that

Ⓐ the performances are worth seeing.

Ⓑ Nashville is easy to get to.

Ⓒ it is where tourists can perform.

Ⓓ the theater is dark and noisy.

2. Performers probably like to be on the Opry show because

Ⓐ they do not have to work too hard.

Ⓑ they all live nearby.

Ⓒ there is no other show in Nashville.

Ⓓ a lot of people listen to and see the show.

3. The fact that Dolly Parton and Garth Brooks sang at the Opry implies that

Ⓐ the show is heard only on Saturday nights.

Ⓑ the performance is six hours long.

Ⓒ you might see other stars when you go.

Ⓓ you will meet Dolly and Garth in person.

4. Most people who go to the Grand Ole Opry probably like

Ⓐ country music.

Ⓑ movie stars.

Ⓒ cowboy boots.

Ⓓ guitar contests.

5. Which sentence best describes the Grand Ole Opry?

Ⓐ It is a television station in Nashville, Tennessee.

Ⓑ It is a live country-music radio show.

Ⓒ It is a music group from Opryland.

Ⓓ It is where Dolly Parton sings.

Vocabulary

Find each vocabulary word in the selection. The words and sentences around it will help you figure out its meaning.

Fill in the letter with the best definition of the underlined word.

1. The theater is dark, and the crowd is noisy.

Ⓐ loud   Ⓒ sad

Ⓑ glad   Ⓓ mean

2. Suddenly the lights go on and a red velvet curtain rises.

Ⓐ large car that brings performers to a show

Ⓑ piece of material hung in front of a stage

Ⓒ clouds that bring rain

Ⓓ small piece of wood

3. The Grand Ole Opry is a part of the musical history of our country.

Ⓐ having to do with music

Ⓑ having to do with movies

Ⓒ country songs

Ⓓ having to do with magic

4. Each section has a different host.

Ⓐ person who directs the band

Ⓑ person who takes the tickets

Ⓒ person who tells what comes next in a show

Ⓓ person who sings the songs

5. You can watch the Opry on television, too.

Ⓐ person who takes pictures

Ⓑ receiver that has a picture and sound

Ⓒ place that hosts concerts

Ⓓ receiver that can only be used for listening to shows

Hi-Lo Nonfiction Passages for Struggling Readers Grades 4-5 • Scholastic Inc.

Name _____ **Date** _____

Word Work

A **suffix** is a word part that comes at the end of a base word. Knowing the meaning of a suffix helps you figure out the meaning of the whole word. The suffix **-ist** means "a person who." The suffix **-ful** means "full of" or "having a lot of."

cartoonist   someone who draws

hopeful   full of hope

Write a word that fits the definition by adding the suffix -ist or -ful to the base word.

1. a person who creates art   art_____
2. full of care   care_____
3. having a lot of color   color_____
4. full of shame   shame_____
5. someone who plays the guitar   guitar_____

Each word on the left contains a base word and a suffix. Complete the definition by writing the correct form of the base word.

6. violinist   someone who plays the _____
7. useful   having a lot of _____
8. fearful   having a lot of _____
9. organist   a person who plays the _____
10. wonderful   full of _____

Write Now

Look at the words in the web shown below. They tell about the Grand Ole Opry.

- Pretend you are at the Grand Ole Opry. Plan to send a greeting card to a friend from there. Look back at the article about the Grand Ole Opry, if needed. Add words to the word web. Think of what you would say to your friend.

- Write your message on the inside of the card. Draw a picture on the outside.

Join the Roller Coaster Club!

adapted by Victor Pinto

Set Your Purpose

Have you ever ridden a roller coaster? Did you like it? Read this article to learn about a special club for people who love roller coasters.

You're sitting in a tiny car. The car is part of a very small train that runs on a narrow track. Slowly, the little train climbs to the top of a huge hill.

You're high above the ground, so high that you can see for miles. Suddenly, you rush toward the ground at a speed that takes your breath away. You're on your way up again, and this time you're upside down!

You go up, down, and around. You're on a roller coaster. Some people think riding a roller coaster is **terrifying**. One ride is more than enough for them. Other people love riding roller coasters. They ride their **favorite** roller coaster over and over again. They also like to try out new roller coasters.

There's a club for people who love roller coasters. It's called ACE. ACE stands for American Coaster Enthusiasts. Steven Reagan and Kevin Lipnicky belong to ACE, and so do their families. Their family vacations often include trips to amusement parks to ride on new roller coasters.

As **members** of ACE, the boys were among the first to ride a new roller coaster at Sea World in Texas. It's called the Great White, which is the name of a kind of shark.

"The Great White has a smooth heart-line," says Steven. "That's when you go upside down on a straight track. Then you go upright." If Steven sounds like he knows what he's talking about, he should. He's ridden more than 150 different roller coasters!

Sometimes, amusement parks close the roller coaster to everyone but ACE members.

"If there's no one in line," says Steven, "we keep our seats and ride again!"

It's not all fun for ACE members. They also have a job to do. They tell owners of new amusement parks where run-down roller coasters are. The owners buy the old roller coasters and move them to new

homes so that they can be fixed instead of **destroyed**.

For ACE members, roller-coaster riding is fun, fun, fun! Thanks to the work they do to save old roller coasters, you can have fun, too.

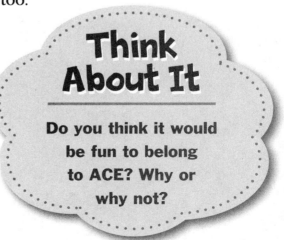

Think About It

Do you think it would be fun to belong to ACE? Why or why not?

Name _____ Date _____

Check Your Understanding

Fill in the letter with the best answer for each question.

1. From this selection you can tell that members of ACE

Ⓐ are all adults.

Ⓑ ride only old roller coasters.

Ⓒ ride only roller coasters with loops.

Ⓓ love to ride roller coasters.

2. What would happen to old roller coasters without the help of ACE members?

Ⓐ They would fall apart or be destroyed.

Ⓑ They would be repaired only once a year.

Ⓒ They would be used in television commercials.

Ⓓ They would be closed to everyone but ACE members.

3. Which statement is probably true about roller coasters?

Ⓐ Roller coasters cannot be moved.

Ⓑ Different roller coasters have different twists and turns.

Ⓒ Roller coasters are all the same.

Ⓓ Old roller coasters cannot be fixed.

4. Which statement would you say is probably true about Steven?

Ⓐ He knows a lot about different roller coasters.

Ⓑ He gets bored after ten rides on a roller coaster.

Ⓒ He likes old roller coasters better than new ones.

Ⓓ He does not enjoy family vacations.

5. What happens after an amusement park buys a run-down roller coaster?

Ⓐ ACE members find out about the old roller coasters.

Ⓑ The old roller coasters are destroyed.

Ⓒ ACE members tell the owners of new parks about old roller coasters.

Ⓓ The owners of the new parks have the old roller coasters fixed.

Vocabulary

Fill in the letter with the best definition of the underlined word.

1. Some people think riding a roller coaster is <u>terrifying</u>.

Ⓐ fun   Ⓒ huge

Ⓑ exciting   Ⓓ scary

2. They ride their <u>favorite</u> roller coaster over and over again.

Ⓐ upside down   Ⓒ slowest

Ⓑ brand new   Ⓓ liked more than others

3. Family vacations often <u>include</u> trips to amusement parks.

Ⓐ find   Ⓒ repeat

Ⓑ share   Ⓓ involve

4. The boys are <u>members</u> of ACE.

Ⓐ amusement park owners

Ⓒ people who belong to a group

Ⓑ people who fix things

Ⓓ people who forget

5. Old rides are fixed, not <u>destroyed</u>.

Ⓐ torn down   Ⓒ cleaned

Ⓑ separated   Ⓓ fixed

Hi-Lo Nonfiction Passages for Struggling Readers Grades 4–5 • Scholastic Inc.

Name _____ Date _____

Word Work

Antonyms are words that have the opposite meanings. For example, *up* and *down* are antonyms.

A **contraction** is two words joined to make one. One or more letters have been left out. The apostrophe (') shows where the letters were left out.

there + is = there's

Read the sentences and the words below. Write the word that means the opposite of the word in dark type.

old   destroyed   give   like   terrifying   low

1. calming A _____ storm hit our school.

2. fixed Parts of the playground were _____ by the storm.

3. new Members of our class helped to fix the _____ playground.

4. dislike We painted the fence yellow which is a color I _____.

5. receive I will _____ you a picture of the new playground.

6. high The diving board is _____.

Fill in the letter of the contraction that is formed by the underlined words.

7. I am so excited about riding the new roller coaster.
- Ⓐ I'd
- Ⓑ I'm
- Ⓒ I've
- Ⓓ I'll

8. My sister, who has always loved roller coasters, is excited, too.
- Ⓐ who'd
- Ⓑ who'll
- Ⓒ what's
- Ⓓ who's

9. We did not have to wait in line for hours.
- Ⓐ doesn't
- Ⓑ don't
- Ⓒ didn't
- Ⓓ hadn't

10. The people in front said they would let us go first.
- Ⓐ they've
- Ⓑ they'd
- Ⓒ they'll
- Ⓓ they're

Write Now

In "Join the Roller Coaster Club," you read about why people belong to the roller coaster club ACE.

- Think of something you like to do, like riding a bike or taking trips. Make up a club for it, and give your club a name. Copy the chart and write down fun things your club can do.

- Write a paragraph explaining what your club does and why people would want to join. Use your chart to help you.

My club can:
_____
_____
_____
_____
_____

Hi-Lo Nonfiction Passages for Struggling Readers: Grades 4–5 • Scholastic Inc.

39

Identifying Main Idea & Details

❖ Identifying the main idea a writer is trying to get across will help you understand and remember the writer's most important points.

- The **main idea** is what the paragraph, article, or story is mostly about.

- To find the **main idea**, think about the most important information.

- If you can't find a sentence that states the main idea, make up a sentence that does.

- Look for **details** that give more information about the main idea.

❖ Read this paragraph. Look for the **main idea** and **details** that support the main idea.

Main Idea

This sentence tells what the whole paragraph is about. It states the **main idea** of the paragraph.

Details

These sentences give **details**. They give more information about the main idea.

Blind as a Bat?

Bats aren't really blind, but they don't use their eyes to find their way around at night. <u>Bats use their sense of hearing to locate the insects that are their food and to avoid objects.</u> <u>Bats send off pulses of sound through their mouths or noses. These pulses echo back, outlining objects in the bat's way. A bat's large ears help it figure out where the echoes are coming from.</u> To find insects, the bat sweeps the room with sound. It sends out pulses faster and faster until it zeroes in on what it is hunting—dinner!

❖ You could chart the **main idea** and **details** in the paragraph like this:

Detail	Detail	Main Idea
Bats send off pulses of sound through their mouths or noses. These pulses echo back, outlining objects in the bat's way.	A bat's large ears help it figure out where the echoes are coming from.	Bats use their sense of hearing to locate the insects that are their food and to avoid objects.

Your Turn

❖ Read this paragraph. Look for the **main idea** and **details**. Make a chart like the one above.

Birds That Can't Fly

In different parts of the world, there are birds that can't fly. That i[...] seems as strange as the idea of a fish that can't swim! However, penguins waddle across the icy shore of Antarctica and swim in its waters. Ostriches race across the deserts of Africa. Kiwis run along the ground in New Zealand. Rheas roam grasslands in South America, and emus do the same in Australia. None of these birds can fly. Penguins are a special kind of flightless bird. Underwater, they use their wings as flippers, and they are very good at "flying" through the water!

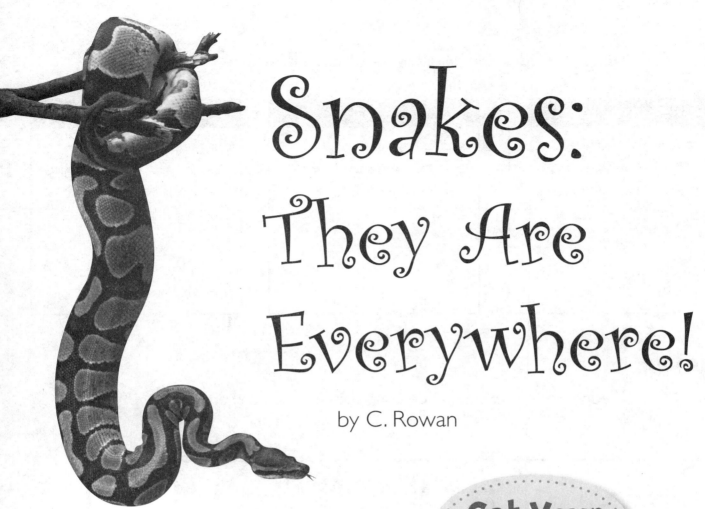

Snakes: They Are Everywhere!

by C. Rowan

Set Your Purpose

Do you like snakes? Read this article to learn interesting facts about snakes.

Some snakes live in **forests**. Some live in hot, dry deserts. Others live in lakes or streams. Some snakes even live in the sea! Some snakes live almost everywhere. But they never live where it is always freezing cold.

Most snakes are **harmless** to people. However, they will attack animals that threaten them. Some snakes have skin patterns that make them **hard** to see. Others make noises to scare off enemies. Certain snakes "play dead" to stop an attack.

Snakes use their long tongues to smell things. They **shed** their skin as they grow. And they never close their eyes to sleep!

Think About It

What did you learn about snakes that you didn't know before?

Name _____   Date _____

Check Your **Understanding**

Fill in the letter with the best answer for each question.

1. What is the main idea of the article?
  Ⓐ Snakes can live in trees.
  Ⓑ Snakes live almost everywhere.
  Ⓒ Snakes do not like freezing cold weather.

2. Which is a detail from the article?
  Ⓐ The author does not like snakes.
  Ⓑ Some snakes live in the sea.
  Ⓒ Snakes never go underground.

3. Snakes cannot live
  Ⓐ where it is always very cold.
  Ⓑ in forests.
  Ⓒ in lakes or streams.

4. If an enemy saw a snake that was not moving, it would probably
  Ⓐ bury it in the ground.
  Ⓑ eat it quickly.
  Ⓒ leave it alone.

Vocabulary

Find each vocabulary word in the selection. The words and sentences around it will help you figure out its meaning.

Fill in the letter with the best definition of the underlined word.

1. Look out for snakes when you hike in <u>forests</u>.
  Ⓐ dry, hot places
  Ⓑ places with many trees
  Ⓒ cold places

2. Garter snakes are <u>harmless</u>.
  Ⓐ will not hurt you
  Ⓑ desert snakes
  Ⓒ snakes that live in the sea

3. Some snakes are <u>hard</u> to find.
  Ⓐ simple
  Ⓑ not strong
  Ⓒ not easy

4. The snake <u>shed</u> its skin.
  Ⓐ removed
  Ⓑ grew
  Ⓒ scraped

Hi-Lo Nonfiction Passages for Struggling Readers: Grades 4–5 • Scholastic Inc.

Name _____   **Date** _____

Word Work

> Some words with a **final *e*** have a long vowel sound.
>
> man + e = mane   hop + e = hope
>
> rip + e = ripe   hug + e = huge

Look at the pictures. Fill in the letter of the picture whose name has a long vowel sound.

1. Ⓐ    Ⓑ

2. Ⓐ   Ⓑ

3. Ⓐ   Ⓑ

4. Ⓐ   Ⓑ

5. Ⓐ   Ⓑ

Make a new word with a long vowel sound by adding a final *e* to each word in dark print. Write your new word to complete each sentence.

6. I did **not** write a _____ .

7. Kim **cut** out a _____ cat.

8. Here is a **kit** to make a _____ .

9. **Tim** knows how to tell _____ .

10. Can you walk with a _____ ?

Write Now

In the article "Snakes: They Are Everywhere!" you read many interesting facts about snakes.

- Plan to make a poster to go with a snake exhibit at the zoo. Copy this word web about snakes. Add information from the article to the web.

- Write your information on a poster. Use ideas from your web. Draw pictures to make your poster fun.

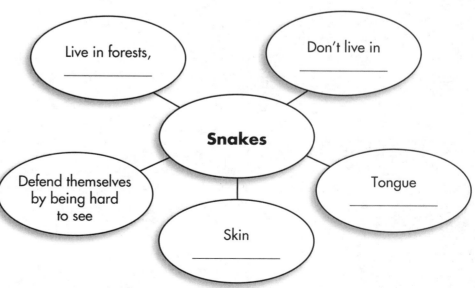

Hi-Lo Nonfiction Passages for Struggling Readers: Grades 4–5 • Scholastic Inc.

45

Desert Life

by Pat Cusick

Would you like to live in a place where it **hardly** rains? That's what a desert is. Deserts are dry. Most deserts are hot, too. The sun beats down, day after day.

All the people, animals, and plants in a desert search for water. The people and animals also try to stay out of the sun. If they can do both, they can survive in the desert. **Otherwise**, they will die.

Desert plants use tricks to get and save water. Bushes and shrubs have long roots. They reach down deep to get every drop of water. Many plants have **waxy** leaves. That helps keep water within the plants. After a rain, cactus plants

Set Your Purpose

What would it be like to live in a desert? Read this article to find out.

drink up the water quickly. They hold water inside for a long time.

Some desert animals live **underground** all day. They never see the sun. Some burrow into cactus plants. That keeps them out of the sun and keeps them wet, too. Desert birds hide in bushes.

What about people? How do they survive? Some desert people wear thin white clothing and stay covered from head to foot. White reflects the sun and stays cooler. Thin clothing **allows** the breezes to blow through. Some desert homes have thick walls. The walls get cool when the sun goes down and stay cool during the day. Usually, desert people live as close as they can to water.

To live in the desert, you need to adapt. That's what desert plants, wildlife, and people do. Their way of living is shaped by where they live.

Think About It

What is the most important thing to remember about living in the desert?

Name _____ Date _____

Check Your **Understanding**

Fill in the letter with the best answer for each question.

1. The main idea of the third paragraph is
- Ⓐ desert plants have long roots.
- Ⓑ some desert plants keep water inside.
- Ⓒ cactus plants drink water quickly.
- Ⓓ desert plants use tricks to get and save water.

2. The main idea of the fourth paragraph is
- Ⓐ desert birds hide in the bushes.
- Ⓑ some desert animals live underground.
- Ⓒ most desert animals stay out of the sun.
- Ⓓ some desert animals burrow into cactus plants.

3. Which sentence states the main idea of the article?
- Ⓐ All who live in the desert must adapt to desert life.
- Ⓑ Birds and animals in the desert adapt to desert life.
- Ⓒ Plants in the desert adapt to desert life.
- Ⓓ People in the desert must adapt to desert life.

4. Why do some animals stay underground during the day?
- Ⓐ to keep out of the sun
- Ⓑ to keep warm
- Ⓒ to keep out of the rain
- Ⓓ to look for food

5. Why do desert people cover themselves from head to toe?
- Ⓐ to protect themselves from cactus plants
- Ⓑ to protect themselves from animals
- Ⓒ to protect themselves from rain
- Ⓓ to protect themselves from the sun

Vocabulary

Find each vocabulary word in the selection. The words and sentences around it will help you figure out its meaning.

Fill in the letter with the best definition of the underlined word.

1. A desert is a dry place where it <u>hardly</u> rains.
- Ⓐ rarely
- Ⓑ very
- Ⓒ likely
- Ⓓ softly

2. Living things in the desert must have water; <u>otherwise</u> they will die.
- Ⓐ if not
- Ⓑ maybe
- Ⓒ surely
- Ⓓ another

3. The <u>waxy</u> leaves of some plants help keep water within the plants.
- Ⓐ smooth and dry
- Ⓑ thick and smooth
- Ⓒ green and fresh
- Ⓓ wavy

4. Some desert animals live <u>underground</u>.
- Ⓐ under a tree
- Ⓑ beneath the earth
- Ⓒ under a tent
- Ⓓ in a box

5. Thin clothing <u>allows</u> breezes to blow through.
- Ⓐ gives
- Ⓑ shakes
- Ⓒ lets
- Ⓓ blows

Hi-Lo Nonfiction Passages for Struggling Readers: Grades 4–5 • Scholastic Inc.

Name _____   Date _____

Word Work

A **compound word** is made of two shorter words. Combining the meanings of the two shorter words often explains the compound word.

rainfall = a **fall** of **rain**

Read the definitions below. Join two words from each definition to make a compound word that fits the definition. Write the new word.

SAMPLE   definition: a **house** for a **dog**
compound word: **doghouse**

Definitions

1. a storm with thunder   _____
2. the rise of the sun   _____
3. the fall of night   _____
4. a boat with a sail   _____
5. a cup for tea   _____

Make compound words by combining each word on the left with a word on the right. Write the compound word that best completes each sentence.

sun	ground
wild	snakes
under	storms
rattle	light
sand	life

6. You might see _____ crawling up the rocks.

7. You will find interesting _____ in the desert.

8. You won't see the desert animals that live _____ during the day.

9. They never see _____.

10. They also avoid blowing _____.

Write Now

This chart lists some of the information from "Desert Life." The first column lists some things people do. The second column tells why.

What People Do	Reason Why
wear white clothing	reflects the sun
stay covered	prevents sunburn
_____	_____
_____	_____

• Pretend that you are in a desert visiting a friend. Plan to write a short letter home telling about your visit. Before writing the letter, copy and complete the chart above.

• Write your letter. Don't forget the greeting and the closing.

The Sneaker Story

adapted by Carole Osterink

Set Your Purpose

What do you know about sneakers? Read this article to find out what new information you can learn.

From high-tops to tennis shoes, sneakers are everywhere! Half the shoes sold in the United States are sneakers. There are shoe stores that sell nothing but sneakers. It used to be that only athletes wore sneakers. If school kids had sneakers, they wore them just for gym. Today just about everybody wears sneakers some of the time. Check out the feet of your classmates. Check out foot **fashion** at the mall. Chances are, you will see a lot of sneakers.

Sneakers come in every **imaginable** size, shape, and color. Some even have air pumps and lights! What will they think of next?

A third-grader from New York thinks that sneakers of the future will be **stretchable** and that they'll grow with your feet. A fourth-grader from Texas thinks future "sneaks" will have built-in telephones.

What do you think?

A Sneak Peek: The History of Sneakers

1868 The first rubber-and-canvas shoes were sold. They were called croquet sandals. Only rich people could **afford** them. They cost $6 a pair.

1873 The word *sneakers* was first used. It came from "sneak thieves." Did people wear these shoes with soft **soles** so they could sneak about like silent spies?

1950s Kids were free to wear what they wanted when many schools got rid of dress codes. Many kids started wearing sneakers to school.

1970s People took up jogging. They wore leather sneakers called running shoes.

1990s–Today Sneakers take off! Kids and grown-ups wear them. More than 90 companies make them.

Think About It

What do you think the sneakers of the future will be like?

51

Name _____   Date _____

Check Your Understanding

Fill in the letter with the best answer for each question.

1. Which sentence tells the main idea of the selection?

Ⓐ Sneakers are the shoes of the future.

Ⓑ Sneakers are kids' favorite shoes.

Ⓒ Sneakers are popular and have a long history.

Ⓓ Sneakers might have telephones some day.

2. Which of these facts supports the idea that sneakers are very popular shoes?

Ⓐ In 1868, only rich people could afford croquet sandals.

Ⓑ Kids wore sneakers only for gym.

Ⓒ Some sneakers have air pumps and lights.

Ⓓ Half the shoes sold in the United States are sneakers.

3. Who used the first rubber-and-canvas shoes?

Ⓐ athletes

Ⓑ kids who went to the gym

Ⓒ people who took up jogging

Ⓓ rich people who could afford them

4. According to the selection, why did kids start wearing sneakers to school in the 1950s?

Ⓐ They cost only $6 a pair.

Ⓑ Many schools got rid of their dress codes.

Ⓒ They had to wear them for gym class.

Ⓓ They did not want to be heard when they walked in the hall.

5. According to the selection, what was the effect of people taking up jogging in the 1970s?

Ⓐ Americans got more exercise.

Ⓑ Kids started wearing sneakers to school.

Ⓒ Companies started making sneakers with lights.

Ⓓ People started wearing leather sneakers called running shoes.

Vocabulary

Find each vocabulary word in the selection. The words and sentences around it will help you figure out its meaning.

Fill in the letter with the best definition of the underlined word.

1. Check out foot <u>fashion</u> at the mall.

Ⓐ style

Ⓑ comfort

Ⓒ problems

Ⓓ powder

2. In 1868, only rich people could <u>afford</u> to buy sneakers.

Ⓐ try

Ⓑ drive a car

Ⓒ have a good reason

Ⓓ have enough money

3. Future sneakers might be <u>stretchable</u> to grow with your feet.

Ⓐ able to learn

Ⓑ able to become larger or longer

Ⓒ able to tell stories

Ⓓ faster and better

4. Sneakers come in every <u>imaginable</u> size, shape, and color.

Ⓐ not a possible idea

Ⓑ able to be pictured in the mind

Ⓒ not popular

Ⓓ pictured on television

5. The soft <u>soles</u> of sneakers let you sneak silently away.

Ⓐ laces

Ⓑ socks

Ⓒ bottoms of the shoes

Ⓓ holes for the laces

Hi-Lo Nonfiction Passages for Struggling Readers: Grades 4–5 • Scholastic Inc.

Name _____ Date _____

Word Work

A **noun** names a person, place, or thing.
A **plural noun** names more than one
person, place, or thing. To make the plural
of most nouns, add *s*.

sneaker ⟶ **sneakers**

If a noun ends in a consonant and *y*,
change the *y* to *i* and add *-es*.

penny ⟶ **pennies**

Write the plural of each word.

1. shoe _____

2. spy _____

3. light _____

4. pump _____

5. athlete _____

Read each sentence. Write the correct plural form of the word in dark type.

6. **company**   More than 90 _____ make sneakers.

7. **classmate**   Check out the feet of your _____.

8. **city**   There are sneaker stores in _____ all over the country.

9. **family**   In many _____, everybody wears sneakers.

10. **school**   Many _____ got rid of their dress codes in the 1950s.

Write Now

In "The Sneaker Story," you learned some of the history behind sneakers. Do you have a favorite pair of sneakers? Have you ever had an adventure that involved your sneakers?

• Plan to write your own amazing or funny story about sneakers. Your story can be something that really happened, or it can be make-believe. Use a web like the one shown to help you decide what you want to write about.

• Write your amazing or funny sneaker story. Draw a picture to go with it if you have the time.

what my favorite pair looks like

what I use them for

sneakers

the day I got my favorite pair

funny stories about them

Hi-Lo Nonfiction Passages for Struggling Readers: Grades 4–5 • Scholastic Inc.

53

Leonardo DaVinci

by William Rockwell

An Amazing Man

Leonardo da Vinci was born in Italy more than 500 years ago. He had many **talents**. He had countless ideas. He was a true **genius**.

Inventor

Leonardo was an **inventor**. He liked to think of new ideas. He drew a picture of a bicycle. At the time, that was a new idea. The first bicycle was built 300 years later. He also drew a picture of an airplane. Leonardo's airplane was another new idea. The first airplane was built 400 years later. Leonardo never ran out of ideas.

Set Your Purpose

Leonardo da Vinci was an amazing man. Read this article to learn about some of the things he created.

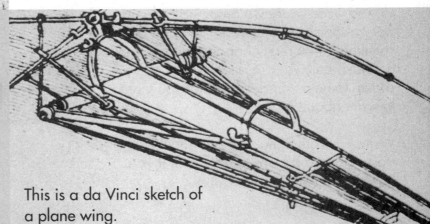

This is a da Vinci sketch of a plane wing.

Artist

Leonardo was a great painter. He painted the Mona Lisa. It is a very famous painting. The woman in the painting has a **puzzling** look on her face. What is she thinking? Why is she smiling? No one knows. As you walk in front of the painting, watch her eyes. It is very strange. Her eyes seem to follow you.

Secret Writing

Leonardo wanted to know how things worked. He studied plants and animals. He studied the stars. He asked questions. Why do waves **form** in water? Why does the moon shine? Leonardo wrote his ideas in a notebook. But he did something strange. He wrote his notes backwards! Why did he do that? No one knows. Maybe he wanted to keep his ideas secret. Maybe he did it for fun. How do people read his writing? They use a mirror!

Think About It

Why is Leonardo da Vinci famous?

Imagine if you did your homework backwards!

Name_____ **Date**_____

Check Your Understanding

Fill in the letter with the best answer for each question.

1. This article is mainly about
ⓐ inventions. ⓒ the Mona Lisa.
ⓑ paintings. ⓓ Leonardo da Vinci.

2. Which of the following best describes Leonardo da Vinci?
ⓐ bicyclist ⓒ airplane pilot
ⓑ original thinker ⓓ painter

3. What did Leonardo have to do with the first bicycle?
ⓐ He rode it.
ⓑ He built it.
ⓒ He drew a picture of it.
ⓓ He bought the first one.

4. The Mona Lisa is
ⓐ one of Leonardo's sisters.
ⓑ a city Leonardo planned.
ⓒ a famous sculpture.
ⓓ a famous painting.

5. Leonardo wrote his ideas
ⓐ on the computer.
ⓑ on a mirror.
ⓒ backwards, in a notebook.
ⓓ on the walls.

Vocabulary

Find each vocabulary word in the selection. The words and sentences around it will help you figure out its meaning.

Fill in the letter with the best definition of the underlined word.

1. Leonardo da Vinci had many <u>talents</u>.
ⓐ tall friends
ⓑ gifts or abilities
ⓒ drawings
ⓓ pieces of work

2. He was a true <u>genius</u>.
ⓐ gentle person
ⓑ person who works
ⓒ unusually smart person
ⓓ person who gives

3. Leonardo was an <u>inventor</u>.
ⓐ fixer of machines
ⓑ maker of light bulbs
ⓒ painter of faces
ⓓ creator of something new

4. Mona Lisa's face has a <u>puzzling</u> expression.
ⓐ sweet
ⓑ hard to figure out
ⓒ unfriendly
ⓓ plain or common

5. Leonardo wondered why waves <u>form</u> in water.
ⓐ fall
ⓑ go far
ⓒ take shape
ⓓ swim

Hi-Lo Nonfiction Passages for Struggling Readers Grades 4–5 • Scholastic Inc.

Name _____ Date _____

Word Work

Antonyms are words that have the opposite meanings. For example, *old* and *new* are antonyms.

Read the sentences and the words below. Write the word that means the opposite of the word in dark type.

strange   famous   first   countless   smiling

1. few   Leonardo had _____ ideas.

2. last   The _____ bicycle was built 300 years after he drew a picture of it.

3. unknown The Mona Lisa is a very _____ painting.

4. frowning She is always _____.

5. common   Leonardo's way of writing was very _____.

A **possessive noun** is a noun that shows ownership. To make a singular noun possessive, add **'s**. To make a plural noun possessive, add an apostrophe after the s **(s')**. Add *'s* to plural nouns that do not end in s.

boy ⟶ boy's

toys ⟶ toys'

Read each pair of sentences. Write the correct possessive noun that completes the second sentence.

6. The painting belongs to Leonardo. It is _____ painting.

7. The smile belongs to the woman. It is the _____ smile.

8. The answers belong to the questions. They are the _____ answers.

9. This is the shape of the waves. It is the _____ shape.

10. The beam belongs to the moon. It is the _____ beam.

Write Now

Leonardo da Vinci dreamed up many new inventions. He drew pictures of his new inventions in his notebook. Then he wrote sentences explaining how the inventions worked.

• Plan to describe a new invention of your own. First, brainstorm some ideas. What will you invent—a new toy, a new machine, a piece of clothing with some special power or ability? Write your ideas in a web like the one shown. Then choose the idea that you like best.

• Write a paragraph describing your invention. If you have time, draw and label a picture of your new invention.

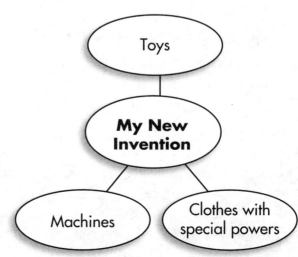

Hi-Lo Nonfiction Passages for Struggling Readers: Grades 4-5 • Scholastic Inc.

57

You Can't Throw a BOOMERANG Away

by Laura E. Crockett

Set Your Purpose

What keeps coming back no matter how often you throw it away? Read this article to find out.

Want to play catch by yourself? You can—with a boomerang! A boomerang is a **weapon** from Australia. Long ago, it was used for hunting. Today, it is used for fun. Try throwing it as hard as you can. If you've done it right, the boomerang circles around and **returns** to you.

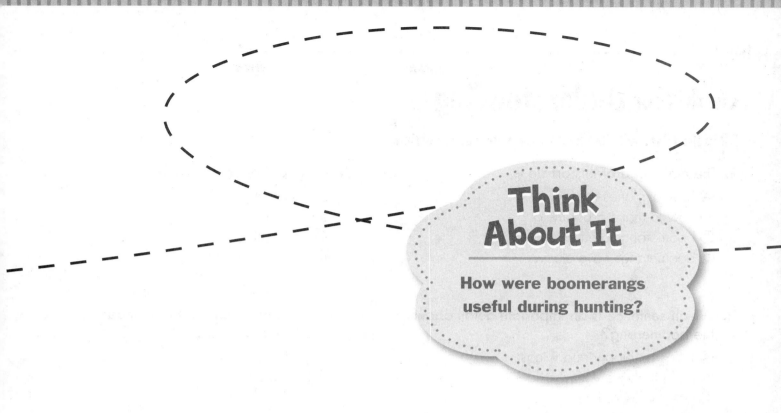

Think About It

How were boomerangs useful during hunting?

The secret is in its shape. Most boomerangs have an **elbow**. That gives it a bend in the middle and two "wings." They work just like airplane wings.

As a boomerang flies through the air, its wings spin. Each wing turns toward the other wing. That makes it fly in a circle. Throwing a boomerang can be tricky. Hold it close to your body, just above the shoulder. Hold the boomerang straight up and down. Now snap your wrist and throw! With practice, you can **release** it and make it come back to exactly the same spot.

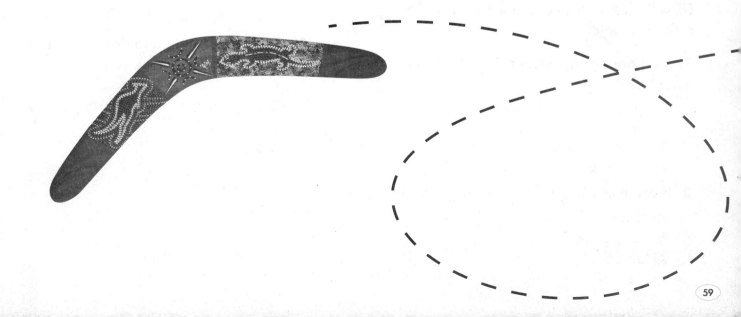

Name _____ **Date** _____

Check Your **Understanding**

Fill in the letter with the best answer for each question.

1. The main idea of this article is
  Ⓐ how airplanes fly.
  Ⓑ how to make a boomerang.
  Ⓒ boomerangs are fun to fly.
  Ⓓ boomerangs have elbows.

2. Which sentence is an important detail about the boomerang?
  Ⓐ It has an elbow and wings.
  Ⓑ Hold it above your shoulder.
  Ⓒ Use it only for hunting.
  Ⓓ It looks just like an airplane.

3. Long ago, boomerangs were used
  Ⓐ for playing games.
  Ⓑ instead of airplanes.
  Ⓒ for hunting.
  Ⓓ to understand how airplanes fly.

4. Boomerangs were probably made to come back so they would
  Ⓐ be hard to throw.
  Ⓑ be more fun.
  Ⓒ fly like airplanes.
  Ⓓ not get lost.

Vocabulary

> Find each vocabulary word in the selection. The words and sentences around it will help you figure out its meaning.

Fill in the letter with the best definition of the underlined word.

1. Long ago, a boomerang was used as a <u>weapon</u>.
  Ⓐ tool for hunting
  Ⓑ toy
  Ⓒ pot for cooking
  Ⓓ way of learning

2. If you throw it right, it should <u>return</u> to you.
  Ⓐ fly away
  Ⓑ come back
  Ⓒ talk back
  Ⓓ give joy

3. The <u>elbow</u> of the boomerang forms two wings.
  Ⓐ path
  Ⓑ bottom of the wing
  Ⓒ top of the wing
  Ⓓ bend in the middle

4. Hold it straight up and down and then <u>release</u> it.
  Ⓐ drop
  Ⓑ let go
  Ⓒ stand on
  Ⓓ bend

Hi-Lo Nonfiction Passages for Struggling Readers: Grades 4–5 • Scholastic Inc.

Name _____ Date _____

Word Work

> The letters **pl** stand for the beginning sounds in *plate*.
>
> The letters **fl** stand for the beginning sounds in *flag*.
>
> The letters **cl** stand for the beginning sounds in *cloud*.

Say each picture name. Complete the word by writing the letters that stand for the beginning sound.

1. ____ ock

2. ____ ug

3. ____ ower

4. ____ ant

5. ____ am

Read the words below. Write the word that completes each sentence.

play   fly   flat   climb   plane

6. Boomerangs are fun to _____ with.

7. They have wings like a _____.

8. The top of the wing is curved and the bottom is _____.

9. I like to _____ a hill and then throw it.

10. Then it can _____ high off the ground!

Write Now

In the article "*You Can't Throw a Boomerang Away,*" you read about an interesting and unusual thing to play with. If you could invent a new, unusual toy, what would it be? What would you call it? How would it work? What's interesting about it?

- Plan to write a description of a new toy. Use a web like the one shown to organize your ideas.

- Write a description of your toy. Use your web to help you. Draw your toy.

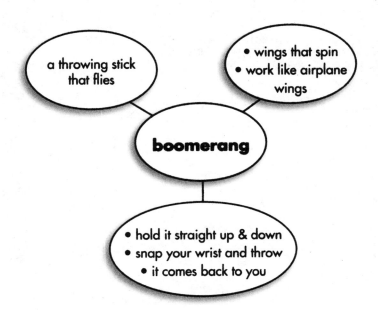

Hi-Lo Nonfiction Passages for Struggling Readers: Grades 4-5 • Scholastic Inc.

61

MEET A
Fine Feathered
DINO!

adapted by Darcy Hanlon

Scientists in China have found a fascinating fossil. A fossil is a very old rock with an **imprint**. The imprint shows the outline of an animal or a plant. Most fossils are millions of years old.

This fossil shows the imprint of a small dinosaur. The dinosaur was about three feet long. It lived about 150 million years ago.

The scientists have named the dinosaur *Sinosauropteryx prima* (sine-ah-sore-OP-terics PREE-ma).

What makes this fossil so special? It shows scientists something new and exciting. This little dinosaur had feathers!

Scientists have found feathers on fossils of birds. Now, the experts think that they may be able to prove that dinosaurs were the ancestors of birds.

Set Your Purpose

Are birds and dinosaurs alike? Read this article to find out.

An intact skeleton of a dinosaur is embedded in a smooth rock.

Fossilized dinosaur footprint

Birds and dinosaurs have a lot in common. **Skeletons** of ancient birds look very much like the skeletons of some dinosaurs. Many dinosaurs stood on two legs, just like birds. Some scientists say that certain dinosaurs look like birds without feathers.

Cathy Forster is a scientist who studies dinosaurs. She **believes** that if dinosaurs had feathers, they probably did not use them for flying. Dinosaurs were probably too heavy to fly. The **purpose** of the feathers may have been to keep the dinosaurs warm.

Scientists will continue to study the feathered fossil. They will search for more fossils in the same area of China. They hope to learn more about how birds and dinosaurs may be **related**.

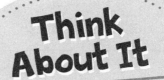

Think About It

Why do scientist think that dinosaurs might be related to birds?

Name _____ Date _____

Check Your **Understanding**

Fill in the letter with the best answer for each question.

1. What is the main idea of this article?
Ⓐ Scientists have found feathers on fossils of birds.
Ⓑ Dinosaurs and birds may be related.
Ⓒ A fossil is usually millions of years old.
Ⓓ Birds are dinosaurs.

2. Which detail supports the idea that the fossil they recently discovered is special?
Ⓐ It was found in China.
Ⓑ It is 150 million years old.
Ⓒ It shows scientists something new.
Ⓓ Scientists have found feathers on fossils of birds.

3. Which detail supports the idea that certain dinosaurs were similar to ancient birds?
Ⓐ Bird fossils were found in China.
Ⓑ They stood on two legs and had a similar skeleton.
Ⓒ Dinosaurs did not use feathers for flying.
Ⓓ They went south for the winter.

4. How do scientists hope to learn more about feathered dinosaurs?
Ⓐ by putting feathers on dinosaur models in museums
Ⓑ by finding more fossils of feathered dinosaurs
Ⓒ by reading more books
Ⓓ by interviewing dinosaurs

5. Cathy Forster thinks the purpose of dinosaur feathers may have been to
Ⓐ make dinosaurs lighter.
Ⓑ help dinosaurs fly.
Ⓒ help dinosaurs find food.
Ⓓ keep dinosaurs warm.

Vocabulary

Find each vocabulary word in the selection. The words and sentences around it will help you figure out its meaning.

Fill in the letter with the best definition of the underlined word.

1. A fossil shows an <u>imprint</u> of something.
Ⓐ movement
Ⓑ color
Ⓒ mark made by pressing something on a surface
Ⓓ letters made with a knife

2. <u>Skeletons</u> of ancient birds look very much like some dinosaur skeletons.
Ⓐ toenails Ⓒ arms and legs
Ⓑ wings Ⓓ frameworks of bones

3. Cathy Forster <u>believes</u> that dinosaurs with feathers probably could not fly.
Ⓐ doubts Ⓒ is sure
Ⓑ senses Ⓓ studies

4. The <u>purpose</u> of the feathers may have been to keep the dinosaurs warm.
Ⓐ color Ⓒ pile
Ⓑ use Ⓓ smoothness

5. Birds and dinosaurs may be <u>related</u>.
Ⓐ exciting Ⓒ exactly the same
Ⓑ different Ⓓ part of the same family

Hi-Lo Nonfiction Passages for Struggling Readers: Grades 4–5 • Scholastic Inc.

Name _____ **Date** _____

Word Work

Many verbs that end in **e** will drop the **e** when **-ed** or **-ing** is added.

share + ed = shared

share + ing = sharing

A **compound word** is made of two shorter words. To understand a compound word, separate it into the two shorter words and think about the meaning of those words.

headache = an **ache** in the **head**

Read each sentence. Add -ed or -ing to the word in dark type. Write the new word.

1. name The dinosaur is _____ *Sinosauropteryx prima.*

2. live It _____ 150 million years ago!

3. save Scientists are _____ the fossil so they can study it.

4. relate Dinosaurs and birds may be _____.

5. hope I keep _____ that I will find a fossil someday!

Read the definitions below. Join two words from each definition to make a compound word that fits the definition. Write the compound word.

Definitions:

6. a house for a bird _____

7. a bird that is blue _____

8. a storm of snow _____

9. like a bird _____

10. a nail on your toe _____

Write Now

In "Meet a Fine Feathered Dino!" you learned that dinosaurs and birds may be related. This Venn diagram shows how they are alike and how they are different.

Dinosaurs
• have long tails
• have 4 legs
• have jaws

Both
• have similar skeletons
• some dinosaurs and all birds stand on 2 legs
• some dinosaurs and all birds have feathers

Birds
• have wings
• have 2 legs
• have beaks

• Plan to write a short paragraph explaining whether you think dinosaurs and birds are related or not. Make a diagram like the one shown. Think of other details you could add to your diagram. Then write down ways in which dinosaurs and birds are alike or different.

• Write your paragraph. Use details from your diagram to help support your opinion.

A turtle hatching from a shell

Mystery on the Beach

by Pat Kenney

Set Your Purpose

The natural world has mysteries that no one can figure out. Read this article to find out about one of them.

One night in Mexico, on a beach lit only by moonlight, a baby is born. In the dark, the baby leaves the beach. She travels hundreds, maybe thousands, of miles away. Fifty years later, she returns to the same place where she was born.

Who is this mysterious female? She is a giant Kemp's ridley sea turtle.

Kemp's ridley turtles feed in the waters all along the **coastline** of North America. During the summer months, many swim as far north as Long Island, New York, to munch on crabs and other local **seafood**. But at nesting time, female Kemp's ridley turtles all head for the same place—the beach on the gulf coast of Mexico where they were born. How

Factoid:

Female sea turtles leave the water only when it's time to nest. Male sea turtles never leave the water.

they get back is a mystery. They have no map. No one points the way or gives them **directions**. Yet they never get lost.

The **arrival** of the Kemp's ridley turtles on this beach is called *arribada* (*arribada* means "arrival" in Spanish). It's an unbelievable show! All at once, all the turtles leave the water! It's as if they had **received** a silent underwater command to go ashore. The turtles dig nests in the sand. Then, as soon as they lay their eggs, they return to the water.

About eight weeks later, the baby turtles hatch. Under the cover of darkness, the babies find their way to the sea on their own. Someday, the females will return to this beach. How will they know when and where to go? That is the mystery!

Think About It

What is the mystery of the ridley turtles?

Name _____ Date _____

Check Your Understanding

Fill in the letter with the best answer for each question.

1. The main idea of the article is that female Kemp's ridley turtles

Ⓐ mysteriously return to the beach where they were born.

Ⓑ travel hundreds, maybe thousands, of miles.

Ⓒ lay eggs on a beach lit only by moonlight.

Ⓓ swim as far north as Long Island, New York.

2. The main idea of the third paragraph is that Kemp's ridley sea turtles

Ⓐ eat crabs and other seafood.

Ⓑ feed all along the coast of North America, up to Long Island.

Ⓒ swim long distances to feed, but return to their birthplace to nest.

Ⓓ live on a beach on the gulf coast of Mexico.

3. Which detail does not describe the nesting habits of ridley turtles?

Ⓐ *Arribada* means "arrival" in English.

Ⓑ All ridley turtles return to the same beach in Mexico to nest.

Ⓒ All at once, the turtles swim ashore.

Ⓓ They lay eggs in nests dug in the sand.

4. You can conclude that

Ⓐ one turtle tells the others what to do.

Ⓑ sea turtles live mostly on land.

Ⓒ sea turtles understand Spanish commands.

Ⓓ baby sea turtles do not need their mothers to survive.

5. The author of this selection wants to

Ⓐ persuade you to visit Mexico.

Ⓑ inform you about a mysterious animal.

Ⓒ tell you a funny story about turtles.

Ⓓ describe how sea turtles swim.

Vocabulary

Find each vocabulary word in the selection. The words and sentences around it will help you figure out its meaning.

Fill in the letter with the best definition of the underlined word.

1. The turtle has no <u>directions</u> to the beach.

Ⓐ light that comes from the moon

Ⓑ babies

Ⓒ instructions that tell how to get somewhere

Ⓓ hundreds of miles

2. Turtles are in the waters all along the <u>coastline</u> of North America.

Ⓐ area of land next to the ocean

Ⓑ summer

Ⓒ animal with a hard shell

Ⓓ food eaten by an animal

3. Turtles eat crabs and other <u>seafood</u>.

Ⓐ sandwiches   Ⓒ sand and wood

Ⓑ plants   Ⓓ fish and shellfish

4. The <u>arrival</u> of the turtles is an incredible show!

Ⓐ coming to a place   Ⓒ something amazing

Ⓑ type of turtle   Ⓓ someone who lives near the sea

5. It is as if the turtles had <u>received</u> a silent command.

Ⓐ dug   Ⓒ sent

Ⓑ gotten   Ⓓ hatched

Name _____   Date _____

Word Work

A **prefix** comes at the beginning of a word and changes the meaning of the word. Knowing the meaning of a prefix helps you figure out the meaning of the whole word. The prefix **re-** means "again." The prefix **un-** means "not." The prefix **under-** means "beneath" or "below."

reappear	to appear again
uncovered	not covered
underwater	beneath the water

Read the definitions below. Add the prefix *re-*, *un-*, or *under-* to the base word to make a new word that fits the definition.

1. turn around and come back again   _____ turn

2. not believable   _____ believable

3. beneath the ground   _____ ground

4. not explained   _____ explained

5. to make new again   _____ new

Synonyms are words that have similar meanings. For example, *big* and *large* are synonyms.

Fill in the letter with the synonym of the word in dark type.

6. No one gave the turtles **directions** to the beach.
Ⓐ instructions   Ⓒ thanks
Ⓑ tickets   Ⓓ questions

7. They only come out of the **sea** to lay their eggs.
Ⓐ lake   Ⓒ ocean
Ⓑ river   Ⓓ beach

8. The turtles are **incredible** to see.
Ⓐ ugly   Ⓒ frightening
Ⓑ amazing   Ⓓ strange

9. The baby turtles are very **small**.
Ⓐ fast   Ⓒ plump
Ⓑ big   Ⓓ little

10. They must move **fast** to get to the safety of the water.
Ⓐ hungry   Ⓒ quickly
Ⓑ dangerous   Ⓓ slowly

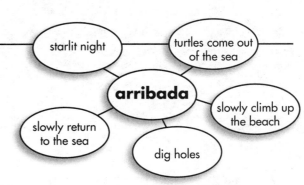

Write Now

"Mystery on the Beach" includes a description of the *arribada*, the arrival of the giant sea turtles on the beach. Skim the passage and try to imagine what it must be like.

- Plan to write a brief postcard message about the arrival of the turtles. First, brainstorm ideas for your message. Imagine yourself on the beach during *arribada*. Then complete a web like the one shown.

- Write your postcard message. Use ideas from your web. Draw a picture to go with your message.

People Take to the Skies

by Carole Osterink

PARIS, France — History was made over Paris today. A huge blue and gold balloon was seen over the city at sunset. It carried two passengers. The two

A twentieth-century hot-air balloon

men rode on a platform underneath the balloon. This is thought to be the first time humans flew.

Amazed **observers** could not believe what they saw. The balloon drifted for about 25 minutes across Paris. It then landed softly about five miles outside the city.

The balloon was seven stories tall. Two brothers, Joseph and Etienne Montgolfier, made it from silk and paper. Under the balloon was a fire. Joseph gave this **explanation** when asked how it worked.

"You can warm your hands over a candle. Why? Hot air moves upward. It forms a bubble over the candle. We made a big bubble of hot air. Then we trapped it in our balloon. We figured it would then rise. If the balloon was big enough, it would lift people up. It worked! We did it!"

A **visiting** American, Benjamin Franklin, watched the flight. He noted the importance of the straw-fed fire under the balloon. "We could see the fire as the balloon drifted **overhead**," he said. "When the passengers were as high as they wanted to be, they made less fire. This stopped the balloon from rising."

His Royal Highness, King Louis XVI of France, was also impressed. "This is a great invention," he **declared**. "I believe balloon flying will become a great sport!"

Think About It

How did the Montgolfier brothers get their balloon to fly?

In 1910, more than one hundred years after the Montgolfier brothers flew the first hot-air balloon over Paris, French spectators gathered to watch a balloon race.

Name _____   Date _____

Check Your Understanding

Fill in the letter with the best answer for each question.

1. What is the main idea of this selection?

   Ⓐ Two brothers used a balloon to achieve the first human flight.

   Ⓑ Two brothers enjoyed science.

   Ⓒ Paris looks beautiful from overhead.

   Ⓓ Silk can be used to make many things.

2. Where did the balloon passengers stand?

   Ⓐ inside the balloon

   Ⓑ on top of the balloon

   Ⓒ on a platform underneath the balloon

   Ⓓ five miles outside the city

3. Which sentence states the main idea of the fourth paragraph?

   Ⓐ Hot air over a candle warms your hands.

   Ⓑ The balloon rose because it contained a bubble of hot air.

   Ⓒ A big balloon could lift a heavy load.

   Ⓓ The brothers put hot air into the balloon.

4. Making the fire smaller makes the balloon fly lower because

   Ⓐ the balloon's silk becomes dry and expands.

   Ⓑ the balloon's silk becomes dry and shrinks.

   Ⓒ a smaller fire makes more hot air to fill the balloon.

   Ⓓ a smaller fire makes less hot air to fill and lift the balloon.

5. The author wrote this article to

   Ⓐ explain how paper, silk, and fire can lift humans.

   Ⓑ prove that Louis XVI was right.

   Ⓒ report the first time humans flew in a balloon.

   Ⓓ entertain readers with a funny story.

Vocabulary

> Find each vocabulary word in the selection. The words and sentences around it will help you figure out the meaning of the new word.

Fill in the letter with the best definition of the underlined word.

1. <u>Observers</u> said the balloon floated overhead for a long time.

   Ⓐ people who see or watch something

   Ⓑ people who ignore something

   Ⓒ people who run from something

   Ⓓ people who eat something

2. Joseph's <u>explanation</u> made perfect sense.

   Ⓐ reason for something

   Ⓑ pictures of something

   Ⓒ fuel used to run something

   Ⓓ people hired to build something

3. A <u>visiting</u> American saw the balloon in flight.

   Ⓐ having good eyesight

   Ⓑ having annoying habits

   Ⓒ living at a place permanently

   Ⓓ only staying for a short time

4. People could see the fire as the balloon drifted <u>overhead</u>.

   Ⓐ too much   Ⓒ high

   Ⓑ above   Ⓓ slowly

5. The king <u>declared</u> his approval of the flight.

   Ⓐ questioned   Ⓒ stated

   Ⓑ whispered   Ⓓ stole

Hi-Lo Nonfiction Passages for Struggling Readers: Grades 4–5 • Scholastic Inc.

Name _____   Date _____

Word Work

Many verbs that end with an **e** drop the e when **-ing** is added.

share → sharing

Add the suffix -ing to each verb. Write the new word.

1. note _____

2. declare _____

3. smile _____

4. like _____

5. hope _____

Synonyms are words that have similar meanings. For example, *large* and *big* are synonyms.

Read the sentences and the words below. Write the word that means almost the same as the word in dark type.

watched   gentle   float   flame   capture

6. Ben Franklin watched the balloon **drift** over the city of Paris. _____

7. The balloon made a **soft** landing in the country. _____

8. We **observed** as the silk balloon slowly filled with hot air. _____

9. The balloonist needed to **trap** hot air in the balloon. _____

10. Onlookers saw the **fire** coming from underneath the balloon. _____

Write Now

In the article "People Take to the Skies," you read about the Montgolfier brothers and their balloon. They achieved the first manned flight ever. It must have been a very exciting experience for Joseph and Etienne Montgolfier.

- Plan to write a journal entry. Imagine that you are Joseph or Etienne Montgolfier. It is November 21, 1783, and you have just returned from your first successful balloon flight. First, copy and complete the chart shown to help you organize your ideas.

- Write your journal entry about the first balloon flight. Remember to write the date: November 21, 1783. Use the notes you have written on your chart.

The First Balloon Flight	
What I saw	_____
How I felt	_____
The most exciting part	_____
The scariest part	_____

Sky Dancers

by Helena Agnew

Set Your Purpose

What do you think about when you see a kite in the sky? Read this article to find out what kites have meant to other people around the world.

They **swoop**. They dip. They toss their tails about. They catch the wind and glide high in the sky. What are these objects dancing in the wind? They are kites.

Kites have a long history. More than three thousand years ago, people in China made the first kites. They used bamboo—light, strong plant stems—to build the **frames**. Then they added silk to make the kite.

The kite became an important symbol in China. People flew kites to celebrate happy events like birthdays. They believed kites could help tell the future. Later, they used kites to study the weather. Some Chinese stories tell of how army generals used kites to **defeat** their enemies.

Soon kites came to other parts of Asia. In Japan, as in China, people believed that kites brought good fortune. However, while Chinese kites had been simple **rectangles**, Japanese kites took the forms of large birds, dragons, and fish.

After a while, the kite found its way from Asia to Europe. In the 1600s, young English children learned to make kites. People named the new toy "kite" because it glided like a kite—a bird of prey. Today, children and grown-ups all over the world enjoy flying kites.

Go Fly a Kite!

Kites can be many different shapes, sizes, and colors. Some kites are flat and diamond shaped. Some look like boxes. Other kites **flit** across the sky in the shapes of butterflies, birds, and even great white sharks. A kite may be one color or a rainbow of colors.

Today, kites are often made of nylon or plastic. Their frames may be a light metal. Some kites are still made of paper and wood. Whatever they look like, kites are fun. So the next time you have a chance, take a break! Go fly a kite!

Think About It

What facts did you learn about kites that surprised you? How will these facts change the way you look at kites?

Name _____ **Date** _____

Check Your **Understanding**

Fill in the letter with the best answer for each question.

1. What is the main idea of this article?
- Ⓐ Kites have a long and interesting history.
- Ⓑ Today, children and grown-ups enjoy flying kites.
- Ⓒ The kite is an important symbol in China.
- Ⓓ In Japan, people believed that kites brought good fortune.

2. What is the main idea of the section, "Go Fly a Kite!"?
- Ⓐ Most kites are very much alike.
- Ⓑ Kites flit across the sky in the shapes of butterflies and birds.
- Ⓒ Kites today are often made of nylon or plastic.
- Ⓓ Kites can be many different shapes, sizes, colors, and materials.

3. Where were the first kites made?
- Ⓐ America
- Ⓒ China
- Ⓑ Japan
- Ⓓ England

4. How do Japanese and Chinese kites differ?
- Ⓐ Chinese kites were rectangles; Japanese kites took different shapes.
- Ⓑ The Japanese made their kite frames from metal instead of bamboo.
- Ⓒ There were no differences.
- Ⓓ Japanese kites did not have long tails.

5. Why did the author write this article?
- Ⓐ to teach you how to make a kite
- Ⓑ to tell the history of kites
- Ⓒ to teach you how to fly a kite
- Ⓓ to help you understand Asia

Vocabulary

Find each vocabulary word in the selection. The words and sentences around it will help you figure out its meaning.

Fill in the letter with the best definition of the underlined word.

1. Kites fly, <u>swoop</u>, and toss their tails about.
- Ⓐ crash
- Ⓒ fall
- Ⓑ dip down
- Ⓓ spin around

2. The Chinese used bamboo to make their kites' <u>frames</u>.
- Ⓐ fronts of the kites
- Ⓑ names given to kites
- Ⓒ things that support and give shape
- Ⓓ things that give color

3. It was said that army generals used kites to <u>defeat</u> their enemies.
- Ⓐ win against in a war
- Ⓑ differ
- Ⓒ make friends with
- Ⓓ fly

4. Chinese kites had been simple <u>rectangles</u>.
- Ⓐ shapes with two sides
- Ⓑ shapes with three sides
- Ⓒ shapes with four sides
- Ⓓ shapes with five sides

5. Some kites <u>flit</u> across the sky in the shape of birds.
- Ⓐ change color quickly
- Ⓑ change into a butterfly
- Ⓒ become flat
- Ⓓ move or fly in a quick, light way

Hi-Lo Nonfiction Passages for Struggling Readers Grades 4-5 • Scholastic Inc.

Name _____ Date _____

Word Work

Synonyms are words that have similar meanings. For example, *happy* and *glad* are synonyms.

Fill in the letter with the synonym of the word in dark type.

1. The American flag is a **symbol** of freedom to Americans.
   Ⓐ history Ⓒ song
   Ⓑ sign Ⓓ enemy

2. The hawk **swooped** down and caught its prey, a small mouse.
   Ⓐ dipped Ⓒ celebrated
   Ⓑ danced Ⓓ chased

3. Butterflies **flit** from flower to flower.
   Ⓐ sit Ⓒ fly
   Ⓑ run Ⓓ sniff

4. Some people think that finding a penny brings good **fortune**.
   Ⓐ money Ⓒ ideas
   Ⓑ food Ⓓ luck

5. I'm sure you will **enjoy** that wonderful book.
   Ⓐ like Ⓒ toss
   Ⓑ hate Ⓓ connect

An **idiom** is a group of words used in a way that has a special meaning. This special meaning is different from the usual meaning of those words.

Read each sentence. The idiom is underlined. Find the meaning of the idiom below. Write the meaning.

clumsy   stop for a while   become
kidding you   be good at

6. Why not take a break from your chores, and fly a kite? _____

7. I'm not pulling your leg when I say that kites are fun to fly. _____

8. At first, you'll be all thumbs. _____

9. You'll soon get the hang of it. _____

10. In fact, flying a kite may turn out to be your favorite activity. _____

Write Now

In "Sky Dancers," you learned about the history of kites and that people all over the world enjoy flying them. What are some activities that you enjoy? Why do you enjoy them? Use the chart to write some ideas.

- Plan to write a paragraph about something you like to do for fun. Pick an idea from your chart and the reasons why this activity is fun for you.

- Write your paragraph. Your paragraph should explain your activity and why it is fun. Encourage others who want to try the activity to do so.

Fun Activities	Why They Are Fun

From Boy to PRESIDENT

adapted by Willena Richards

Do you know any 9-year-olds who have started their own museums? When Theodore Roosevelt was only nine, he and two of his cousins opened the "Roosevelt Museum of Natural History." The museum was in Theodore's bedroom. It had a total of 12 specimens. On display were a few seashells, some dead insects, and some birds' nests. Young Roosevelt took great pride in his small museum.

Set Your Purpose

What was one of our most popular presidents like as a child? Read this article to find out.

Born in New York in 1858, Theodore Roosevelt was not always healthy. "I was a sickly, **delicate** boy," he once wrote. Roosevelt had a health condition called asthma. He often found it hard to breathe. Instead of playing, he observed nature and then read and wrote about it.

Roosevelt's interest in nature sometimes got him into trouble. Once, his mother found **several** dead mice in the icebox. She demanded that the mice be thrown out. This was indeed "a loss to science," Roosevelt said later.

Because Roosevelt was often sickly as a boy, his body was small and frail. When he was about 12, his father **urged** him to improve his body. Roosevelt began working out in a gym. He didn't become strong quickly. But he did **decide** to face life's challenges with a strong spirit. That determination stayed with Roosevelt his whole life. And eventually his body did get strong. As an adult, he was an **active**, healthy person. He enjoyed adventures, and he loved the outdoors!

In 1900, at the age of 41, Roosevelt was elected Vice President. A year later, President McKinley was shot and killed. Roosevelt became our 26th President. At 42, he was the youngest leader the country had ever had.

Think About It

How would you describe young Theodore Roosevelt?

A toy company named the teddy bear for Theodore "Teddy" Roosevelt after it was learned that Roosevelt refused to shoot a baby bear while hunting.

Name _____ Date _____

Check Your **Understanding**

Fill in the letter with the best answer for each question.

1. What is the main idea of the first paragraph?
  Ⓐ Roosevelt had a natural history museum in his bedroom when he was a boy.
  Ⓑ The museum had 12 specimens.
  Ⓒ Roosevelt had two cousins.
  Ⓓ Roosevelt was a brave man.

2. Which sentence best tells the main idea of the second paragraph?
  Ⓐ Roosevelt loved the outdoors.
  Ⓑ Asthma makes it hard to run around and have fun.
  Ⓒ Roosevelt did not like to play.
  Ⓓ Roosevelt was a sickly child.

3. Which detail does not tell about Roosevelt as a boy?
  Ⓐ He opened his own natural history museum.
  Ⓑ He became President in 1901.
  Ⓒ He had asthma and often found it difficult to breathe.
  Ⓓ He once left a collection of dead mice in the icebox.

4. From the selection, you can draw the conclusion that
  Ⓐ Roosevelt's mother liked mice.
  Ⓑ Roosevelt respected his father's advice.
  Ⓒ everyone with asthma is small and frail.
  Ⓓ working out in a gym is a waste of time.

5. In which book might you find this selection?
  Ⓐ Small Nature Museums
  Ⓑ Living with Asthma
  Ⓒ The Childhoods of America's Presidents
  Ⓓ How the Teddy Bear Got Its Name

Vocabulary

Find each vocabulary word in the selection. The words and sentences around it will help you figure out its meaning.

Fill in the letter with the best definition of the underlined word.

1. "I was a sickly, <u>delicate</u> boy," he once wrote.
  Ⓐ not strong   Ⓒ not interested
  Ⓑ not happy   Ⓓ not friendly

2. Once, his mother found <u>several</u> dead mice in the icebox.
  Ⓐ some   Ⓒ hundreds of
  Ⓑ only one   Ⓓ exactly two

3. His father <u>urged</u> him to improve his body.
  Ⓐ created   Ⓒ buried
  Ⓑ suggested to   Ⓓ studied

4. He did <u>decide</u> to face life's challenges with a strong spirit.
  Ⓐ say angrily   Ⓒ make up one's mind
  Ⓑ refuse   Ⓓ confuse

5. We think of President Roosevelt as an <u>active</u>, healthy person.
  Ⓐ weak   Ⓒ interesting
  Ⓑ angry   Ⓓ busy and full of energy

Hi-Lo Nonfiction Passages for Struggling Readers: Grades 4–5 • Scholastic Inc.

Name _____   Date _____

Word Work

> Many one-syllable verbs that end with an **e** will drop the e when **-ed** or **-ing** is added.
>
> **race   raced   racing**

Add the suffix *-ed* to each verb. Write the new word.

1. place _____

2. bake _____

3. urge _____

4. work _____

5. stay _____

Read each sentence. Add the suffix *-ed* or *-ing* to the word in dark type.

6. **play**   Yesterday, I _____ outdoors.

7. **walk**   I saw a bear _____ near the river.

8. **hunt**   It was _____ for something to eat.

9. **move**   I _____ closer to take a picture.

10. **look**   When it _____ at me, I ran away.

Write Now

This list shows items Theodore Roosevelt had in the "Roosevelt Museum of Natural History."

> seashells
> dead insects
> birds' nests

- Plan to write a flyer inviting people to the opening of your own museum. What will you display? Look at the list shown. Then make a list of specimens, or items from nature, that your museum will contain.

- Write your flyer. Tell when and where the museum will open. Give examples of what will be on display. Use your list for ideas. You may wish to draw pictures of some of these items.

Hi-Lo Nonfiction Passages for Struggling Readers: Grades 4-5 • Scholastic Inc.

81

IT CAME FROM MARS!

adapted by Brendon O'Donnell

Set Your Purpose

Does life as we know it exist on Mars? Read this article to find out.

Not long ago, scientists **announced** that they had found tiny fossils inside a rock. (Fossils are the hardened remains of animals or plants that lived long ago.)

So? What was so important about this discovery? After all, scientists have been finding fossils in rocks on Earth for years.

The amazing part of this story is that the rock wasn't from Earth. It came from Mars, and the fossils could **prove** that there was life on Mars!

Does that mean that Martians exist? Well, the answer to that is "maybe," but not in the way you may have read about in science-fiction stories or seen in movies. Here's what scientists believe.

About 16 million years ago, a comet or asteroid slammed into Mars, causing an explosion. A **fragment** of rock broke off Mars and came flying toward Earth. A researcher found it in Antarctica in 1984.

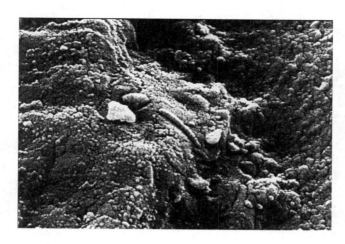

Is it a worm? Is it a bug? Whatever it is, this fossil came from Mars!

In 1993, scientists examined the rock with a powerful new microscope. They could tell that the rock came from Mars because of what they already knew about the surface of Mars. Then they made a **startling** discovery! Inside the rock, they found hardened traces of what looked like a very tiny worm! Did this mean that Mars could support life?

In July of 1997, scientists got a possible answer. That was when the spacecraft *Pathfinder* landed on Mars. It sent out a small robot car called a rover. Scientists **steered** the rover from Earth, by remote control, across Mars's surface. The rover discovered a place on Mars that showed signs of once having been filled with water. Since water is needed for life, this discovery might help prove what the fossils in the rock showed— life may have existed on Mars long, long ago!

Scientists continue to study the rock and the discoveries from the *Pathfinder* mission. Someday they hope to send a human to Mars to do more exploring! Maybe it will be you!

Think About It

What new information did you find out about possible life on Mars?

This robot car is called Mars Rover. It studied rocks on the planet Mars.

Name _____ Date _____

Check Your **Understanding**

Fill in the letter with the best answer for each question.

1. What is the main idea of "It Came From Mars!"?
- Ⓐ Scientists often find fossils.
- Ⓑ A piece of Mars slammed into Earth many years ago.
- Ⓒ Scientists may have proof that there once was life on Mars.
- Ⓓ Scientists continue to study Mars to look for fossils.

2. Which detail does <u>not</u> support the idea that there may have been life on Mars?
- Ⓐ A rock from Mars contained a tiny worm fossil.
- Ⓑ A rover is a robot car.
- Ⓒ Scientists found a place on Mars that was once filled with water.
- Ⓓ Water is needed for life.

3. Why was the discovery of fossils inside a rock important?
- Ⓐ A human may be sent to Mars someday.
- Ⓑ Weak microscopes can study fossils.
- Ⓒ The spacecraft explored Mars.
- Ⓓ It might be evidence that life once existed on Mars.

4. Which of these events happened first?
- Ⓐ A comet slammed into Mars.
- Ⓑ A researcher found a rock from Mars.
- Ⓒ Scientists found a fossil inside a Mars rock.
- Ⓓ The spacecraft *Pathfinder* landed on Mars.

5. What conclusion can you draw about life on Mars from the story?
- Ⓐ Life exists on Mars just as it does on Earth.
- Ⓑ No living things ever existed on Mars.
- Ⓒ Life may have existed on Mars once.
- Ⓓ Living things exist on all the planets.

Vocabulary

Find each vocabulary word in the selection. The words and sentences around it will help you figure out its meaning.

Fill in the letter with the best definition of the underlined word.

1. Scientists <u>announced</u> that they had found tiny fossils inside a rock.
- Ⓐ found
- Ⓒ looked for
- Ⓑ let people know
- Ⓓ put inside

2. Fossils could <u>prove</u> there was life on Mars.
- Ⓐ show to be true
- Ⓒ live
- Ⓑ ask
- Ⓓ come from

3. A rock <u>fragment</u> from Mars flew to Earth.
- Ⓐ something soft
- Ⓑ scientist that studies planets
- Ⓒ piece that has broken off
- Ⓓ event from the past

4. The scientists made a <u>startling</u> discovery.
- Ⓐ boring
- Ⓒ useless
- Ⓑ already known
- Ⓓ surprising

5. Scientists <u>steered</u> the rover by remote control.
- Ⓐ guided its direction
- Ⓑ discovered by scientific study
- Ⓒ built or created
- Ⓓ filled with water

Name _____ **Date** _____

Word Work

> **Synonyms** are words with similar meanings. For example, *tiny* and *small* are synonyms.

Read the sentences and the words below. Write the word that means almost the same as the underlined word.

piece   guided   surprising   crashed   found

1. Scientists <u>steered</u> the vehicle and its camera on the distant planet. _____

2. What they saw was <u>startling</u>. _____

3. They <u>discovered</u> a deep hole on the surface of the planet. _____

4. Inside the hole was a large <u>fragment</u> of rock. _____

5. A rock had <u>slammed</u> into the planet and made the hole. _____

> The letters **ar** stand for the sound you hear in c<u>ar</u>. The letters **er** stand for the sound you hear in ladd<u>er</u>. The letters **or** stand for the sound you hear in c<u>or</u>n.
>
> **c<u>ar</u>**   **ladd<u>er</u>**   **c<u>or</u>n**

Each sentence below has an incomplete word. Add *or*, *er*, or *ar* to complete the word.

6. M_____s is the fourth planet from the sun.

7. It is much small_____ than Earth.

8. It is twice as f_____ from the sun as Earth.

9. Nothing can live on Mars now because all its wat_____ is frozen.

10. No animals are being b_____n there now.

Write Now

Look at the chart. It shows some details from "It Came From Mars!"

- Plan to write a short essay about Mars. Copy and complete the chart on the right.

- Write your essay. Use the facts in your chart. Tell about the discoveries scientists have made.

16 million years ago	A piece of rock broke off from Mars and landed on Earth.
1984	
1993	
1997	Scientists studied the rock and found tiny worm fossils.

Set Your Purpose

Who is M.C. Escher?
What did he do?
Read this biography
to find out.

MEET M.C. ESCHER

by Barbara Linde

M.C. Escher is an **artist** who is famous for drawings that play tricks on your eyes. He was born in Holland in 1898. When he was in school, Maurits (MORE-its) Cornelis (cor-NEL-is) did not do well at most subjects, but he was skillful at drawing. His father thought M.C. might become an architect, a person who draws and designs buildings. In 1922, M.C. went to school to be an architect, but he and his teacher decided he should make drawings **instead**.

M.C. was a graphic artist. He drew pictures in pencil on paper. Sometimes he carved his pictures with a knife on a special block of wood. Then he would put ink on the block and **print** the block on paper. Escher was not a successful artist at first. He worked hard, but not many people **bought** his works. Even when he was not selling his drawings, he kept working.

M.C. Escher created drawings with puzzles and **visual** tricks in them because

Escher used patterns like this. You can probably see the dark birds. But do you also see the light ones?

he wanted people to inspect his drawings carefully. Many of Escher's works show animals or other images locked together like pieces of a puzzle. Half of the images might be drawn in a bright color, making them easy to see. However, the other half might be drawn in a different color that is not as easy to see. Drawings like Escher's are called optical illusions because they play tricks on your eyes.

By 1960, M.C. was making a lot of money, and he gave some of it to people who needed help. M.C. Escher died in 1972, but his artwork is still very popular.

You might wish to look at more of M.C. Escher's works. Maybe a museum near you has some of his prints. Check the library for books about him. Whenever you look at his prints, remember that M.C.'s drawings are puzzles and visual tricks. Try to solve the puzzles. It's a fun challenge!

Think About It

How would you describe M.C. Escher's works? What makes them special?

Name _____ Date _____

Check Your **Understanding**

Fill in the letter with the best answer for each question.

1. This selection tells about a famous
- Ⓐ artist.
- Ⓒ architect.
- Ⓑ teacher.
- Ⓓ engineer.

2. M.C. Escher went to school to become
- Ⓐ a graphic artist.
- Ⓒ an architect.
- Ⓑ a printer.
- Ⓓ like his father.

3. Which sentence supports the idea that M.C. Escher created pictures with visual tricks in them?
- Ⓐ He worked hard, but not many people bought his works.
- Ⓑ He drew pictures in pencil on paper.
- Ⓒ By 1960, M.C. was making a lot of money.
- Ⓓ Half of Escher's drawing might be in a color that is not so easy to see.

4. Escher kept drawing even when he was not making money. This shows that he had a
- Ⓐ good friend.
- Ⓑ strong will.
- Ⓒ lot of anger.
- Ⓓ family.

5. The author of the selection wants to
- Ⓐ buy some of M.C. Escher's artwork.
- Ⓑ learn to draw like M.C. Escher.
- Ⓒ tell about M.C. Escher's life and work.
- Ⓓ read about M.C. Escher at the library.

Vocabulary

Find each vocabulary word in the selection. The words and sentences around it will help you figure out its meaning.

Fill in the letter with the best definition of the underlined word.

1. Have you ever heard of an <u>artist</u> named M.C. Escher?
- Ⓐ person who plays sports
- Ⓑ person who writes news reports
- Ⓒ person who paints, makes things, or acts
- Ⓓ person who makes food

2. <u>Instead</u> of drawing buildings, M.C. drew puzzles.
- Ⓐ rather than
- Ⓒ the same as
- Ⓑ interested
- Ⓓ in a place

3. He would put ink on a block of wood and <u>print</u> the block on paper.
- Ⓐ color
- Ⓑ write
- Ⓒ tell in the news
- Ⓓ stamp or press on

4. M.C. worked hard, but not many people <u>bought</u> his works.
- Ⓐ looked at
- Ⓒ paid money for
- Ⓑ brought
- Ⓓ copied

5. Look closely at the <u>visual</u> tricks in M.C.'s drawings.
- Ⓐ having to do with hearing
- Ⓑ having to do with seeing
- Ⓒ having to do with smelling
- Ⓓ having to do with feeling

Hi-Lo Nonfiction Passages for Struggling Readers: Grades 4–5 • Scholastic Inc.

Name _____   Date _____

Word Work

> Many one-syllable verbs ending with an **e** will drop the e when **-ed** or **-ing** is added.
>
> **bake   baked   baking**

Add the suffix -ed to each verb. Write the new word.

1. carve   _____

2. talk   _____

3. like   _____

4. state   _____

5. smile   _____

Read each sentence. Add the suffix -ed or -ing to the word in dark type.

6. **draw**   M.C. Escher enjoyed _____ pictures.

7. **work**   Even when no one bought his prints, he _____ hard.

8. **make**   By 1960, M.C. Escher was _____ a lot of money.

9. **want**   He _____ people to look at his drawings carefully.

10. **stand** Parts of his drawings seem to be _____ up on the paper.

Write Now

This web shows words to describe M.C. Escher's work.

- Plan to write a short speech about M.C. Escher's work. Pretend that your class will soon go to a museum to see some of his art. What should you tell your classmates about Escher before they go? First, copy the word web. Then brainstorm words that describe Escher's art to finish the web.

- Write your speech. Use your word web to help you.

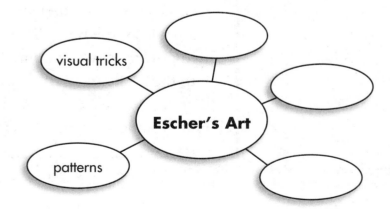

visual tricks

Escher's Art

patterns

Hi-Lo Nonfiction Passages for Struggling Readers: Grades 4–5 • Scholastic Inc.

89

Recognizing Cause & Effect

❖ When reading a story or an article, it's helpful to think about events and what caused them.

- As you read, ask yourself: **"What happened?"** and **"Why?"**

- The answer to **"What happened?"** tells you the **effect**.

- The answer to **"Why?"** tells you the **cause**.

❖ Read this paragraph. Look for the **cause** and **effect**.

Effect
The first sentence tells you **what happened**: *Plants wilt and die.*

Cause
The second sentence tells **why**: *Plants lose water through their leaves.*

Thirsty Plants

In dry times when there is little water, plants wilt and die. This happens because plants lose water through their leaves. To replace this water, they need a constant supply from the roots. This process serves two purposes. Water going from the leaves into the air helps keep the plant cool. Water flowing up the stem from the roots brings with it important minerals from the soil.

❖ You could chart the **cause/effect** in this article like this:

Cause: Why?	Effect: What Happened?
Plants lose water through their leaves.	Plants wilt and die.

Your Turn

❖ Read this article. Look for **causes** and **effects**. Make a chart like the one above.

High Waters

Floods happen most often in the spring. Snow melts off the mountains and turns to water. The water runs down into rivers. Rainstorms may add even more water to the rivers. The water rises and overflows the riverbanks. These high waters can flood fields and towns.

Some floods are called flash floods. They quickly form and can be fast and dangerous. Storms with a lot of rain can cause flash floods. Hard ground can't soak up the rain fast enough. Rivers run wild! Sometimes rushing waters sweep away houses and trees. Cars float down watery streets.

Wild, Wild Snowstorm

by Theresa Froberg

Set Your Purpose

Have you ever seen a
blizzard? Read this article
to find out about these
wild storms.

Think About It

What is the difference between a regular snowstorm and a blizzard?

A blizzard is a wild snowstorm. It snows for hours and hours. Sometimes, it snows for days! The air is freezing cold. Strong gusts of wind make trees **sway** and cause high snowdrifts. These **drifts** can bury cars. It might take days, even weeks, to uncover them!

Swirling snows cause whiteouts. That's when the sky and ground look like a big white sheet! It's easy to get lost in a whiteout.

Protect yourself and your pets during a blizzard. Stay inside until the snow stops. Then go out and have some fun!

Name _____   Date _____

Check Your Understanding

Fill in the letter with the best answer for each question.

1. Why do trees bend in a snowstorm?

   Ⓐ because the air is too hot

   Ⓑ because the wind is very strong

   Ⓒ because the sky is not bright

2. It is easy to get lost in a whiteout because

   Ⓐ you can see far ahead of you.

   Ⓑ cars can be buried under snow.

   Ⓒ everything looks white.

3. What causes a blizzard?

   Ⓐ freezing air, strong winds, and snow

   Ⓑ warm air, strong winds, and rain

   Ⓒ cool air, light winds, and ice

4. The word that best describes a blizzard is

   Ⓐ hot.

   Ⓑ silly.

   Ⓒ dangerous.

Vocabulary

> Find each vocabulary word in the selection. The words and sentences around it will help you figure out its meaning.

Fill in the letter with the best definition of the underlined word.

1. The wind made the trees <u>sway</u>.

   Ⓐ break into small pieces

   Ⓑ move from side to side

   Ⓒ jump up and down

2. Cars get buried in <u>drifts</u> of snow.

   Ⓐ boxes

   Ⓑ balls

   Ⓒ piles

3. <u>Swirling</u> snow causes whiteouts.

   Ⓐ moving in circles

   Ⓑ standing still

   Ⓒ going backwards

4. Stay inside to <u>protect</u> yourself.

   Ⓐ get sick

   Ⓑ keep safe

   Ⓒ learn new things

Name_____   Date_____

Word Work

The letters **dr** stand for the beginning sound in <u>dr</u>um.

The letters **fr** stand for the beginning sound in <u>fr</u>uit.

The letters **gr** stand for the beginning sound in <u>gr</u>ass.

drum   **fruit**   **grass**

Look at each picture. Write *dr*, *fr*, or *gr* to complete each picture name.

1. ___ apes
2. ___ og
3. ___ ess
4. ___ own
5. ___ agon

Read the words below. Write the word that completes each sentence.

fresh   drift   ground   friend   group

6. The blizzard left three feet of snow on the _____.

7. Everything looked _____ and new.

8. My best _____ and I went sledding at the park.

9. There was a big _____ of kids on the hill.

10. Our sled ran into a _____ of soft, fluffy snow.

Write Now

In the article "Wild, Wild Snowstorm," you read about blizzards. This chart shows some of the causes and effects of these wild storms.

Cause		Effect
strong winds	➡	swaying trees
swirling snow	➡	whiteout, easy to get lost
snowdrifts	➡	buried cars

- Plan to write a weather report about another kind of weather event, such as a very windy day, a long hot summer without rain, or a thunderstorm. Make a chart like the one you see here. Write the causes and effects.

- Write your weather report. Use your chart to help you tell what happens and why it happens. Use words such as *because*, *cause*, and *so*.

Hi-Lo Nonfiction Passages for Struggling Readers: Grades 4-5 • Scholastic Inc.

95

SHARK:
Friend or Enemy?

adapted by Jennifer Jasper

Set Your Purpose

What do you know about sharks? Read to find out more about these special creatures of the sea.

Swift, sleek sharks are among the most feared creatures of the sea. In the past, humans stayed away from them. Now humans who like to eat fish are eating sharks. Scientists worry that some kinds of sharks will disappear. They may soon be **endangered**.

Saving the shark is a challenge. Other fish lay hundreds of eggs at one time. Sharks might give birth to only one baby a year. Shark populations take years to grow.

Sharks have been around for 400 million years. Still, scientists do not know much about them. That is why there are many **myths** about sharks.

For instance, people think sharks love to eat humans. Sharks rarely **attack** humans. When they do, it may be because they think the human is a seal. Most sharks prefer seafood. Some eat only fish. Others eat sea mammals.

> **Shark Myth**
Sharks don't see well.

> **Shark Fact**
Sharks have powerful eyes. They can see better than humans can.

> **Shark Myth**
Sharks use their nostrils to breathe.

> **Shark Fact**
Like all fish, sharks use their nostrils to smell. They breathe through gills.

Sharks are at the top of the **ocean** food chain. They help keep sea life balanced. People need to learn more shark facts. If we do, we'll **discover** that sharks help the whole earth. We may even try harder to save them.

> **Shark Myth**
Sharks have peanut-size brains. They are not very smart.

> **Shark Fact**
Shark brains are quite large. Sharks can be trained.

> **Shark Myth**
Sharks will eat anything—even humans.

> **Shark Fact**
Sharks are picky eaters.

Think About It

What did you learn about sharks? Did this selection help you look at sharks in a different way? How?

Name _____   Date _____

Check Your Understanding

Fill in the letter with the best answer for each question.

1. Why are scientists worried that the shark will die out?

Ⓐ There isn't enough oxygen left in the oceans for the sharks to breathe.

Ⓑ Sharks lay hundreds of eggs, but most of them do not live.

Ⓒ Humans are now eating sharks.

Ⓓ People are eating the fish that sharks like to eat.

2. Why does it take a long time for the shark population to grow?

Ⓐ Sharks are picky eaters.

Ⓑ Sharks attack and kill each other in large numbers.

Ⓒ Sharks don't take care of their babies.

Ⓓ Sharks give birth to only one baby each year.

3. According to the article, what could happen if people learn more about sharks?

Ⓐ They might try harder to save them.

Ⓑ They might figure out better ways to catch them.

Ⓒ They might start keeping them as pets.

Ⓓ They might find out that sharks are harmful.

4. Which of the following is an opinion?

Ⓐ Sharks have powerful eyes.

Ⓑ Sharks are beautiful animals.

Ⓒ Sharks can be trained.

Ⓓ Sharks have gills.

5. Why did the author write this article?

Ⓐ to tell a funny story about sharks

Ⓑ to encourage people to hunt sharks

Ⓒ to teach people to eat sharks

Ⓓ to convince people to protect sharks

Vocabulary

Find each vocabulary word in the selection. The words and sentences around it will help you figure out its meaning.

Fill in the letter with the best definition of the underlined word.

1. Some kinds of sharks will disappear. They may soon be <u>endangered</u>.

Ⓐ changed   Ⓒ at risk of being wiped out

Ⓑ popular   Ⓓ at risk of becoming too many

2. There are many <u>myths</u> about sharks.

Ⓐ reptiles   Ⓒ books containing information

Ⓑ commands   Ⓓ ideas or beliefs that are not true

3. Sharks rarely <u>attack</u> humans.

Ⓐ ask for   Ⓒ try to hurt or kill

Ⓑ connect to   Ⓓ make a hole by poking

4. Sharks are at the top of the <u>ocean</u> food chain.

Ⓐ the desert

Ⓑ areas with many trees

Ⓒ an area too cold for anything to grow

Ⓓ a large body of salt water

5. People will <u>discover</u> that sharks help the whole earth.

Ⓐ be angry   Ⓒ learn or find out

Ⓑ leave open   Ⓓ worry about

Word Work

Antonyms are words that have opposite meanings. For example, *true* and *false* are antonyms.

A **noun** names a person, place, or thing. A **plural noun** names more than one person, place, or thing. To form the plural of most nouns, add *-s*.

Singular	Plural
creature	creatures
human	humans

Write the word that means the opposite of the underlined word.

truths   slow   easy   protect   often

1. Scientists don't want people to <u>attack</u> the shark.

_____

2. Most stories about sharks are <u>myths</u>.

_____

3. A shark will <u>rarely</u> approach a person.

_____

4. Most people find it <u>hard</u> to forget myths about sharks.   _____

5. A shark is <u>swift</u> and powerful.

_____

Write the plural form of the word that best completes each sentence.

eye   water   tiger   hammer   stripe

6. Hammerhead sharks live in warm ocean

_____.

7. Their heads are shaped like _____.

8. Their _____ and nostrils are on the ends of their hammer-shaped heads.

9. Tiger sharks have _____ on their bodies.

10. The markings are like those on _____.

Write Now

Read this list of facts about sharks.

Shark populations are slow to grow.
Sharks rarely attack humans.
Sharks keep sea life balanced.

• Plan to write a letter to a newspaper about saving sharks. First, make a list of facts about sharks. You can begin by copying this list. Add other ideas from the selection and what you already know about sharks.

• Use the facts from your list to write a letter to a newspaper. Explain why you think people should try to protect and save sharks. Use strong language that will make readers agree with you. Include words such as *must, should, have to,* and so on.

Titanic!

by Pat Cusick

Set Your Purpose

Why is the *Titanic* such a famous ship? Read this article to find out.

People said it was the safest ship ever built. It was the largest, for sure. How was it for the first-class passengers? No other ship could top its style. It had a big **gym**, tennis courts, and a huge swimming pool. There were elegant dining rooms and ballrooms. They called it a "floating palace."

It set sail for New York with about 2,000 people on board. Imagine all the food and drink on that ship! There were over 40 tons of potatoes and over 6,000 pounds of butter. There were more than two tons of coffee to drink.

Not long into the trip, the *Titanic* **struck** an iceberg. The "safest ship" began to sink. In that **moment**, the captain knew what would happen. Many people would die. Why? There were not enough lifeboats. The ship and its passengers sank to the bottom of the sea.

About 1,500 people died that night. How could something so **awful**, so terrible, happen? Why weren't there enough lifeboats? Some people say the builders took shortcuts. They wanted the ship to sail even though it wasn't ready.

In 1986 the **wreck** of the *Titanic* was found. Divers removed and brought up more than 5,000 artifacts. These included jewelry and coins. Postcards and magazines were found, too. The wreckage told the real story. The ship had split in two and scattered pieces of people's lives all over the ocean floor. What was believed to be the safest ship is now famous for a very sad ending.

"All the News That's Fit to Print."

The New York Times.

THE WEATHER.
Unsettled Tuesday; Wednesday, fair, cooler; moderate southerly winds, becoming variable.

VOL. LXI...NO. 19,806. NEW YORK, TUESDAY, APRIL 16, 1912.—TWENTY-FOUR PAGES. ONE CENT In Greater New York, Jersey City, and Newark. Elsewhere TWO CENTS

TITANIC SINKS FOUR HOURS AFTER HITTING ICEBERG; 866 RESCUED BY CARPATHIA, PROBABLY 1250 PERISH; ISMAY SAFE, MRS. ASTOR MAYBE, NOTED NAMES MISSING

M. Astor and Bride, dor Straus and Wife, nd Maj. Butt Aboard.

ULE OF SEA" FOLLOWED

nen and Children Put Over Lifeboats and Are Supposed to be Safe on Carpathia.

KED UP AFTER 8 HOURS

ent Astor Calls at White Star fice for News of His Father and Leaves Weeping.

NKLIN HOPEFUL ALL DAY

ager of the Line Insisted anic Was Unsinkable Even fter She Had Gone Down.

AD OF THE LINE ABOARD

Bruce Ismay Making First Trip on Gigantic Ship That Was to Surpass All Others.

admission that the Titanic, the st steamship in the world, had sunk by an iceberg and had gone bottom of the Atlantic, probably ing more than 1,400 of her pas-ers came with her, was made the White Star Line offices, 9 dway, at 8:20 o'clock last night. P. A. S. Franklin, Vice President General Manager of the Inter-al Mercantile Marine, conceded that ably only those passengers who picked up by the Cunarder Car-ta had been saved. Advices re-ed early this morning tended to ase the number of survivers by

admission followed a day in h the White Star Line officials been optimistic in the extreme. At time was the admission made that y one aboard the huge steamer was safe. The ship itself, it was confi-ly asserted, was unsinkable, and irers were informed that she would h port, under her own steam prob-, but surely with the help of the e liner Virginian, which was re-ed to be towing her.

the day passed, however, with no authentic reports from the Titanic ny of the ships which were known ave responded to her wireless call help, it became apparent that au-tic news of the disaster probably d come only from the Titanic's sis-ship, the Olympic. The wireless e of the Olympic is 500 miles. That e Carpathia, the Parisian, and the inian is much less, and as they ed the position of the Titanic they further and farther out of shore e. From the Titanic's position at time of the disaster it is doubtful iy of the ships except the Olympic d establish communication with

nic Sank at 2:20 A. M. Monday. the White Star offices the hope held out all day that the Parisian the Virginian had taken off some the Titanic's passengers, and efforts made to get into communication these liners. Until such commu-tion was established the White officials refused to recognize the ibility that there were none of the nic's passengers aboard them. by nightfall came the message Capt. Haddock of the Olympic at Race, Newfoundland, telling of rescue of 655 of the passengers by Cunarder Carpathia, which the eless message said, reached the posi-of the Titanic at daybreak. All found there, however, was life-s and wreckage. The biggest ship

Franklin admitted late last night

The Lost Titanic Being Towed Out of Belfast Harbor.

CAPT. E. J. SMITH,
Commander of the Titanic.

hours before the expected arrival of the Virginian and the Parisian.

It is unbelievable, so White Star Line officials were compelled to concede finally, that the Carpathia should have failed to pick up every lifeboat which still floated on the waves. If they failed to pick up more than 655 passen-gers, it was because the others of the ship's complement had gone with her to the bottom.

But it was not until nearly night-fall that the extent of the disaster was realized. Before that the reas-suring nature of the bulletins issued by the White Star line was sufficient to quiet the fears of those who had

THE PROBABLE LOSS.
Number Aboard.

First cabin	825
Second cabin	285
Steerage	710
Crew, (estimated)	900
Total	2,120
Saved.	
By the Carpathia	806
Probably drowned	1,254

1,465 Lives Lost First Report.

layed immediately to the White Star offices, but Mr. Franklin positively declined to make the text of the mes-sage public. He offered still the hope that passengers were aboard the Pari-sian and the Virginian, and even

and when Capt. Haddock's message proved this to be untrue only the ad-mission was made at the White Star offices that the Titanic had sunk. Mr. Franklin said that Capt. Haddock's message was brief and "neglected to say that all the crew had been saved." But the inference was not that all the passengers had been saved. Rather it was that many of them had died, and presently Mr. Franklin admitted the fear that there had been a terrible loss of life on the Titanic.

As far as we know the situation tanic is less, however, ... this statement, declaring ... At 9 o'clock, however ... concerning this ... We have heard from Halifax that three steamers were at the scene of the Titanic's sinking, namely, the Virgin-ian, the Parisian, and the Carpathia. We have heard from Capt. Haddock of the Olympic, who says that the Ti-tanic sank at 2:20 o'clock this morning. Haddock also informs us that the Car-pathia has 675 survivors on board. This version of Capt. Haddock's ... ourselves whether or not any of the Titanic's passengers are aboard the Allan liners.

We are hopeful that the rumors which have reached us by telegraph from Hali-fax that there are passengers aboard the Virginian and the Parisian will prove to be true, and that these vessels will turn up with some of the passen-gers. It is the loss of life of the passen-gers. It is very difficult to say whether this thing or any ...

Biggest Liner Plunged to the Bottom at 2:20 A.M.

RESCUERS THERE TOO LATE

Except to Pick Up the Few Hun-dreds Who Took to the Lifeboats.

WOMEN AND CHILDREN FIRST

Cunarder Carpathia, Rushing to New York with the Survivors.

SEA SEARCH FOR OTHERS

The Californie Stands By on Chance of Picking Up Other Boats or Rafts.

OLYMPIC SENDS THE NEWS

Only Ship to Flash Wireless Mes-sages to Shore After the Disaster.

LATER REPORT SAVES 866.

BOSTON, April 15.—A wireless message picked up late to-night, relayed from the Olympic, says that the Carpathia is on her way to New York with 866 passengers from the steamer Titanic aboard. They are mostly women and chil-dren, the message said, and it con-cluded: "Grave fears are felt for the safety of the balance of the passengers and crew."

Special to The New York Times.

CAPE RACE, N. F., April 1 —The White Star liner Olymp reports by wireless this evenin that the Cunarder Carpath reached, at daybreak this morn ing, the position from which wire less calls for help were sent ou last night by the Titanic after he collision with an iceberg. Th Carpathia found only the lifeboa and the wreckage of what ha been the biggest steamship afloa

The Titanic had foundered a about 2:20 A. M., in latitud 41:16 north and longitude 50:1 west. This is about 30 minute of latitude, or about 34 miles, du south of the position at which sh struck the iceberg. All her boa accounted for; about 655 ... ve been saved of the cre ... gers, most of the latt ... women and childre about 2,100 person ... Titanic.

nyland liner California ... and searching the pos ... disaster, while the Ca ... returning to New Yor ... survivors.

be positively state tha ... 11 o'clock to-night noth ng whatever had been receiv at or heard by the Marconi sta tion here to the effect that the Parisian, Virginian or any othe ships had picked up any surviv ors, other than those picked by the Carpathia.

First News of the Disaster.

PARTIAL LIST OF THE SAVED.

Includes Bruce Ismay, Mrs. Widener, Mrs. H. B. Harris, and an Incomplete name, suggesting Mrs. Astor's.

CAPE RACE, N. F., Tuesday, April 16.—Following is a partial list of survivors among the first-class passengers of the Titanic, received by the Marconi wireless station this morning from the Carpa-thia, via the steamship Olympic:

Mrs. JACOB P. ——— and maid.
Mr. HARRY ANDERSON.
Mrs. ED. W. APPLETON.
Mrs. ROSE ABBOTT.
Miss G. M. BURNS.
Mrs. D. D. CASSEBERE.
Mrs. WM. M. CLARKE.
Mrs. B. CHIBINACE.
Miss E. G. CROSSBIE.
Miss H. ROSEBIE.
Miss JEAN HIPACK.
Mrs. HY. B. HARRIS.
Mrs. ALEX. HALVERSON.
Miss MARGARET BATS.
Mr. BRUCE ISMAY.
Mr. and Mrs. ED. KIMBERLEY.
Mr. P. A. KENNYMAN.
Miss EMILE KENCHEN.
Miss G. F. LONGLEY.
Mrs. A. F. LEADER.
Miss BERTHA LAVORY.
Mrs. ERNEST LIVES.
Miss MARY CLINES.
Mrs. SINGRID LINDSTROM.
Mr. GUSTAVE J. LESNEUR.
Miss GIORGETTA A. MADILL.
Mme. MELICARD.
Mrs. TUCKER and maid.
Mr. J. B. THAYER.
Mr. J. B. THAYER, Jr.
Mr. HENRY WOOLMER.
Mrs. ANNA WARD.
Mr. RICHARD M. WILLIAMS.
Miss HELEN A. WILSON.
Miss WILLARD.
Miss MARY WICKS.
Mrs. GEO. D. WIDENER and ma
Mrs. J. STEWART WHITE.
Mrs. MARIE YOUNG.
Mrs. THOMAS POTTER, Jr.
Mrs. EDNA S. ROBERTS.
Countess of ROTHES.

Mr. C. ROLMANE.
Mrs. SUSAN P. ROGERSON. (Prob-ably Ryerson).
Miss EMILY B. ROGERSON.
Mrs. ARTHUR ROGERSON.
Master ALLISON and nurse.
Miss K. T. ANDREWS.
Miss NINETTE PANHART.
Mr. E. W. ALLEN.
Mr. and Mrs. D. BISHOP.
Mr. H. BLANK.
Miss A. BASSINA.
Mrs. JAMES BAXTER.
Mr. GEORGE A. BAYT——
Miss C. BONNELL.
Mrs. J. M. BROWN.
Mrs. G. C. BOWEN.
Mr. and Mrs. R. J.
Miss RUTH ——
Miss ELL——
Mr. and ——
GILBE——
M——

Mrs. WILLIAM BUCKNELL.
Mrs. O. H. BARKWORTH.
Mrs. H. B. STEFFASON.
Mrs. ELSIE BOWERMAN.

The Marconi station reports that it missed the word after "Mrs. Jacob P." In a list received by the Associated Press this morning this name appeared well down, but in THE TIMES list it is first, suggesting the name of Mrs. John Jacob Astor is intended. This sup-position is strengthened by the fact that, except for Mrs. H. J. Allison, Mrs. Astor is the only lady in the "A" col-'s pasenger list attended

BOSTON, ...

Think About It

Why do we remember the *Titanic*?

Name _____ **Date** _____

Check Your Understanding

Fill in the letter with the best answer for each question.

1. The *Titanic* started to sink because it had
- Ⓐ sailed too fast.
- Ⓑ hit an iceberg.
- Ⓒ rained so hard.
- Ⓓ no lifeboats.

2. Because there were not enough lifeboats
- Ⓐ people died.
- Ⓑ people swam for shore.
- Ⓒ people complained to the captain.
- Ⓓ people did nothing.

3. Because the wreck of the *Titanic* was found
- Ⓐ workers are starting to rebuild the ship.
- Ⓑ more than 5,000 artifacts have been brought up.
- Ⓒ we learned how much food was on board.
- Ⓓ traveling by ship is safer today.

4. What shape was the *Titanic* in when the divers found it?
- Ⓐ It was ready to set sail.
- Ⓑ It was hitting an iceberg.
- Ⓒ It was split in two.
- Ⓓ It was not there.

5. The *Titanic* had been called a "floating palace" because it
- Ⓐ belonged to the king and queen.
- Ⓑ was very old.
- Ⓒ had a huge house on it.
- Ⓓ was big and elegant.

Vocabulary

Find each vocabulary word in the selection. The words and sentences around it will help you figure out its meaning.

Fill in the letter with the best definition of the underlined word.

1. Passengers could work out in a big <u>gym</u>.
- Ⓐ room with many windows
- Ⓑ room for doing exercises and playing games
- Ⓒ place where people eat dinner
- Ⓓ room that has lifeboats in it

2. The *Titanic* sank because it <u>struck</u> an iceberg.
- Ⓐ destroyed
- Ⓑ went through
- Ⓒ went around
- Ⓓ hit with force

3. It took only a <u>moment</u> for the boat to break apart.
- Ⓐ key
- Ⓑ hour
- Ⓒ short time
- Ⓓ long year

4. It was an <u>awful</u> disaster.
- Ⓐ wonderful
- Ⓑ small
- Ⓒ exciting
- Ⓓ terrible

5. The <u>wreck</u> of the *Titanic* was found in 1986.
- Ⓐ place to hang coats
- Ⓑ food
- Ⓒ remains of something that has been destroyed
- Ⓓ game room

Name _____ Date _____

Word Work

A **prefix** comes at the beginning of a word and changes the meaning of the word. Knowing the meaning of a prefix helps you figure out the meaning of the whole word. The prefix **re-** means "again." The prefix **dis-** means "not."

reopen   to open again

disbelief   the state of not believing

Read the definitions below. Add the prefix **re-** or **dis-** to each base word to make a new word that fits the definition.

1. not to continue   _____ continue

2. paint again   _____ paint

3. not to favor   _____ favor

4. heat again   _____ heat

5. not honest   _____ honest

Fill in the letter with the correct definition of the word in dark type.

6. redo
  Ⓐ not do   Ⓒ done wrong
  Ⓑ do again   Ⓓ done correctly

7. disagree
  Ⓐ agree again   Ⓒ do not agree
  Ⓑ agree after   Ⓓ agree

8. renew
  Ⓐ not new   Ⓒ very new
  Ⓑ make new again   Ⓓ make old

9. dislike
  Ⓐ like a lot   Ⓒ do not like
  Ⓑ like again   Ⓓ like a little

10. disappeared
  Ⓐ went out of sight   Ⓒ appeared
  Ⓑ was seen again   Ⓓ was soon seen

Write Now

In the selection "Titanic!" you learned that the divers found many jewels and coins. They found personal belongings, too. Imagine that a diary was found in an airtight box on the *Titanic*. The last entry in the diary might look like the one on the right.

I have just heard a loud cracking sound. I wonder what it is . . .

- Plan to complete the journal entry. Imagine what a passenger on the *Titanic* might have heard, seen, and felt immediately after the ship hit the iceberg.

- Write the rest of the diary entry. Use details from the article and what you already know to help you.

Hi-Lo Nonfiction Passages for Struggling Readers: Grades 4-5 • Scholastic Inc.

103

BALLOONS GALORE!

by Martina Hanson

Set Your Purpose

Where can you see dogs and cats fly? Read this article to find out about a festival called the Balloon Fiesta.

Can dogs fly? How about cows? They can when they are hot-air balloons, like these! They are from the Balloon Fiesta in Albuquerque, New Mexico.

For nine days every year, Albuquerque has a big balloon party. Hundreds of balloons go up in the air at the same time. It looks wonderful!

Look! Over there! It's a giant floating piggy bank! There is a cat! Oh, there is a bird! Look at the dragon! It's the Special Shape Rodeo. These balloons are very, very big. It looks like a **zoo** in the air.

Now it's twilight at the Balloon Fiesta. So why isn't it dark? It is time for the Balloon Glow. Hundreds of balloons are tied to the ground. That way, they cannot **rise**. People put special lights in the balloons. They light up the night. The Balloon Glow is so popular that it is now held on two nights instead of just one.

Some people like their balloons to be **swift**. They race their balloons in contests. In 1998, a team flew 1,388 miles. They flew almost to the North Pole. That's a long way!

The Albuquerque Balloon Fiesta **lasts** for nine days. You will **relive** the good times you have there for many years.

Think About It

What are some of the things you can see at the Balloon Fiesta?

Name _____ Date _____

Check Your **Understanding**

Fill in the letter with the best answer for each question.

1. The balloons look wonderful because they
Ⓐ are all red.
Ⓑ all go up at the same time.
Ⓒ are all wet.
Ⓓ all look like birds.

2. It is not dark in the evening because
Ⓐ there is a full moon.
Ⓑ people have flashlights.
Ⓒ it is time for the Balloon Glow.
Ⓓ people have candles.

3. Now there are two Balloon Glow nights because
Ⓐ the people like it so much.
Ⓑ there are too many balloons for one night.
Ⓒ the fiesta needs the lights.
Ⓓ the city needs the lights.

4. During the Special Shape Rodeo, the sky looks
Ⓐ dark.
Ⓑ cloudy.
Ⓒ like a giant zoo.
Ⓓ like a giant toy box.

5. The Balloon Fiesta
Ⓐ does not go on if it rains.
Ⓑ happens two times every year.
Ⓒ has a lot of music.
Ⓓ goes on for nine days.

Vocabulary

Find each vocabulary word in the selection. The words and sentences around it will help you figure out its meaning.

Fill in the letter with the best definition of the underlined word.

1. With so many animal shapes flying, it looked like a <u>zoo</u> in the air.
Ⓐ large airplane
Ⓑ place where animals are kept
Ⓒ field to grow crops
Ⓓ place where birds can fly

2. Tied to the ground, the balloons cannot <u>rise</u>.
Ⓐ come down   Ⓒ move
Ⓑ ripen   Ⓓ go up

3. Some people like their balloons to be <u>swift</u> so that they can win races.
Ⓐ fast   Ⓒ slow
Ⓑ sweet   Ⓓ first

4. The balloon festival <u>lasts</u> for nine days.
Ⓐ ends fast   Ⓒ goes on
Ⓑ loses   Ⓓ is fun

5. You will <u>relive</u> the good times you had at the Balloon Fiesta.
Ⓐ live out   Ⓒ forget
Ⓑ return   Ⓓ remember

Name _____   Date _____

Word Work

Some words have more than one meaning. You can often figure out the meaning of a word by looking at how the word is used in a sentence. For example, the word *row* has two different meanings—"a line" and "to paddle."

Decide if each underlined word has meaning A or B. Fill in the letter with the correct answer.

1. Can dogs <u>fly</u>?
   Ⓐ to go through the air
   Ⓑ a bug with two wings

2. Some balloons look like piggy <u>banks</u>.
   Ⓐ land on the side of a river
   Ⓑ places to keep money

3. Wouldn't the balloon race be fun to <u>watch</u>?
   Ⓐ to look at
   Ⓑ a small clock

4. Hundreds of balloons are <u>tied</u> to the ground.
   Ⓐ held down with ropes
   Ⓑ having the same score

5. The balloons <u>light</u> up the night.
   Ⓐ not heavy
   Ⓑ to make bright

A **contraction** is two words joined to make one. One or more letters have been left out. The apostrophe (') shows where the letters were left out.

could + not = couldn't

Fill in the letter of the contraction formed by the two words in dark type.

6. would not
   Ⓐ wouldn't   Ⓑ weren't

7. it is
   Ⓐ it'll   Ⓑ it's

8. that is
   Ⓐ that'll   Ⓑ that's

9. you will
   Ⓐ you'll   Ⓑ you'd

10. do not
   Ⓐ doesn't   Ⓑ don't

Write Now

In the article "Balloons Galore!" you learned about the fun things to do at the Balloon Fiesta. If you could suggest an event for the fiesta, what would it be?

• Plan to write a description of a new balloon event at the Balloon Fiesta. Look back in the article to see how the events are described. Use a web like the one shown to help you organize your thoughts.

• Write your description of a new event for the Balloon Fiesta. Use your web to help you.

Hi-Lo Nonfiction Passages for Struggling Readers: Grades 4–5 • Scholastic Inc.

107

Why Are the Fish Swimming in the Forest?

by Rona Laird

Set Your Purpose

What is a kelp forest? Where does a kelp forest grow?

You are in a forest. Huge green plants surround you. From the corner of your eye, you sense movement. You look toward a pile of rocks. There, you see bright orange fish **darting** in and out of the rocks.

Fish! What are fish doing in the forest? Where are you, anyway?

You are under the ocean in a kelp forest. Kelp is a kind of seaweed that grows big and tall. It grows best and fastest in seas that are clear and cool. When a **cluster** of these plants grow together they make a kelp forest. Like forests on land, a large variety of creatures live in the beautiful kelp forests, including the garibaldi fish, sea otter, and octopus.

Garibaldi Fish

Garibaldi (gar-uh-BAWL-dee) fish live and nest in kelp. These colorful orange fish lay eggs on the sea floor in the kelp. The fish guard the nest until the eggs **hatch**. Their bright orange color warns enemies to stay away.

Sea Otter

Sea otters sleep and eat in kelp. They wrap strands of kelp around their bodies. This keeps the otters from **drifting** away. Sea otters find their favorite food in kelp— clams and sea urchins. Urchins live in kelp, but urchins eat kelp. They eat lots and lots of it. If there were no sea otters to eat urchins, the urchins would eat too much kelp. The kelp forests would start to die. The animals that live in kelp might die, too.

Octopus

An octopus can change color to hide from its enemies. Octopuses that live in kelp change color to **blend** in with the bottom of the kelp plants.

Think About It

How are kelp forests different from land forests? How are they like land forests?

Name_____   Date_____

Check Your **Understanding**

Fill in the letter with the best answer for each question.

1. Why do sea otters wrap kelp around their bodies?
- Ⓐ to hide from clams and sea urchins
- Ⓑ to scare off their enemies
- Ⓒ to keep from drifting away
- Ⓓ to cool themselves off

2. What could happen if sea otters did not live in the kelp forests?
- Ⓐ The sea urchins would eat too much kelp.
- Ⓑ They would not be able to hide there.
- Ⓒ Kelp would stop growing.
- Ⓓ Octopuses would eat all the fish eggs.

3. What may happen if a kelp forest dies?
- Ⓐ Otters would eat the garibaldi fish.
- Ⓑ Sea urchins would not be able to hide from octopuses.
- Ⓒ The sea would not stay clear and cool.
- Ⓓ The animals that live in that kelp forest might die, too.

4. What is kelp?
- Ⓐ a kind of seaweed that grows big and tall
- Ⓑ a bright orange fish
- Ⓒ a rocky area with small plants and few animals
- Ⓓ a kind of clam that otters eat

5. How are the garibaldi fish and octopus alike?
- Ⓐ They can both change colors.
- Ⓑ Their coloring helps keep them safe from enemies.
- Ⓒ They are both brightly colored.
- Ⓓ They both blend in with their surroundings.

Vocabulary

Find each vocabulary word in the selection. The words and sentences around it will help you figure out its meaning.

Fill in the letter with the best definition of the underlined word.

1. A bright orange fish is <u>darting</u> in and out.
- Ⓐ moving quickly
- Ⓑ swimming slowly
- Ⓒ eating
- Ⓓ dancing

2. A large <u>cluster</u> of kelp plants makes a kelp forest.
- Ⓐ one thing
- Ⓑ something that grows up
- Ⓒ things growing together
- Ⓓ a type of animal

3. The fish guard the nests until the eggs <u>hatch</u>.
- Ⓐ float away
- Ⓑ come out of an egg
- Ⓒ guard
- Ⓓ warn enemies

4. Sea otters wrap strands of kelp around their bodies to keep from <u>drifting</u> away.
- Ⓐ floating
- Ⓑ walking
- Ⓒ eating
- Ⓓ feeling

5. An octopus changes its colors to <u>blend</u> in.
- Ⓐ be noticeable
- Ⓑ look like part of the surroundings
- Ⓒ hunt for food
- Ⓓ attract attention

Hi-Lo Nonfiction Passages for Struggling Readers Grades 4–5 • Scholastic Inc.

Name _____   Date _____

Word Work

> Some words have more than one meaning. You can often figure out the meaning of a word by looking at how the word is used in a sentence. For example, the word *spring* has several different meanings.
>
> **1. spring** *(noun)* – the time of year after winter and before summer
>
> **2. spring** *(verb)* – to jump up quickly

Decide if each underlined word has meaning A or B. Fill in the letter with the correct answer.

1. Everyone watched the fish eggs <u>hatch</u>.
  Ⓐ an opening on the floor or deck of a boat
  Ⓑ to come out of an egg

2. Close the <u>hatch</u> when it starts to rain.
  Ⓐ an opening on the floor or deck of a boat
  Ⓑ to come out of an egg

3. Dolphins would <u>dart</u> through the water.
  Ⓐ to move suddenly or quickly
  Ⓑ a thin pointed object that is thrown

4. Jean's <u>dart</u> landed in the center of the board.
  Ⓐ to move suddenly or quickly
  Ⓑ a thin pointed object that is thrown

> The letter combinations **sh**, **th**, and **ch** each stand for a special sound that is different from the sounds of the two individual letters.
>
> fi<u>sh</u>   <u>th</u>ree   bea<u>ch</u>

Each sentence below has an incomplete word. Add *sh*, *th*, or *ch* to complete the word.

5. I love going to the **bea**____ in the summer.

6. I enjoy hearing the **cra**____ of the waves.

7. I watch ____**ips** go by.

8. I like to walk along the sand and look for ____**ells**.

9. I keep the ones that I ____**ink** are really neat.

10. When I get home, I ____**eck** in a book to see what they are called.

Write Now

Look at the chart. It tells about a kelp forest.

- Plan to write your own description of a place in nature. Make a chart like the one shown to the right. Think of a place that you have been to or have read about where different kinds of animals live. In your description, tell what makes this place special.

- Write your description. Use your chart to help you write. Add details that will help readers see this place in their minds.

A Kelp Forest		
Where is it?	**What does it look like?**	**What lives there?**
• under the ocean • in clear, cool water	• tall, green seaweed that grows in clusters	• bright orange garibaldi fish • sea otters • urchins • octopuses

INTO THE CAVES

by Anna Nunes

Set Your Purpose

What would you expect to see in a cave? Read this newspaper article to find out what people see in Carlsbad Caverns.

Soda straws, popcorn, lily pads, and pearls make an **odd** list of items. Is this a scavenger hunt?

No, it's a trip to one of the most spectacular underground caves in the world—Carlsbad Caverns in New Mexico.

Shining forms called stalactites hang from the ceiling of these caves. The water dripping from them has created other forms called stalagmites. These **sprout** from the floor like a stone forest. Each form has a nickname to describe its **particular** shape, like *soda straws* and *popcorn*.

There are miles of caves to explore at Carlsbad Caverns, and the stone formations are great. But they're not the only attraction at this National Park.

Every day during the summer, people gather near an outside theater at sunset. As they wait, they watch

Stalagmites and stalactites form unusual shapes inside this cave.

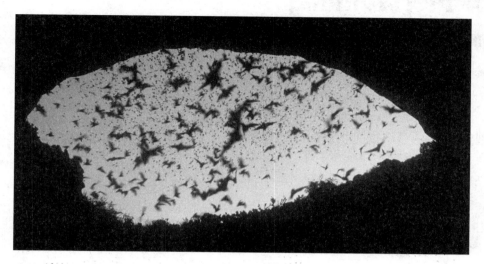
Thousands of Free-Tail Bats fly out of the cave at night to feed.

the mouth of the cave. A faint sound of flapping wings echoes from inside the cave. In moments, the sound grows louder. Then, "Whoosh!"—thousands and thousands of bats swoop from the cave. Like a large black cloud, they rise up into the **dusky** sky and fly off to hunt insects in the desert. When they return, they fold back their wings and shoot into the cave like dark rockets.

About one million Free-Tail Bats from Mexico spend spring and summer in the Bat Cave. The cave is cool (the temperature, that is). It stays under 54 degrees—perfect for bats. All day long, they hang from the cave ceilings. Mother bats even give birth on the ceiling. The babies **cling** to their mothers for three or four months. By the middle of summer, the baby bats are ready to join their mothers for the nightly show at the Bat Cave.

It is a truly great show. Visit Carlsbad Caverns yourself someday, and you're sure to agree.

Think About It

Would you like to visit Carlsbad Caverns? Why or why not?

Name _____   Date _____

Check Your **Understanding**

Fill in the letter with the best answer for each question.

1. Dripping water from stalactites caused
   - Ⓐ forms called stalagmites to grow on the cave floor.
   - Ⓑ huge puddles.
   - Ⓒ a "whoosh" sound.
   - Ⓓ bats to fly into the cave at night.

2. The nickname of each form in the caves is
   - Ⓐ made by drops of water.
   - Ⓑ to help people remember where they are.
   - Ⓒ there for people to take home.
   - Ⓓ given to match its shape.

3. Why do the bats leave the cave?
   - Ⓐ to hunt insects
   - Ⓑ to give birth
   - Ⓒ to get warm
   - Ⓓ for exercise

4. What do the bats in the caves attract?
   - Ⓐ insects
   - Ⓑ people who want to watch them
   - Ⓒ stalagmites
   - Ⓓ soda straws, popcorn, lily pads, and pearls

5. The author would like you to
   - Ⓐ have bats for pets.
   - Ⓑ visit Carlsbad Caverns.
   - Ⓒ make popcorn.
   - Ⓓ learn what bats like to eat.

Vocabulary

Find each vocabulary word in the selection. The words and sentences around it will help you figure out its meaning.

Fill in the letter with the best definition of the underlined word.

1. Popcorn, lily pads, and pearls make up an <u>odd</u> list of items.
   - Ⓐ ugly
   - Ⓑ secret
   - Ⓒ smart
   - Ⓓ strange

2. Forms <u>sprout</u> from the floor like a stone forest.
   - Ⓐ grow
   - Ⓑ disappear
   - Ⓒ bounce
   - Ⓓ slide

3. A form's nickname, like popcorn or pearl, matches its <u>particular</u> shape.
   - Ⓐ invisible
   - Ⓑ mysterious
   - Ⓒ special
   - Ⓓ dangerous

4. The bats fly up into a <u>dusky</u> sky.
   - Ⓐ bright
   - Ⓑ rainy
   - Ⓒ large black cloud
   - Ⓓ starting to get dark

5. The baby bats <u>cling</u> to their mothers for three or four months.
   - Ⓐ hold tight
   - Ⓑ argue with
   - Ⓒ wait
   - Ⓓ wonder about

Hi-Lo Nonfiction Passages for Struggling Readers Grades 4–5 • Scholastic Inc.

Name _____ Date _____

Word Work

A **contraction** is two words joined
to make one. One or more letters have
been left out. The apostrophe (') shows
where the letters were left out.

**Fill in the letter of the contraction formed by the two
words in dark type.**

1. it is
Ⓐ it'll   Ⓑ isn't   Ⓒ it's   Ⓓ it'd

2. they are
Ⓐ they're   Ⓑ they've   Ⓒ they'll   Ⓓ they'd

3. that is
Ⓐ that'll   Ⓑ that'd   Ⓒ there's   Ⓓ that's

4. you are
Ⓐ you'd   Ⓑ you're   Ⓒ you've   Ⓓ you'll

5. we have
Ⓐ we've   Ⓑ we'd   Ⓒ we'll   Ⓓ we're

**Read each sentence. Write the contraction that can
be formed by the two underlined words.**

6. <u>I have</u> never seen a bat.

_____

7. This <u>book is</u> full of pictures of bats.

_____

8. I <u>did not</u> know that bats had thumbs.

_____

9. Bats <u>do not</u> see well, so they use their other
senses.

_____

10. A bat <u>does not</u> suck people's blood.

_____

Write Now

In the article "Into the Caves," you read a description of the Carlsbad Caverns in New Mexico. Look at the chart.

What I see	What I hear	What I feel
stalactites on the ceiling and stalagmites on the floor	flapping wings	cool air inside the cave
thousands of bats swoop from cave	whoosh	
bats fold back their wings and shoot back into cave		

- Plan to write a one-page travel brochure that describes Carlsbad Caverns. Make a chart like the one shown above. Use information from the article and your own imagination to list what you see, hear, and feel.

- Write your travel brochure. Use the details in your chart.

Those Shoes Are a Crime!

by Margaret Ryan

Set Your Purpose

Why was it once a crime to wear certain kinds of shoes? Read this article to find out.

Some shoes sparkle. Some glitter and some light up when you walk in them. They can be **plain** or fancy. They can be made of leather or cloth. Some are worn for **comfort**, others for style. There are special ones for different sports and for different types of dancing. Like the feet they cover, they come in all shapes, sizes, and styles. But no matter what they look like or why they're worn, shoes are a sensible way to **protect** your feet.

Long ago, shoes weren't always so helpful. In fact, some were so silly, they were just plain ridiculous!

In the early 1400s, in countries all over Europe, shoes with long toes became popular. Everyone wanted a pair. People could tell how important you were by how long your shoes were.

Just to show off, some important men wore shoes over two-and-one-half feet long! The toes of these shoes had to be lifted off the ground with chains just so the men could walk! The chains were attached to the front of the shoes and tied to the men's knees. What a sight that must have been!

Later, it became popular to wear shoes that were very wide in the toe area. These shoes looked like a duck's bill, which is how they got the name "duckbills." Soon, shoes got even wider—as wide as nine inches across the toe!

Because of their incredible length and width, these shoes made it nearly impossible to get anywhere. People were stepping on one another **constantly**. They tripped and fell all the time. Can you imagine trying to walk up or down the stairs in shoes like that?

It soon became **obvious** that these shoes were dangerous. Something had to be done. So laws were passed in countries all over Europe. People could no longer make, buy, sell, or wear shoes that were so big. It's a good thing, too. Without those laws, the shoes we wear today might be so long and so wide, we'd never get out the door!

Think About It

Do you think it was a good idea to make long, wide shoes illegal? Why or why not?

Name _____   Date _____

Check Your **Understanding**

Fill in the letter with the best answer for each question.

1. What is the main reason people wear shoes?

- Ⓐ for fun
- Ⓑ to protect their feet
- Ⓒ to run and hike
- Ⓓ for dancing

2. Why did people begin to wear big, long shoes?

- Ⓐ to keep their feet warm
- Ⓑ to walk more easily
- Ⓒ to match their clothes
- Ⓓ to show they were important

3. Why were laws passed to stop people from wearing big, long shoes?

- Ⓐ People were hurting themselves.
- Ⓑ No one liked the way they looked.
- Ⓒ They cost too much.
- Ⓓ Poor people had started wearing them.

4. How did people solve the problem of walking in very long shoes?

- Ⓐ They used chains to hold up the toes of the shoes off the ground.
- Ⓑ They held the toes of the shoes in their hands.
- Ⓒ Only smart, important men were allowed to wear long shoes.
- Ⓓ People practiced walking up and down stairs.

5. Which of these statements is true, based on what you read?

- Ⓐ Important people always make smart and sensible choices.
- Ⓑ People who make shoes often commit crimes.
- Ⓒ Dancers wear silly shoes.
- Ⓓ Just because something is popular doesn't mean it makes sense.

Vocabulary

Find each vocabulary word in the selection. The words and sentences around it will help you figure out its meaning.

Fill in the letter with the best definition of the underlined word.

1. Shoes can be <u>plain</u> or fancy.

- Ⓐ without decoration
- Ⓑ uneven and rough
- Ⓒ not safe
- Ⓓ beautiful

2. Some are worn for <u>comfort</u>, others for style.

- Ⓐ cool
- Ⓑ home
- Ⓒ ease
- Ⓓ work

3. Shoes are a sensible way to <u>protect</u> your feet.

- Ⓐ cover
- Ⓑ hurt
- Ⓒ ease
- Ⓓ put

4. People wearing wide shoes were stepping on one another <u>constantly</u>.

- Ⓐ on purpose
- Ⓑ carefully
- Ⓒ for no reason
- Ⓓ all the time

5. It soon became <u>obvious</u> that huge shoes were dangerous.

- Ⓐ funny
- Ⓑ illegal
- Ⓒ easily understood
- Ⓓ surprising

Hi-Lo Nonfiction Passages for Struggling Readers Grades 4–5 • Scholastic Inc.

Name _____   Date _____

Word Work

A **prefix** comes at the beginning of a word and changes the meaning of the word. Knowing the meaning of a prefix helps you figure out the meaning of the whole word. The prefix **in-** means "not." The prefix **re-** means "again."

<u>in</u>active	not active
<u>re</u>open	to open again

Read the definitions below. Add the prefix *in-* or *re-* to the base word to make a new word that fits the definition.

1. not complete   _____ complete

2. do again   _____ do

3. not visible   _____ visible

4. arrange again   _____ arrange

5. not accurate   _____ accurate

Fill in the letter with the correct definition of the word in dark type.

6. inappropriate
  Ⓐ sometimes appropriate   Ⓒ not appropriate
  Ⓑ very appropriate   Ⓓ always appropriate

7. recapture
  Ⓐ to capture with help   Ⓒ to never capture
  Ⓑ to capture again   Ⓓ to set free

8. incorrect
  Ⓐ not correct   Ⓒ making corrections
  Ⓑ almost correct   Ⓓ always correct

9. repay
  Ⓐ to pay late   Ⓒ to not pay
  Ⓑ to pay early   Ⓓ to pay again

10. inexpensive
  Ⓐ too expensive   Ⓒ not expensive
  Ⓑ very expensive   Ⓓ more expensive

Write Now

Look at the web. It gives details that describe shoes worn in the 1400s.

• Plan to write a paragraph about something that is popular with children your age. It may be a type of clothing, jewelry, toy, or game. Make a web like the one shown. Add details that describe what it looks like, how it is used, and why it is popular.

• Write a paragraph about your subject. Tell why you think the item became so popular. Use your web to help you write. Include a drawing if you wish.

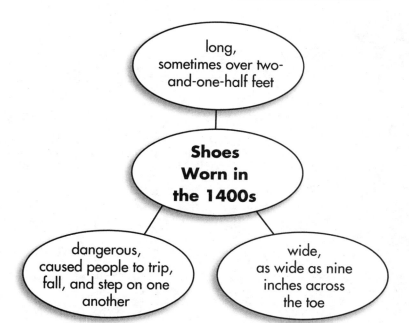

long, sometimes over two-and-one-half feet

Shoes Worn in the 1400s

dangerous, caused people to trip, fall, and step on one another

wide, as wide as nine inches across the toe

Sick frogs may be sending a **message** to humans: Take better care of our Earth!

A Frog Mystery

by Jeremy Watkins

Set Your Purpose

Scientists are trying to solve a mystery about sick frogs. Read this article to find out what they have discovered.

"Hey!" one student yelled. "Look at these weird frogs!"

"Yuck!" "Weird!" other students shouted.

What was so strange about the frogs the kids found?

They had three back legs!

Since then, frogs like these have been found all over North America. Other frogs are missing eyes or have grown tails. Animals that do not grow normally are called **deformed** or mutant.

Why are there so many deformed frogs? Scientists want to solve this mystery. They also want to know why there are fewer frogs than ever before.

Scientists have learned that nature causes some problems. Humans cause more and bigger problems.

Natural Causes

Drought and disease are some natural causes of the frog problems.

- During a drought it doesn't rain for a long time. The ground becomes very dry. Since frogs lay their eggs in water, this means fewer frogs are born.

- Scientists also have found a type of worm that can enter tadpole eggs. These worms may be causing some of the deformed frogs.

Human Causes

There are also some human causes for the frog problems.

- People sometimes let dangerous chemicals get into our water **supply**. Water that has dangerous chemicals in it is called polluted water. Because frogs are so sensitive, polluted water can easily enter their bodies. This can make adult frogs sick. This can also cause deformed baby frogs.

- Ultraviolet rays from the sun can kill baby frogs before they **hatch**. More of these harmful rays are getting through to Earth because of some products people use. Because of the harmful rays, fewer baby frogs are hatching.

- When people build roads and houses, they take over the places where frogs live.

Think About It

Why do scientists think frogs are getting sick and becoming fewer?

Name _____ Date _____

Check Your **Understanding**

Fill in the letter with the best answer for each question.

1. What has caused so many deformed frogs?

Ⓐ Some have three back legs and some are missing eyes.

Ⓑ Scientists are trying to solve a mystery about frogs.

Ⓒ Nature and humans cause problems.

Ⓓ There are fewer frogs than ever before.

2. Which of these problems are not caused by humans?

Ⓐ Dangerous chemicals get into our water supply.

Ⓑ More harmful rays are getting through to Earth.

Ⓒ Roads and houses take over the places where frogs live.

Ⓓ Worms enter tadpole eggs.

3. How do the sun's ultraviolet rays affect frogs?

Ⓐ Frogs die of thirst.

Ⓑ The tadpoles die of thirst.

Ⓒ Many baby frogs are killed before they hatch.

Ⓓ The eggs grow faster.

4. What happens when the ground dries up?

Ⓐ Farmers use chemicals to kill worms.

Ⓑ The sun's rays cause pollution.

Ⓒ Frogs grow extra tails.

Ⓓ Frogs have fewer wet places to lay eggs.

5. What effect can polluted water have on frogs?

Ⓐ It can cause deformed frogs.

Ⓑ It can result in a drought.

Ⓒ Frogs can't lay eggs.

Ⓓ Tadpoles will not get enough to drink.

Vocabulary

Find each vocabulary word in the selection. The words and sentences around it will help you figure out its meaning.

Fill in the letter with the best definition of the underlined word.

1. Sick frogs may be sending a <u>message</u> to humans.

Ⓐ pollution from cars

Ⓑ worm that enters tadpole eggs

Ⓒ information sent to someone

Ⓓ chemicals in the water

2. A <u>deformed</u> animal is one that doesn't look the way it should.

Ⓐ not normal   Ⓒ disruptive

Ⓑ intelligent   Ⓓ discovered

3. During a <u>drought</u>, the ground becomes very dry.

Ⓐ sponge   Ⓒ worm that enters frog eggs

Ⓑ wet day   Ⓓ time of little or no rainfall

4. Dangerous chemicals are getting into our water <u>supply</u>.

Ⓐ forests

Ⓑ amount of something that is available for use

Ⓒ rays

Ⓓ roads and houses

5. Harmful rays from the sun can kill baby frogs before they <u>hatch</u>.

Ⓐ come out from an egg

Ⓑ something that will cause hurt or injury

Ⓒ catch with bait

Ⓓ lay eggs in water

Hi-Lo Nonfiction Passages for Struggling Readers: Grades 4–5 • Scholastic Inc.

Name _____ **Date** _____

Word Work

> **Synonyms** are words that have similar meanings. For example, *wet* and *rainy* are synonyms.

Fill in the letter with the synonym of the word in dark type.

1. The **mutant** frog had three back legs.
- Ⓐ normal
- Ⓒ deformed
- Ⓑ large
- Ⓓ missing

2. This frog is **strange** because it has two sets of legs.
- Ⓐ tired
- Ⓒ healthy
- Ⓑ wet
- Ⓓ unusual

3. The number of frogs will **decline** if the problem is not solved.
- Ⓐ drop
- Ⓒ rise
- Ⓑ fight
- Ⓓ spin

4. Sunlight and worms can **ruin** frog eggs.
- Ⓐ tickle
- Ⓒ destroy
- Ⓑ grow
- Ⓓ eat

5. Pesticides and other chemicals are **harmful** to frogs.
- Ⓐ warm
- Ⓒ helpful
- Ⓑ damaging
- Ⓓ special

> A **suffix** is an ending that changes the meaning of a base word. The suffix **-er** can mean "a person who." The suffix **-ly** can mean "in a certain way."
>
> **build<u>er</u>**   a person who builds
>
> **normal<u>ly</u>**   in a normal way

Write a word that fits the definition by adding the suffix *-er* or *-ly* to the base word.

6. someone who teaches   teach____

7. in a quick way   quick____

8. someone who farms   farm____

9. someone who paints   paint____

10. in a quiet way   quiet____

Write Now

Look at the list of questions about frogs that "A Frog Mystery" answers.

- Plan to write a letter to the president persuading him to act on the message that sick frogs may be telling us. Look at the information in the chart. What do you think the president could do to help?

- Write your letter to the president. Explain the problem. Suggest some things the president could do to help.

Questions	Answers
What do scientists think is making frogs sick?	Nature is causing some problems. Humans are causing bigger problems.
Why are there fewer frogs?	One reason: Drought makes the ground too dry for frogs to lay eggs.
How do people hurt frogs?	They pollute water with harmful chemicals. Their houses and roads are taking over places where frogs live.

Identifying Problem & Solution

❖ When you read a story, it's helpful to think about the characters' problems and how they solve them.

- As you read, ask yourself: "What is the problem in the story?"

- Next, ask: "What steps are taken to solve the problem?"

- Then ask: "How is the problem finally solved?"

❖ Read this story. Look for the answers to these **problem/solution** questions:

- What is Florence Nightingale's problem?

- How did she try to solve her problem?

- How was the problem finally solved?

Problem
These sentences tell you the problem.

Steps
These sentences tell you the ways Nightingale tried to solve the problem.

Solution
This sentence tells you the solution.

The Lady With the Lamp

Florence Nightingale wanted to be a nurse. In 1854, Nightingale helped men who were fighting a war. She took care of the wounded. There were too few cots. Sick men slept on the floor. There was no soap or towels. The hospital was old and dirty. Nightingale took charge. She wrote letters asking for supplies. She tried to keep the hospital and the sick men clean. At night, she carried a lamp as she worked. She went from bed to bed checking on the men. Thanks to Florence Nightingale, hospitals improved. Many lives were saved.

❖ You could diagram the **problem** and **solutions** in this story like this:

Problem		Steps		Solution
There were too few cots. Sick men slept on the floor. There was no soap or towels. The hospital was old and dirty.	**+**	Nightingale wrote letters asking for supplies. She tried to keep the hospital and the sick men clean. She went from bed to bed checking on the men.	**=**	Thanks to Nightingale's efforts, hospitals improved and many lives were saved.

Your Turn

❖ Read this article. Look for the **problem**, the steps taken to solve it, and the **solution**. Make a chart like the one above.

Hilltown to Start Recycling

Hilltown has tons of trash to deal with. Too much trash is bad for our town. Trash takes up space. Hilltown needs to recycle its trash and clean its town. When you recycle things, you use them again instead of just throwing them away. It takes lots of energy to make things like paper and glass. Making new products from recycled things also take energy, but it takes much less. The more we recycle, the fewer trees we need to cut down. Trees provide homes for many animals. Trees also help to clean the air, so we can breathe easier. We will start to recycle paper and cardboard. This includes newspapers and boxes. Next month we will start to recycle glass jars and bottles. Later on, we will recycle cans.

A 7,000-Mile Shortcut!

by Amelia Johnson

Set Your Purpose

What is the Panama Canal? Where is it? Read this article to find out.

Suppose a ship wants to sail from New York to California. One **route** takes many weeks. Another sails through the Panama Canal. It is a 7,000-mile shortcut for ships!

The Panama Canal is only about 50 miles long. But it took ten years to build! Workers had to dig all **across** Panama. They **hauled** away tons of dirt. It was not easy to dig through jungles, hills, and swamps.

Insects were a big **problem**. Some spread yellow fever and other diseases. To kill the insects, workers drained swamps and cleared brush. It was a hard job, but it worked! In 1914, workers finished the canal.

Think About It

How does the Panama Canal make trips by ship faster?

Did You Know?

Some parts of the canal are higher than others. So workers built "locks." They are like steps filled with water. They raise or lower ships that travel through the canal.

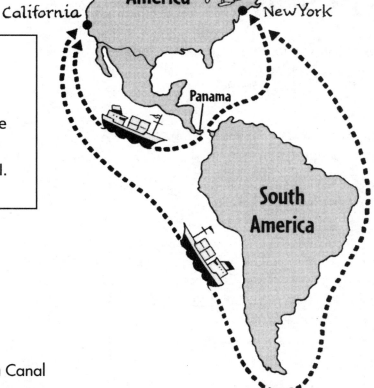

The Panama Canal

Name _____ Date _____

Check Your **Understanding**

Fill in the letter with the best answer for each question.

1. Why was the Panama Canal built?
Ⓐ to give workers something to do
Ⓑ to have tons of dirt to haul away
Ⓒ to make a shorter way for ships to travel

2. Insects were a problem because they
Ⓐ spread disease to workers.
Ⓑ drank water.
Ⓒ didn't want the canal finished.

3. How did workers get rid of harmful insects?
Ⓐ They drowned them.
Ⓑ They drained swamps and cleared brush.
Ⓒ They dug them up.

4. Which statement is true?
Ⓐ The Panama Canal is a shorter route.
Ⓑ The Panama Canal is a longer route.
Ⓒ The Panama Canal is a more dangerous route.

Vocabulary

Find each vocabulary word in the selection. The words and sentences around it will help you figure out its meaning.

Fill in the letter with the best definition of the underlined word.

1. Some ships take the short <u>route</u> through the canal.
Ⓐ path
Ⓑ fence
Ⓒ car

2. Workers dug all the way <u>across</u> Panama.
Ⓐ a piece of writing
Ⓑ from one side to the other
Ⓒ in the middle of

3. They <u>hauled</u> away tons of dirt.
Ⓐ buried
Ⓑ carried
Ⓒ locked

4. Insects were a big <u>problem</u>.
Ⓐ a small pool of water
Ⓑ large area of land
Ⓒ something that causes trouble

Name _____ Date _____

Word Work

The letter **i** stands for the **short-i** sound in *pig*.

Look at the pictures. Find the picture whose name has the short-*i* sound. Fill in the letter of that picture.

1. Ⓐ Ⓑ Ⓒ

2. Ⓐ Ⓑ Ⓒ

3. Ⓐ Ⓑ Ⓒ

4. Ⓐ Ⓑ Ⓒ

5. Ⓐ Ⓑ Ⓒ

Read the words below. Write the word that completes each sentence.

insects   ships   sick   fill   trip

6. Many _____ sail through the canal.

7. It makes the _____ shorter.

8. The locks _____ with water.

9. When the canal was built, there were many _____.

10. They made some workers _____.

Write Now

In the article "A 7,000-Mile Shortcut!" you learned how the Panama Canal solved a problem for people who travel by ship.

- Plan to write about a problem you had and the way you solved it. Write your ideas on a chart like the one shown.

- Write about your problem. Tell why you wanted to solve it. Tell how you solved it and who helped you. Tell how you felt before and after you solved the problem.

Problem	How It Was Solved
Insects spread yellow fever and other diseases.	• drained swamps • cleared brush

THANK YOU, BENJAMIN BANNEKER!

adapted by Nick Mercouri

Set Your Purpose

Who was Benjamin Banneker? How did he rescue Washington, D.C.? Read this article to find out.

Benjamin Banneker helped draw up plans for the new capital.

Washington, D.C., is our nation's **capital**. Our President lives there. Our laws are made there. It's one of the most beautiful cities in the world. But without a man named Benjamin Banneker, it might not have been built!

Banneker was born in 1731 in Maryland. His parents were free blacks. As a boy, Ben loved to learn. But going to school back then was almost unheard of for black children. Ben's mother finally **persuaded** a white teacher to take Ben into his class. Soon, Ben was the best student.

After Banneker finished school, he continued to read and learn. When he was about 30, a friend lent him a watch. Banneker took it apart. He was fascinated by how it worked. He put the watch back together. Then he built his own clock. It was a masterpiece. It even **chimed** on the hour. The clock made Banneker famous.

Banneker didn't stop there. When a friend gave him a telescope, he taught himself about the stars. He found mistakes in a book about the movement of the stars. So he learned the difficult math needed to **correct** the mistakes.

Benjamin Banneker soon began work on another exciting new project. He helped draw up plans for the new capital city. Charles L'Enfant had been **hired** to plan the city. But

L'Enfant was stubborn. He made everyone mad, including President George Washington. L'Enfant was fired. He left town and took his plans with him!

The country's leaders had a problem. How could they build the city? That's when Banneker spoke up. He offered to redraw the map—from memory! Using Banneker's plans, workers turned swampy land into our beautiful capital—Washington, D.C.

These plans for Washington, D.C., were drawn in 1791.

Think About It

How did Benjamin Banneker rescue our nation's capital?

Name_____ Date_____

Check Your Understanding

Fill in the letter with the best answer for each question.

1. To educate her son, Banneker's mother
   Ⓐ taught him what she knew at home.
   Ⓑ found a white teacher who would let Benjamin into his class.
   Ⓒ sent him to France, where black children could go to school.
   Ⓓ hired a black teacher to come to their home.

2. When Banneker found mistakes in a book about the stars, he
   Ⓐ borrowed a telescope from a friend.
   Ⓑ wrote a letter to the author to tell him to fix the mistakes.
   Ⓒ learned the math necessary to correct the mistakes.
   Ⓓ asked his friend Charles L'Enfant to rewrite the book.

3. What problem did Charles L'Enfant cause the country's leaders?
   Ⓐ He made too many mistakes in his plans.
   Ⓑ He lost the plans.
   Ⓒ He refused to draw the plans.
   Ⓓ He left town and took the plans with him.

4. How did Banneker solve the problem L'Enfant caused?
   Ⓐ He drew L'Enfant's plans for Washington from memory.
   Ⓑ He made a new design for the city.
   Ⓒ He fixed all the mistakes L'Enfant made in his plans.
   Ⓓ He found the lost plans.

5. Which did Benjamin Banneker not do?
   Ⓐ attended school when it was unheard of for black children to do so
   Ⓑ built a clock that chimed
   Ⓒ learned about the movements of stars
   Ⓓ built the White House

Vocabulary

Find each vocabulary word in the selection. The words and sentences around it will help you figure out its meaning.

Fill in the letter with the best definition of the underlined word.

1. Our nation's <u>capital</u> is in Washington, D.C.
   Ⓐ letter   Ⓒ money
   Ⓑ government   Ⓓ fort

2. She <u>persuaded</u> a teacher to help Benjamin.
   Ⓐ studied   Ⓒ convinced
   Ⓑ believed   Ⓓ fixed

3. The clock <u>chimed</u> every hour on the hour.
   Ⓐ became famous   Ⓒ taught
   Ⓑ built   Ⓓ rang a bell

4. Banneker learned the math needed to <u>correct</u> mistakes.
   Ⓐ fix or repair   Ⓒ speed up
   Ⓑ make beautiful   Ⓓ find

5. Charles L'Enfant had been <u>hired</u> to plan the city.
   Ⓐ given a paying job   Ⓒ angered
   Ⓑ mistaken   Ⓓ tired

Hi-Lo Nonfiction Passages for Struggling Readers: Grades 4–5 • Scholastic Inc.

Name _____ Date _____

Word Work

A **suffix** is a word part that comes at the end of a base word. Knowing the meaning of a suffix helps you figure out the meaning of the whole word. The suffix **-er** means "a person who." The suffix **-ful** means "full of."

Each word on the left contains a base word and a suffix. Complete the definition by writing the correct form of the base word.

1. leader   a person who _____

2. cheerful   full of _____

3. builder   a person who _____

4. writer   a person who _____

5. careful   full of _____

Add the suffix -er or -ful to each base word below to make a new word. Write the new word.

6. paint   _____

7. clean   _____

8. respect   _____

9. hope   _____

10. sing   _____

Write Now

In "Thank You, Benjamin Banneker!" you learned how Benjamin Banneker saved our nation's capital.

- Plan to write a short scene for a play. Base your play on an event in Benjamin Banneker's life. Copy the chart shown. Add details that tell about each event. Make a check next to the event you will use for your play scene.

Event	Details About What Happened
Banneker's mother wants her son to be educated.	
Banneker borrows a watch from a friend.	
A friend gives Banneker a telescope.	
Banneker helps build the city of Washington.	

- Write your scene. Use your chart to help you.

Where Is LONDON BRIDGE?

by Bob Santos

Set Your Purpose

Do you know where London Bridge is? Read this article to find the answer. You might be surprised.

Have you heard of London Bridge? You probably know this nursery **rhyme**:

> *London Bridge is falling down,*
> *Falling down, falling down.*
> *London Bridge is falling down,*
> *My fair lady.*

London Bridge has a long history. The first London Bridge was built almost a thousand years ago. It arched across the Thames River in London, England. For years, London Bridge was the only way for people to cross the river without getting in a boat or getting wet!

London Bridge was a very lively place. Houses and shops lined both sides of the bridge. People **flocked** to the bridge. They came on foot and in horse-drawn carriages. They came to shop, to visit, and to chat. Of course, they also came to cross the river.

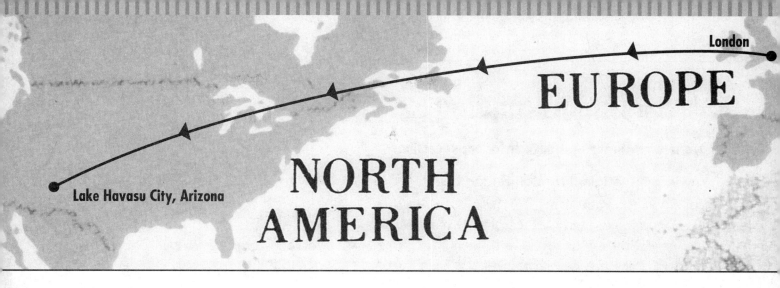

Lake Havasu City, Arizona

NORTH AMERICA

EUROPE

London

Years passed. London Bridge was repaired and rebuilt several times. People no longer traveled in horse-drawn carriages. They crossed the bridge in trucks and cars.

In 1962, engineers discovered an alarming fact. London Bridge really was falling down. Heavy traffic had weakened the old bridge. Cracks were developing. The bridge was no longer safe. Plans were made to build a new, **modern** bridge.

What happened to the old London Bridge? An American named Robert McCulluch bought it! He wanted to bring the bridge to his hometown. McCulluch lived in Lake Havasu City, Arizona.

Workers took London Bridge apart, stone by stone. They numbered each stone. Then they **shipped** the stones to Arizona. Workers in Arizona studied the original plan for the bridge. They matched the numbers on each stone. Then they put the bridge back together again.

When the bridge was built, they dug a channel under it. The channel filled with water. London Bridge was back in business.

Now when **tourists** want to see London Bridge, they don't go to England. They visit Arizona!

Think About It

Where is the old London Bridge now? How did it get there?

Name _____ Date _____

Check Your Understanding

Fill in the letter with the best answer for each question.

1. Why was the original London Bridge built?
   Ⓐ as a tourist attraction
   Ⓑ to give people a way to cross the Thames River
   Ⓒ to make work for local bridge builders
   Ⓓ to handle the heavy automobile traffic across the Thames River

2. Why did London Bridge have problems in the early 1960s?
   Ⓐ Traffic had damaged the bridge; it was falling apart.
   Ⓑ People no longer used the bridge; it had become useless.
   Ⓒ The Thames River overflowed and the bridge sank.
   Ⓓ The stones began to break apart and the bridge fell down.

3. To move London Bridge to Arizona, workers first had to
   Ⓐ cut it into three large pieces.
   Ⓑ take it apart stone by stone.
   Ⓒ lift the whole bridge with a crane.
   Ⓓ find a ship large enough to carry the bridge.

4. Workers were able to put London Bridge back together because
   Ⓐ they had good clear photographs.
   Ⓑ they had seen postcards of the bridge.
   Ⓒ the pieces were painted.
   Ⓓ they had the original plans, and each stone was numbered.

5. The main idea of the selection is that
   Ⓐ London Bridge was a lively place where Londoners shopped.
   Ⓑ heavy traffic has caused many important bridges to collapse.
   Ⓒ London Bridge, now in Arizona, has an interesting history.
   Ⓓ Arizona, the home of London Bridge, is a fun place to visit.

Vocabulary

Find each vocabulary word in the selection. The words and sentences around it will help you figure out its meaning.

Fill in the letter with the best definition of the underlined word.

1. The nursery <u>rhyme</u> about London Bridge is very old.
   Ⓐ room   Ⓒ short poem
   Ⓑ animal   Ⓓ riddle

2. People <u>flocked</u> to the bridge.
   Ⓐ flew by   Ⓒ scattered quickly
   Ⓑ walked away   Ⓓ went to as a group

3. They decided to build a new, <u>modern</u> bridge.
   Ⓐ up-to-date   Ⓒ very long
   Ⓑ without problems Ⓓ fancy

4. They <u>shipped</u> the stones to Arizona.
   Ⓐ took apart   Ⓒ sent
   Ⓑ found   Ⓓ built again

5. <u>Tourists</u> go to Arizona to see London Bridge.
   Ⓐ people who travel for pleasure   Ⓒ people who buy old things
   Ⓑ people who build things with stones   Ⓓ people who ride horses

Hi-Lo Nonfiction Passages for Struggling Readers Grades 4–5 • Scholastic Inc.

Hi-Lo Nonfiction Passages for Struggling Readers: Grades 4-5 • Scholastic Inc.

Name _____ **Date** _____

Word Work

Synonyms are words that have similar meanings. For example, *little* and *small* are synonyms.

Antonyms are words that have opposite meanings. For example, *hot* and *cold* are antonyms.

Fill in the letter of the synonym of the word in dark type.

1. The bridge was made of **stones**.
   - Ⓐ wood
   - Ⓒ rocks
   - Ⓑ metal
   - Ⓓ plastic

2. The newest London Bridge was **completed** in 1973.
   - Ⓐ begun
   - Ⓒ planned
   - Ⓑ destroyed
   - Ⓓ finished

3. There is **heavy** traffic on the bridge.
   - Ⓐ little
   - Ⓒ slow
   - Ⓑ much
   - Ⓓ fast

4. Trucks and **cars** drive across it.
   - Ⓐ motorcycles
   - Ⓒ automobiles
   - Ⓑ trailers
   - Ⓓ vans

5. People **enjoy** the view.
   - Ⓐ like
   - Ⓒ invent
   - Ⓑ ignore
   - Ⓓ dislike

Read the sentences and the words below. Write the word that means the opposite of the word in dark type.

dry   lively   new   heavy   down

6. This bridge is not **old**. It is _____.

7. These rocks are not **light**. They are _____.

8. The crowd was not **still**. It was very _____.

9. Walk **up** the stairs to cross the bridge. Walk _____ the stairs on the other side.

10. Don't get **wet**. Stay _____.

Write Now

"Where Is London Bridge?" tells how a famous nursery rhyme began to come true.

- Plan to write new verses for the nursery rhyme "London Bridge." Your song will tell the story of how London Bridge came to Arizona. Make a list of the things that happened. Then circle the ideas you will write about in your new song verses. The new verse on the chart may help you get started.

- Write your new verses for "London Bridge." If you wish, draw a picture to go with your song.

London Bridge is falling down,
  falling down, falling down.
London Bridge is falling down,
  my fair lady.

The bridge was bought by an American,
  an American, an American.
The bridge was bought by an American,
  named Robert McCulloch.

137

Replanting the Past

by Isabelle Santos

In the 1800s, American pioneers traveled from the East to the Midwest to **settle** the land. They **journeyed** in covered wagons across wide, open grassy areas known as prairies. The prairies once covered vast stretches of the American landscape. Birds

Set Your Purpose

Read this newspaper article to find out about some children who turned back time in their neighborhood.

flew over them. Large animals **roamed** the land. Bugs lived there. Deer, foxes, and wild turkeys made their home in the tall grasses. All these creatures lived in **harmony** with each other and with nature.

More and more settlers arrived. Towns and small farms spread across the land. The prairies and the creatures that made their homes there began to **vanish**.

Then, in 1994, children in Cedar Rapids, Iowa, decided to save the prairie. First, they had to tear down an old farm. It took 2,600 kids to pull down the old empty buildings. They worked for two years.

The land was finally ready for replanting. The kids planted the seeds of prairie flowers and grasses. Soon the animals came back. They began to make their homes in the new prairie land. Wild turkeys brought their chicks to the grass to feed on bugs. Deer and foxes returned, too.

The children knew that not all animals would be able to find the new prairie. So they planned to release

The prairie now has grass and flowers that are waist high.

river otters into a nearby creek. They also planned to release ground squirrels. These animals would help bring the prairie back to life.

Pioneer days are gone, but one prairie has returned.

Think About It

Do you think it was a good idea for the children to bring back part of the prairie? Why or why not?

Name _____ Date _____

Check Your Understanding

Fill in the letter with the best answer for each question.

1. What problem did the children try to solve?
Ⓐ A farm needed to be repaired.
Ⓑ The prairie was disappearing.
Ⓒ Travel in a covered wagon was difficult.
Ⓓ Buffalo were eating the prairie grasses.

2. What did the children do first?
Ⓐ plant seeds of prairie grasses and flowers
Ⓑ release 15 river otters into a creek
Ⓒ bring bugs for wild turkey chicks to eat
Ⓓ clear the land of old farm buildings

3. Why did the children plan to put river otters in the creek?
Ⓐ The otters may not have found the new prairie on their own.
Ⓑ The otters were eating the grass and destroying the prairie.
Ⓒ The otters would eat some of the extra fish in the creek.
Ⓓ The otters were ruining a farm.

4. What happened after American pioneers came to the Midwest?
Ⓐ They planted the prairies.
Ⓑ They got lonely and returned to their families in the East.
Ⓒ They tore down abandoned farms.
Ⓓ They built farms and towns.

5. Which of the following statements is an opinion?
Ⓐ In the 1800s, pioneers journeyed across the prairie.
Ⓑ Kids in Iowa replanted a prairie.
Ⓒ Replanting the prairie is a great thing to do.
Ⓓ Millions of buffalo once roamed prairie land.

Vocabulary

Find each vocabulary word in the selection. The words and sentences around it will help you figure out its meaning.

Fill in the letter with the best definition of the underlined word.

1. Pioneers traveled from the East to the Midwest to settle the land.
Ⓐ break
Ⓑ make a home in a new place
Ⓒ plant
Ⓓ bring

2. They journeyed in covered wagons across the prairies.
Ⓐ sat still
Ⓑ wrote in a book
Ⓒ traveled
Ⓓ committed a crime

3. Large animals roamed the prairie.
Ⓐ went away
Ⓑ wandered around
Ⓒ liked
Ⓓ ran

4. All these creatures lived in harmony with each other and with nature.
Ⓐ open grassy areas
Ⓑ fear of danger
Ⓒ ponds
Ⓓ agreement

5. As towns and small farms spread across the land, the prairies began to vanish.
Ⓐ disappear
Ⓑ disagree
Ⓒ grow
Ⓓ decide

Name _____   Date _____

Word Work

Some words have more than one meaning. You can often figure out the meaning of a word by looking at the way it is used in a sentence.

1. tear (*noun*) – a drop of liquid that comes from the eye

I saw my brother wipe a *tear* from his eye.

2. tear (*verb*) – to rip into pieces

They had to *tear* down the old building.

A **noun** names a person, place, or thing. A **plural noun** names more than one person, place, or thing. To make the plural of most nouns, add -*s*. Add -*es* if the noun ends with *s, ss, x, sh, ch,* or *tch.*

glass → glasses   watch → watches

Read each sentence below. Fill in the letter with the meaning of the word in dark type.

1. The animals came **back** to the prairie.
 Ⓐ rear part of your body
 Ⓑ where something was before

2. The child's **back** hurt.
 Ⓐ rear part of your body
 Ⓑ where something was before

3. The city built office buildings on that **land**.
 Ⓐ an area of the ground
 Ⓑ to set down on a surface

4. There is even going to be a place for a helicopter to **land**.
 Ⓐ an area of the ground
 Ⓑ to set down on a surface

Complete each sentence by writing the correct plural form of the word on the left.

5. ranch   Many people who settled the West started _____.

6. horse   They raised and sold _____ and cows.

7. patch   The animals grazed on large _____ of grass.

8. dress   Pioneer women wore _____.

9. box   They stored food in _____.

10. wagon   Families rode to town in _____.

Write Now

Look at the chart. It shows how problems were solved in "Replanting the Past."

- Plan to write an article about a problem that you would like to solve in your school or your neighborhood. Make a chart like the one shown.

Problem	Solution
Prairie land and the animals that lived there were disappearing.	Children decided to plant a new prairie.
There were old farm buildings on the land that the children wanted to use.	2,600 children tore down the buildings.
Some animals would not find the new prairie on their own.	The children planned to release river otters into a creek and squirrels on the land.

- Write your article. Use your chart to help you write. Add words that help connect ideas, such as *and, so, because, first, then,* and *next.*

Hi-Lo Nonfiction Passages for Struggling Readers: Grades 4-5 • Scholastic Inc.

141

Categorizing

❖ When reading a story or an article, it's helpful to put things that are similar into the same category or group. Categorizing helps you organize and remember important information.

- As you read, think about how things are alike.
- Put the things that are alike in the same group.
- Think of a title or label for each group.

❖ Read this paragraph. Look for things that are alike in some way. How can you **categorize** them?

Members of a Category

These things belong in the same group.

Category Name

This tells you the group names: _team sports, stick-and-ball sports, court sports, and target ball sports._

Ball Sports

How many sports are played with balls? A lot! <u>Volleyball, basketball, soccer, and football</u> are just four <u>team sports</u> that use balls. Yes, baseball is a team sport that uses a ball. But it's classified as a <u>stick-and-ball sport</u> along with softball and cricket. Then there are <u>court sports</u>, such as tennis, handball, and squash. <u>Target ball sports</u> include bowling, golf, and billiards. How many others can you think of?

❖ You could **categorize** these sports like this:

Type of Sport	Sports in this Group
Team	volleyball, basketball, soccer, football
Stick-and-ball	baseball, softball, cricket
Court	tennis, handball, squash
Target ball	bowling, golf, billiards

Your Turn

❖ Read this passage. Look for ways the information can be **categorized**. Make a chart like the one above.

Insect Helpers

Believe it or not, many bugs are helpful to people. Praying mantises eat grasshoppers and other bugs that hurt plants. Farmers and gardeners love these insects. Ladybugs are another insect that helps keep gardens free of insect pests.

Just about everyone loves the sweet taste of golden honey made by bees. Another insect, the silkworm, gives us the beautiful cloth we call silk. Silkworms are actually caterpillars. The silkworm spins a thread around itself and forms a cocoon. Left

alone, it will turn into a moth. Silk factories unwind silkworm cocoons and spin the thread to make silk.

SAVE OUR WETLANDS

by Derrick Wu

Set Your Purpose

What do you think soggy places are good for? Read this article to find out.

Wetlands are low, wet places like marshes and swamps. There are many kinds of wetlands. Some lie at the edges of lakes and streams. Others are on the coast, near the ocean. But they all have one thing in common. They are flooded with water at least part of the time.

People used to think that wetlands were useless. They thought that they were just **soggy** places. Now we know that's not true. Wetlands are home to many birds and other animals. Some of them are endangered species. That means that very **few** of them are left on Earth. How can we make sure that they don't disappear?

One way is to protect the places where **wildlife** lives. Laws now make it **illegal** to use wetlands as garbage dumps. Also, roads can't be built through wetlands. If we're careful, wetland animals will be around for a long time.

Think About It

What else can people do to protect wetlands?

145

Name_____ Date_____

Check Your **Understanding**

Fill in the letter with the best answer for each question.

1. In which category do swamps and marshes belong?
- Ⓐ Kinds of Wetlands
- Ⓑ Wetland Plants
- Ⓒ Wetland Animals
- Ⓓ Wetland Laws

2. Which does not tell where wetlands are found?
- Ⓐ at the edge of streams
- Ⓑ at the edge of rivers
- Ⓒ next to oceans
- Ⓓ wherever animals live

3. Endangered species are animals that
- Ⓐ there are too many of.
- Ⓑ there are very few of.
- Ⓒ are dangerous to people.
- Ⓓ are dangerous to wetlands.

4. The best way to protect wetlands is to
- Ⓐ keep them clean.
- Ⓑ remove the animals.
- Ⓒ dig them up.
- Ⓓ drain the water out.

Vocabulary

Find each vocabulary word in the selection. The words and sentences around it will help you figure out its meaning.

Fill in the letter with the best definition of the underlined word.

1. Marshes and swamps are <u>soggy</u> places.
- Ⓐ high
- Ⓑ dry
- Ⓒ wet
- Ⓓ strange

2. There are <u>few</u> of those animals still on Earth.
- Ⓐ not many
- Ⓑ millions of kinds
- Ⓒ too many to count
- Ⓓ the last one

3. We need to protect wetland <u>wildlife</u>.
- Ⓐ buildings
- Ⓑ highways
- Ⓒ animals
- Ⓓ foods

4. It is <u>illegal</u> to dump garbage in wetlands.
- Ⓐ helpful
- Ⓑ against the law
- Ⓒ a good idea
- Ⓓ not greedy

Hi-Lo Nonfiction Passages for Struggling Readers: Grades 4–5 • Scholastic Inc.

Name _____   Date _____

Word Work

A **suffix** is a word part that is added to the end of a base word. Knowing what a suffix means will help you figure out the meaning of the whole word.

The suffix **-less** means "without any."

fear<u>less</u> = without fear

The suffix **-ful** means "full of."

care<u>ful</u> = full of care

Read each definition. Add the suffix -less or -ful to each base word to match the definition.

1. full of harm _____

2. without joy _____

3. without power _____

4. full of hope _____

5. without color _____

Add the suffix −less or −ful to the word in dark type to complete the sentence. Write the new word.

6. color   The parrot is
a _____ bird.

7. home   I found
a _____ cat.

8. forget   Take your books home. Don't be
_____.

9. respect   You should be
_____ of your parents.

10. fear   That brave woman
is _____.

Write Now

In the article "Save Our Wetlands," you read why wetlands are important. Pretend that a company in your town wants to build a factory right next to a wetland.

• Plan to write a letter to the mayor. Ask that the town government stop the factory from building near the wetland. Make a chart like this to show your ideas.

• Write your letter. Use details from your chart.

Main Idea

The town should not allow _____.

Reason 1

The wetland is home to many _____.

Reason 2

Some endangered animals might _____.

Hi-Lo Nonfiction Passages for Struggling Readers: Grades 4–5 • Scholastic Inc.

Video Games

PAST AND PRESENT

by Hannah Bok

Set Your Purpose

What's your favorite video game? Read this article to find out how these games have changed over time.

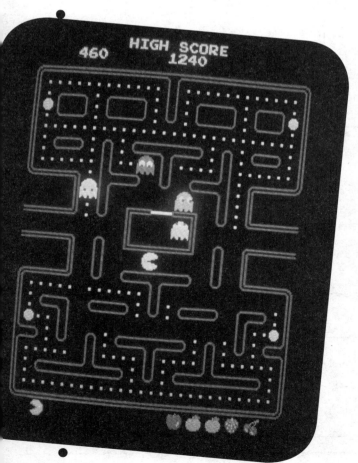

HIGH SCORE
460   1240

In 1930, pinball machines were the closest thing to video games. These machines were very large. People had to go to restaurants and bowling alleys to play them.

In 1970, the game Pong® was invented. Pong had a computer in it. People liked this new game. It was a lot like Ping-Pong. But this machine was big, too. Pong was played **mostly** in arcades.

One year later, a new game was made. This game could be put on home computers. People loved being able to play video games at home.

One of the first video-game characters was Pac Man®. Pac Man looked like a yellow smiling face. He chased little **figures** around the screen and then ate them!

Many other games **followed** Pac Man. Today, video games have better **graphics** and sounds. Some even fit in your hand!

What do you think will be the next step in video games?

Think About It

How have video games changed? What changes do you recommend for future video games?

149

Name _____   Date _____

Check Your Understanding

Fill in the letter with the best answer for each question.

1. In which group do video games belong?

Ⓐ board games

Ⓑ water games

Ⓒ electronic games

Ⓓ outdoor games

2. The game Pac Man does not fit in the group of

Ⓐ games with moving figures.

Ⓑ games that look like Ping-Pong.

Ⓒ games that are played on screens.

Ⓓ games that are played indoors.

3. Why did people like Pong?

Ⓐ They could press a button.

Ⓑ They could play it at home.

Ⓒ It was like football.

Ⓓ It was like Ping-Pong.

4. Why do you think so many people play video games today?

Ⓐ They have nothing else to do.

Ⓑ They can play these games only at home.

Ⓒ They can play these games almost anywhere.

Ⓓ They don't like other kinds of games.

Vocabulary

Find each vocabulary word in the selection. The words and sentences around it will help you figure out its meaning.

Fill in the letter with the best definition of the underlined word.

1. Pong was played <u>mostly</u> in arcades.

Ⓐ only

Ⓑ rarely

Ⓒ almost never

Ⓓ almost always

2. Pac Man chased little <u>figures</u> around the screen!

Ⓐ shapes

Ⓑ cars

Ⓒ trees

Ⓓ animals

3. Many games <u>followed</u> Pac Man.

Ⓐ came before

Ⓑ came after

Ⓒ copied

Ⓓ looked like

4. Today, video games have better <u>graphics</u> and sounds.

Ⓐ rules

Ⓑ sizes

Ⓒ pictures

Ⓓ pieces

Name _____   Date _____

Word Work

A **contraction** is a short way of writing two words as one. In a contraction, one or more letters are left out. An apostrophe (') takes the place of the missing letters.

> **did + not = didn't**
>
> **he + would = he'd**
>
> **she + will = she'll**
>
> **we + have = we've**
>
> **that + is = that's**

Fill in the letter of the contraction that is formed by the two words in dark type.

1. what is
  Ⓐ what's   Ⓑ whats'   Ⓒ what'is

2. do not
  Ⓐ doesn't   Ⓑ don't   Ⓒ didn't

3. she would
  Ⓐ she'll   Ⓑ she's   Ⓒ she'd

4. I will
  Ⓐ I'd   Ⓑ I'll   Ⓒ I've

5. they have
  Ⓐ they'd   Ⓑ they'll   Ⓒ they've

Read each sentence. Look at the underlined contraction. Write the two words that have been joined together to form the contraction.

6. Pac Man <u>wasn't</u> too big for homes. _____

7. <u>I've</u> never played Pong. _____

8. I think <u>you'd</u> like Pac Man. _____

9. <u>It's</u> fun to play video games. _____

10. Do you think <u>we'll</u> have new games soon? _____

Write Now

In the article "Video Games—Past and Present," you learned how video games have changed over time. The chart shown lists information about Pac Man, one of the earliest video games.

- Plan to compare Pac Man to another video game. Fill in the chart with information about a different video game.

- Write your comparison. Use your chart to explain how the two games are alike and how they are different. Tell which game you like better and why.

Pac Man	Video Game
yellow smiling face	
chases figures around screen	
tries to eat as many figures as possible	

WHAT'S INSIDE A ROBOT?

adapted by Pauline Snyder

Would you like a robot to serve you snacks or help with your chores? You might be in luck. Scientists are creating robots to perform these and other jobs.

Robots are not a new **concept**, or idea. They have **starred** in movies and TV shows for years. Do you remember C-3PO in *Star Wars*? Did you ever catch reruns of *The Jetsons*? One of its stars was Rosie, the robot housekeeper.

Over the years, many robots have been created to help humans. In Tokyo, Japan, a spider-shaped robot checks gas tanks for leaks and cracks. In some American hotels, robots

Set Your Purpose

What would you find inside a robot? Read this article to find out.

clean and vacuum. Scientists have even sent robots into space to study the **planets**.

Most people would agree that robots are amazing machines. But what exactly is inside a robot? How does it **operate**?

Like all machines, robots are made of some **basic** parts. These parts are called simple machines. The chart below lists some of the simple machines you will find inside many robots.

With so many simple machines inside, robots can help you do your chores and perform many other difficult jobs. Having a robot at your beck and call may soon be a dream come true!

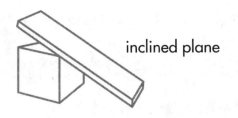
inclined plane

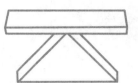
lever

Think About It

What simple machines inside a robot would help it move from place to place?

SIMPLE MACHINE	WHAT IT DOES	EVERYDAY EXAMPLE
inclined plane	helps move heavy loads	playground slide
lever	helps lift things	seesaw
wheel and axle	spins around to get you from place to place	wagon
pulley (rope attached to a wheel)	used for pulling and lifting	elevator
gear (a wheel with ridges, or teeth)	helps turn wheels	bicycle

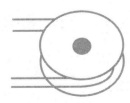
pulley

gear

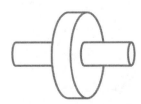
wheel and axle

Name _____ Date _____

Check Your Understanding

Fill in the letter with the best answer for each question.

1. Which simple machines help you lift heavy things?

   Ⓐ wheel and axle   Ⓒ lever and pulley

   Ⓑ wheel and gear   Ⓓ square and triangle

2. An axle, a wheel, and a gear are all

   Ⓐ things that turn.   Ⓒ complicated machines.

   Ⓑ things with teeth.   Ⓓ things that lift other things.

3. According to the article, which of these has been done by a robot?

   Ⓐ check gas tanks for leaks and cracks

   Ⓑ sing at a concert

   Ⓒ cook and serve in a restaurant

   Ⓓ climb into an active volcano

4. What conclusion can you draw from the second paragraph?

   Ⓐ In the future, all actors will be replaced by robots.

   Ⓑ The robots in movies all have women's names.

   Ⓒ Robot housekeepers have been available for a long time.

   Ⓓ Robots have been popular in movies and television for a while.

5. What is a pulley?

   Ⓐ a wheel with teeth

   Ⓑ an inclined plane that helps you move heavy loads

   Ⓒ a wheel with a rope attached that can lift things

   Ⓓ something that holds two things together

Vocabulary

> Find each vocabulary word in the selection. The words and sentences around it will help you figure out its meaning.

Fill in the letter with the best definition of the underlined word.

1. Robots are not a new <u>concept</u>.

   Ⓐ concert   Ⓒ maker of something new

   Ⓑ machine   Ⓓ idea

2. Robots have <u>starred</u> in movies and TV shows.

   Ⓐ played an important role

   Ⓑ climbed up

   Ⓒ looked at for a long time

   Ⓓ blinked on and off

3. Scientists have sent robots into space to study the <u>planets</u>.

   Ⓐ eight large bodies circling the sun

   Ⓑ plants in outer space

   Ⓒ stars around the moon

   Ⓓ space travelers

4. Simple machines inside the robot make it <u>operate</u>.

   Ⓐ open   Ⓒ run

   Ⓑ close   Ⓓ stop

5. Robots are made up of some <u>basic</u> parts.

   Ⓐ expensive and rare

   Ⓑ simple and important

   Ⓒ careful

   Ⓓ mysterious

Hi-Lo Nonfiction Passages for Struggling Readers: Grades 4–5 • Scholastic Inc.

Name_____ Date_____

Word Work

> **Synonyms** are words that have similar meanings. For example, *some* and *several* are synonyms.

Fill in the letter of the synonym of the underlined word.

1. Yeast makes dough rise. It is one of dough's <u>basic</u> ingredients.
- Ⓐ unimportant
- Ⓒ wrong
- Ⓑ necessary
- Ⓓ only

2. I was too tired to <u>perform</u> my tasks.
- Ⓐ answer
- Ⓒ join
- Ⓑ waste
- Ⓓ do

3. The <u>concept</u> of the wheel was thought of more than 5,000 years ago.
- Ⓐ destruction
- Ⓒ idea
- Ⓑ middle
- Ⓓ party

4. A Japanese robot <u>checks</u> for gas tank leaks.
- Ⓐ looks
- Ⓒ cracks
- Ⓑ teeth
- Ⓓ stars

5. I thought it was <u>amazing</u> that a robot could learn sign language.
- Ⓐ scary
- Ⓒ sticky
- Ⓑ unfortunate
- Ⓓ incredible

> Many one-syllable verbs that end with an **-e** will drop the e when **-ed** or **-ing** is added.
>
> **move   moved   moving**

Read each sentence. Add *-ed* or *-ing* to the word in dark type.

6. live I'm _____ next door to a woman who is an inventor.

7. invite One day, she _____ me over to see the machine she made.

8. staple It looked like a pole with lights _____ to it and a dish on top.

9. make "I'm _____ a new toy," the inventor said.

10. raise When she _____ the pole, the lights blinked and the dish slowly floated upward.

Write Now

In the article "What's Inside a Robot?" you read about several things robots today can do.

- Plan to create your own robot. Make a list of things you would want a robot to do for you.

- Use your list of ideas and your imagination to draw a picture or diagram of your own personal robot. Label the parts of your diagram to let people know all the things your robot can do.

Things Robots Can Do
- check gas tanks
- clean and vacuum

155

Animals of Australia

by Louise Tidd

Australia

Set Your Purpose

What unusual animals live in Australia? Read this article to learn about them.

Can you find Australia on a world map? It is a very large **island**. It is also one of the seven **continents**. Most of its people live near the coast. The middle of the island is very dry. Some of it is desert. Not too many people live there. But many unusual animals do!

You may **recognize** Australia's most famous animals. They are kangaroos. They have **powerful** back legs for hopping. Kangaroos are big, but they can hop very fast! Kangaroo babies are called joeys. Joeys spend their first few months riding in their mothers' pouches.

Think About It

Which animal from Australia would you like to learn more about?

You may also know koalas. Some people think they look like teddy bears! But they're not bears at all. Koalas spend almost all their time in trees. They stay there to avoid bigger animals below. Baby koalas are called joeys. These joeys ride in their mothers' pouches for seven months! After that, mother koalas carry their joeys on their backs.

Another tree animal is the kookaburra (koo kuh BUR uh). It's a large bird. It sounds like someone laughing out loud!

Now look to the water to find the platypus. Its webbed feet and flat bill make it look like a duck with fur!

There are many unique animals living in Australia. Which would you like to meet?

Name _____ **Date** _____

Check Your Understanding

Fill in the letter with the best answer for each question.

1. Which does not belong in the category "Animals of Australia"?
Ⓐ kangaroo
Ⓑ kookaburra
Ⓒ platypus
Ⓓ teddy bear

2. In which category does the platypus belong?
Ⓐ desert animals
Ⓑ tree animals
Ⓒ water animals
Ⓓ pouched animals

3. In which category do kookaburras belong?
Ⓐ animals that live in deserts
Ⓑ animals that live in trees
Ⓒ animals that have pouches
Ⓓ animals that have joeys

4. From this article, you can tell that koalas probably eat
Ⓐ fish.
Ⓑ leaves.
Ⓒ kangaroos.
Ⓓ platypuses.

Vocabulary

Find each vocabulary word in the selection. The words and sentences around it will help you figure out its meaning.

Fill in the letter with the best definition of the underlined word.

1. Australia is a very large <u>island</u>.
Ⓐ land that has strange animals
Ⓑ land that is faraway
Ⓒ land that has water on all sides
Ⓓ land that is hard to find

2. Australia is also one of the seven <u>continents</u>.
Ⓐ small areas
Ⓑ big groups of animals
Ⓒ large masses of land
Ⓓ city parks

3. Now that I've seen a kangaroo, I'll <u>recognize</u> its picture.
Ⓐ get to know better
Ⓑ be sure to thank
Ⓒ call on the phone
Ⓓ be able to identify

4. Kangaroos' back legs are big and <u>powerful</u>.
Ⓐ weak
Ⓑ strong
Ⓒ brown
Ⓓ tasty

Hi-Lo Nonfiction Passages for Struggling Readers: Grades 4–5 • Scholastic Inc.

Name _____ **Date** _____

Word Work

> The letters **ow** and **ou** can stand for the same sound.
>
> The letters **ow** can stand for the last sound in _cow_.
>
> The letters **ou** can stand for the middle sound in _mouse_.

Say the picture names. Fill in the letter of the picture whose name contains the sound you hear at the end of _cow_.

1. Ⓐ   Ⓑ
2. Ⓐ   Ⓑ
3. Ⓐ   Ⓑ
4. Ⓐ   Ⓑ
5. Ⓐ   Ⓑ

Read the words below. Write the word that completes each sentence.

brown pouches down loud ground

6. Australia is also called "the land _____ under."

7. Some kangaroos are _____ and some are gray.

8. Joeys are carried in their mothers' _____.

9. The kookaburra sounds like it's laughing out _____.

10. Kookaburras spend almost no time on the _____.

Write Now

In the article "Animals of Australia," you read about some very unusual animals. Pretend that you are a scientist who has discovered a new animal in Australia. What do you call it? What does it look like? Where does it live? What is unusual about it?

- Plan to write a newspaper article about your discovery. First, copy the chart shown here and complete it. You can use what you know about Australian animals to describe the new one.

- Write your newspaper article. Draw a picture to go with your article.

Animal	Description
kangaroo	• big, strong back legs • can hop fast • baby called "joey" • mother has a pouch
koala	
kookaburra	
platypus	

159

What's FUNNY About the FUNNY Bone?

by Emily LaRoche

Set Your Purpose

Do you know you have a funny bone? Can you locate your ticker? Read this article to find out about some other strange and funny names for parts of your body.

Sometimes, when people bang their elbow at a certain spot, they say that they hit their funny bone. Have you ever banged your elbow? Can you **recall** the pain you felt? There's nothing funny about it!

Some people call the heart their ticker. Listen to the beat of your own heart. Ticker is a pretty good nickname for a **healthy** heart. It beats with a rhythm that is like the tick-tock of a clock.

Another strange name is the one for a **navel**. Lots of folks call their navel a belly button, and if you have a navel that sticks out, you can see where that name came from. If your navel goes in, belly button may not work for you.

Some real names for body parts can create strange pictures in your mind. For example, look at the back of your leg, below your knee. Do you see a baby cow **attached**? Of course you don't. However, that part of your leg is called the calf, which is also the name for a young cow.

Now picture the hamstring at the back of your knee. It's not really a string used to tie hams. The hamstring is a **tendon**. A tendon is a thick, strong band of tissue that connects muscles to bones. When the muscle moves, the tendon pulls the bone with it.

It's a good thing that some parts of the body are not what they sound like. For instance, what if shoulder blades were actually sharp steel blades? They would hurt! Can you imagine how noisy it would be inside your head if the eardrum were a real drum? And who would want to shake hands if our fingernails were the kinds of nails you hammer?

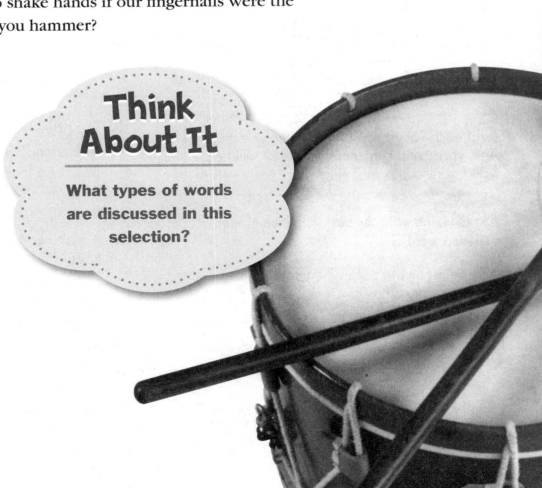

Think About It

What types of words are discussed in this selection?

Name _____   Date _____

Check Your **Understanding**

Fill in the letter with the best answer for each question.

1. Belly button, funny bone, and ticker are all
- Ⓐ artists.
- Ⓒ nicknames of body parts.
- Ⓑ tools.
- Ⓓ musical instruments.

2. Calf, hamstring, shoulder blades, eardrum, and fingernails are all
- Ⓐ types of birds.
- Ⓑ names of body parts that sound like something else.
- Ⓒ parts of the body that you can't see because they are on the inside.
- Ⓓ tendons.

3. Which of these is a tendon?
- Ⓐ a hamstring
- Ⓒ a fingernail
- Ⓑ an elbow
- Ⓓ a belly button

4. Which of the following states an opinion?
- Ⓐ A tendon is a thick, strong band of tissue.
- Ⓑ A healthy heart beats with a steady rhythm.
- Ⓒ I think "belly button" is an odd name.
- Ⓓ The back part of the lower leg is called the calf.

5. What is the main idea of the selection?
- Ⓐ Some parts of the body are sharp and painful.
- Ⓑ Ticker is a pretty good name for the heart.
- Ⓒ People don't like it when they bang their funny bones.
- Ⓓ Some body parts have odd or funny names.

Vocabulary

Find each vocabulary word in the selection. The words and sentences around it will help you figure out its meaning.

Fill in the letter with the best definition of the underlined word.

1. I can <u>recall</u> the pain when someone banged my elbow.
- Ⓐ remember
- Ⓒ not call
- Ⓑ call aloud
- Ⓓ receive

2. Ticker is a good name for a <u>healthy</u> heart.
- Ⓐ without disease or other problems
- Ⓑ broken
- Ⓒ without movement or noise
- Ⓓ angry

3. The <u>navel</u> doesn't always look like a button.
- Ⓐ anything colored dark blue
- Ⓑ having to do with the ocean
- Ⓒ back of the knee
- Ⓓ bump or hole in the middle of your belly

4. A baby calf is not <u>attached</u> below your knee.
- Ⓐ burst or blew up
- Ⓑ bag used to carry papers
- Ⓒ connected or joined
- Ⓓ spun or turned wildly

5. When a muscle moves, a <u>tendon</u> pulls the bone with it.
- Ⓐ waiter or waitress
- Ⓑ band that connects muscles to bones
- Ⓒ top of your head
- Ⓓ vessel that blood flows through

Hi-Lo Nonfiction Passages for Struggling Readers Grades 4–5 • Scholastic Inc.

Name _____ Date _____

Word Work

A **compound word** is made of two shorter words. To understand a compound word, separate it into the shorter words and think about the meaning of those words.

chalk + board   = chalkboard
ham + string   = hamstring

Make compound words by combining each word on the left with a word on the right. Write the compound word.

1. eye   cap   _____

2. knee   drum   _____

3. ear   nail   _____

4. back   lid   _____

5. finger   bone   _____

Look at the compound words below. Write the word that best completes each sentence. Then draw a line between the two shorter words that make up the compound word.

newspaper   eyeglasses   weekend
overtime   hamstring

6. To see better, I put on my _____.

7. I read in the _____ that our best soccer player got injured.

8. The game was in _____.

9. She limped off the field with a pulled _____.

10. She won't be able to play this _____.

Write Now

The selection discussed nicknames people use to talk about parts of the body. In this chart, you can read funny terms used for body parts, sleeping, and cars.

Nicknames for body parts	funny bone, ticker
Nickname for sleeping	catching a few z's
Nickname for a car	wheels

• Plan to write a conversation between two people using nicknames and funny expressions. First, copy the chart. Add other nicknames and funny expressions to each category. Add other topics if you want.

• Write the conversation. Use some of the expressions listed on your chart.

Sequencing

❖ When reading a story or an article, it's helpful to think about the order of events.

- As you read, ask yourself: "What happened first? What happened after that?"

- Look for dates and signal words such as *first*, *then*, *next*, and *finally* for clues to the **sequence** of events.

- If there are no signal words, look for story and picture clues.

❖ Read this paragraph. Look for the answers to these **sequence** questions:

- Which event happened first?
- Which event happened next?
- What was the last thing that happened?

Clue
The first sentence tells the first thing that happened.

Clue
The second sentence tells the next thing that happened. The words *after that* are a clue.

Clue
This sentence tells the last thing that happened.

The Mystery of Flight 19

One December afternoon in 1945, five Navy planes took off from their base in Florida. Some time after that, the leader radioed that they were lost. Flight 19 and its 14 crew members were never seen again. The plane vanished without a trace over a part of the Atlantic Ocean now known as the Bermuda

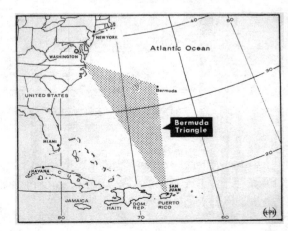

❖ You could chart the **sequence** of events in this paragraph like this:

| Five planes took off from their base. | → | The leader radioed that they were lost. | → | The planes vanished over the Bermuda Triangle. |

Your Turn

❖ Read this passage. Look for the **sequence** of events. Make a chart like the one above.

The First Video Game

Video games are common now, but in 1961 there were none. That year, three young men at Massachusetts Institute of Technology were working with a new computer. They thought it would be fun to create a game to play on the computer.

First, they talked about the kind of game it should be. Then they thought up a name for the game—Spacewar! Two enemy spaceships would fire missiles at each other. After that, the team set up the basic rules for the game. Finally, they added a starry background and other features to make the game more interesting and challenging.

Spacewar! was a big hit. It was fun to play, and it also showed what a computer could do.

Planting a Vegetable Garden

adapted by Barbara Lieff

Set Your Purpose

Do you like vegetables? Read this article to find out how you can grow them in your own garden.

Summer is the time to plant **vegetables** like peas, corn, and peppers. These children are planting a vegetable garden. You can, too! Here's how:

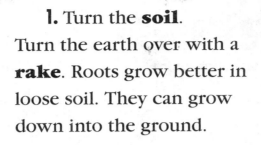

1. Turn the **soil**. Turn the earth over with a **rake**. Roots grow better in loose soil. They can grow down into the ground.

2. Plant the seeds. Plant the seeds in rows. Cover the seeds with soil.

3. Water the plants. Plants need water and sunlight to grow. Water you plants when the soil is dry.

4. Pull the **weeds**. Pull out any wild, unwanted plants. They use soil and water that your other plants need to grow.

5. Pick and eat your vegetables!

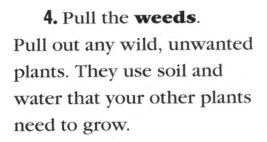

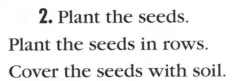

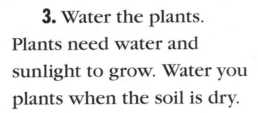

Think About It

If you planted a vegetable garden, what vegetables would you grow?

Name _____ Date _____

Check Your **Understanding**

Fill in the letter with the best answer for each question.

1. What is the first thing the children do?
- Ⓐ pick the vegetables
- Ⓑ turn over the soil
- Ⓒ plant the seeds

2. After putting the seeds in rows, what is the next step?
- Ⓐ watering the plants
- Ⓑ covering the seeds with soil
- Ⓒ picking and eating the vegetables

3. What helps the vegetable plants grow?
- Ⓐ water and sunlight
- Ⓑ weeds and bugs
- Ⓒ milk and eggs

4. The main thing this story tells about is
- Ⓐ life on a farm.
- Ⓑ big, funny vegetables.
- Ⓒ how to grow vegetables.

Vocabulary

Find each vocabulary word in the selection. The words and sentences around it will help you figure out its meaning.

Fill in the letter with the best definition of the underlined word.

1. Summer is the time to plant <u>vegetables</u>.
- Ⓐ wild flowers
- Ⓑ plants that can be eaten
- Ⓒ food for birds

2. First, turn the <u>soil</u>.
- Ⓐ pile of clay
- Ⓑ hole in the ground
- Ⓒ top layer of earth

3. You can use a <u>rake</u> to turn the soil.
- Ⓐ garden tool with a long handle
- Ⓑ garden tool used to water plants
- Ⓒ kitchen tool used for cooking

4. <u>Weeds</u> use soil and water that other plants need.
- Ⓐ pretty leaves
- Ⓑ unwanted plants
- Ⓒ branches and twigs

Name _____   Date _____

Word Work

> The letter **p** stands for the beginning sound in *potato*.
>
> The letter **z** stands for the beginning sound in *zucchini*.
>
> The letter **v** stands for the beginning sound in *vine*.
>
> The letter **m** stands for the beginning sound in *melon*.

Look at each picture. Write the picture name. Use *p, z, v,* or *m* to complete each word.

1.   ____onkey

2.   ____ebra

3.   ____oon

4.   ____ase

5.   ____izza

Read the words below. Write the word that completes each sentence.

visit   May   potatoes   zoo   vegetable

6. We planted peas in April and

_____.

7. Our _____ garden has rows of corn.

8. Carrots and _____ grow underground.

9. Some _____ animals eat peanuts.

10. Let's _____ our neighbor's flower garden.

Write Now

In the article "Planting a Vegetable Garden," you read the five steps for growing a vegetable garden.

| First, turn the soil. | → | Next, plant the seeds. | → | Then, water the plants. | → | Pull out the weeds. | → | Last, pick the vegetables. |

- Plan to write about a snack you like to make. Draw a chart like the one shown above. Write all the steps needed to make a snack.

- Write how to make the snack. Use your chart to help you write the steps in order. Use words such as *first, next,* and *last* to show the order.

Hi-Lo Nonfiction Passages for Struggling Readers: Grades 4–5 • Scholastic Inc.

169

Carving a Cameo

by Barbara A. Donovan

Set Your Purpose

What do cameos have in common with the beach? Read the article to find out.

Did you know that cameos are made from **seashells?** Most cameos show a face.

To make a cameo, first get a thick shell from the sea. Cut off a round piece. Then, find the top, **middle**, and bottom layers of the shell. The middle layer is white. The bottom may be a **peach** color.

Glue the bottom of the shell to a stick, and hold it as your work. Use a tool to **scrape** away the top layer of the shell. Next, draw a face on the middle. Then carve out the face. The peach color shows where the white is cut away.

At last, you have a cameo.

Think About It

Are all cameos the same? Why do people make cameos?

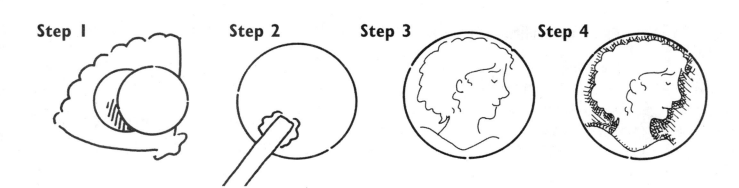

Step 1   Step 2   Step 3   Step 4

Name _____   Date _____

Check Your **Understanding**

Fill in the letter with the best answer for each question.

1. To make a cameo, the first thing you need is
- Ⓐ a face.
- Ⓑ a round hole.
- Ⓒ a thick shell.

2. After you cut a round piece of shell, you
- Ⓐ cut a hole in the shell.
- Ⓑ find all the layers.
- Ⓒ scrape off the top of the shell.

3. What do you do just before you carve out the face?
- Ⓐ glue the shell to a stick
- Ⓑ draw the face on the middle
- Ⓒ paint the bottom of the shell

4. What is another good title for "Carving a Cameo"?
- Ⓐ Making a Seashell
- Ⓑ Kids, Cars, and Cameos
- Ⓒ From Seashell to Cameo

Vocabulary

Find each vocabulary word in the selection. The words and sentences around it will help you figure out its meaning.

Fill in the letter with the best definition of the underlined word.

1. Cameos can be made from <u>seashells</u>.
- Ⓐ hard covering of nuts
- Ⓑ hard covering of eggs
- Ⓒ hard covering of sea animals

2. You will see white in the <u>middle</u>.
- Ⓐ the part in between
- Ⓑ a small piece of land
- Ⓒ a large number

3. The bottom is <u>peach</u>, not white.
- Ⓐ an animal
- Ⓑ a pinkish-orange color
- Ⓒ a game

4. Use a tool to <u>scrape</u> the top of the shell.
- Ⓐ throw out
- Ⓑ glue together
- Ⓒ rub off

Hi-Lo Nonfiction Passages for Struggling Readers: Grades 4–5 • Scholastic Inc.

Name _____ Date _____

Word Work

> The letter *i* stands for the **short-i** sound in *pig*.

Look at the pictures in each row. Find the one whose name has the short-*i* sound. Fill in the letter of that picture.

1. Ⓐ   Ⓑ   Ⓒ

2. Ⓐ  Ⓑ   Ⓒ

3. Ⓐ   Ⓑ   Ⓒ

4. Ⓐ   Ⓑ   Ⓒ

5. Ⓐ   Ⓑ   Ⓒ

Read each sentence. Write the short-*i* word that completes the sentence.

6. The man will _____ my cameo. (*five, fix*)

7. He _____ some glue on the stick. (*drips, hides*)

8. He _____ on the chair and works. (*sits, slides*)

9. He holds the _____ in his hand. (*tie, stick*)

10. He _____ it over to work on it. (*flips, wipes*)

Write Now

In the article "Carving a Cameo," you read about making a cameo. Cameos were made to celebrate special people. Some were scenes of special events. What special person or event would you like to see as a cameo?

- Plan to write a letter telling who or what you think would make a good cameo. Explain your choice. Then tell how you would make the cameo. Copy and complete a chart like this one.

- Use your chart to write your letter. Draw a picture of the finished cameo.

Who: My aunt

Why: She took care of us when mother was ill.

How to Make a Cameo

Step 1: Find a thick shell.

Step 2: Cut a round piece of shell.

Step 3:

Step 4:

SLEDDING: NOT JUST FOR KIDS

by Andrew Seligsohn

Set Your Purpose

Many people think sledding is something kids do for fun. But can sledding also be a sport? Read this article to find out.

In the winter months, many kids enjoy riding sleds quickly down a snowy hill on a clear, **crisp** day. Very few have raced on an icy sled going 60 miles an hour!

The sled that moves that fast is called a luge. *Luge* is the French word for "sled." These high-tech sleds race on icy **tracks**. To ride them, lugers lie on their backs.

They steer with their shoulders. The race is against time. The luge that gets down the hilly course fastest wins.

Luge became an Olympic sport in 1964. Since 1990, the U.S. Luge Association has been getting kids interested in luge. They visit different cities. They hold summer **clinics**. They bring luges with wheels for kids to try. They show them how to steer correctly. Kids who show **promise** get to go to special winter sessions. There they can drive a luge down a real ice run.

Cindy Jenkins was part of the program in 1991. She was 13 when she first tried luge. "It was scary at first," she **recalled**, "because of the speed."

Adam Heidt was in the program, too. He thought luge looked exciting. It was. But he admitted, "The sled was much harder to drive than I thought it would be."

Think About It

How does luge compare with the kind of sledding many people do for fun?

The program paid off. In 2002, the U.S. won two medals in luge at the Winter Olympics in Salt Lake City, Utah. The U.S. team won the silver medal. They also won the bronze medal. Both medals were for a luge event called the men's doubles.

Name _____ **Date** _____

Check Your Understanding

Fill in the letter with the best answer for each question.

1. Which event happened first?
- Ⓐ The U.S. won two Olympic medals in luge.
- Ⓑ Luge became an Olympic sport.
- Ⓒ Cindy Jenkins first tried luge.
- Ⓓ The U.S. Luge Association started a program for kids.

2. Kids who do well in summer clinics
- Ⓐ go to the Olympics.
- Ⓑ get to go to special winter sessions.
- Ⓒ go to clinics in different cities.
- Ⓓ win bronze medals.

3. Which event happened last?
- Ⓐ The U.S. won two Olympic medals in luge.
- Ⓑ The U.S. Luge Association was founded.
- Ⓒ Adam Heidt entered the luge program.
- Ⓓ Luge became an Olympic sport.

4. Why do you think the U.S. Luge Association has kids try sleds on wheels during the summer?
- Ⓐ They get tired of cold weather and snow.
- Ⓑ They enjoy the chance to travel.
- Ⓒ They want to make luge a summer sport.
- Ⓓ They want to get kids interested in luge.

5. Which detail does <u>not</u> support the idea that luge is different from ordinary sledding?
- Ⓐ Lugers lie down on their backs on the sleds.
- Ⓑ The sled moves on an icy track.
- Ⓒ The sled goes down a hill.
- Ⓓ The sled goes 60 miles an hour.

Vocabulary

Find each vocabulary word in the selection. The words and sentences around it will help you figure out its meaning.

Fill in the letter with the best definition of the underlined word.

1. It was a clear, <u>crisp</u> winter day.
- Ⓐ fresh, cool, and dry
- Ⓒ hot and windy
- Ⓑ warm and damp
- Ⓓ cold and rainy

2. A luge races down icy <u>tracks</u> at 60 miles an hour.
- Ⓐ hills
- Ⓒ vans or trucks
- Ⓑ paths or courses
- Ⓓ rinks

3. The U.S. Luge Association holds summer <u>clinics</u>.
- Ⓐ training camps
- Ⓒ ways of raising money
- Ⓑ resort hotels
- Ⓓ health-care centers

4. Kids who show <u>promise</u> get to go to special winter sessions.
- Ⓐ sign that gives reason for future success
- Ⓑ word to keep
- Ⓒ better grades in school
- Ⓓ worse actions than before

5. "It was scary at first," she <u>recalled</u>.
- Ⓐ laughed
- Ⓒ coughed
- Ⓑ remembered
- Ⓓ whispered

Hi-Lo Nonfiction Passages for Struggling Readers: Grades 4–5 • Scholastic Inc.

Name _____   Date _____

Word Work

A **suffix** is a word part that comes at the end of a base word. Knowing the meaning of a suffix helps you figure out the meaning of the whole word. The suffix **-y** means "having." The suffix **-ly** means "in a certain way."

cloud<u>y</u>	having clouds
quiet<u>ly</u>	in a quiet way

Add the suffix -y or -ly to each base word below to make a new word.

1. in a wrong way   wrong_____

2. having snow   snow_____

3. having sand   sand_____

4. in a quick way   quick_____

5. in a bright way   bright_____

Add the suffix -y or -ly to the base word in dark type to complete the sentence.

6. You need to learn how to steer the sled **correct**_____.

7. We couldn't sled because the day was very **rain**_____.

8. If you go sledding, you need to go down the hill **safe**_____.

9. The luge moved so fast because the course was very **hill**_____.

10. You'll need to wear a scarf because it is getting **wind**_____.

Write Now

"Sledding: Not Just for Kids" tells about events that happened over a period of time. In what order did the events that relate to luge happen?

- Plan to create a timeline using the story events. First, organize the dates and events in the article in a table like the one shown to the right.

- Write your timeline. Make it go from left to right. Place the first thing that happened at the left and the last thing at the right.

Date	What Happened?
1964	Luge became an Olympic sport.
_____	_____
_____	_____
_____	_____

Hi-Lo Nonfiction Passages for Struggling Readers: Grades 4-5 • Scholastic Inc.

177

AN ACTOR'S DAY

by Pat Cusick

Set Your Purpose

What's it like to be an actor? See what a day with Rishi Bhat is like by reading this article.

Is acting all fun and games? Ask Rishi Bhat. This young actor can tell you what it's like.

"It's fun seeing how movies get made," Rishi says. "But it's not all glamour. It's long hours of work. You have to start work very early."

Getting up early is **rough**. But Rishi knows that's what it takes to be in a movie. Rishi's mom drives him to the movie set. She drops him off at his own trailer on the set.

The first thing Rishi does is change clothes. He gets into the **wardrobe** he will be wearing on the set. Next is makeup

call. Rishi can spend up to an hour in the makeup chair! He uses the time wisely. He studies his lines for the day while his makeup is being done. After makeup, Rishi **reports** to the set. He will act in a scene from the movie that's being **shot** today.

It's a good thing he studied his lines!

Around noon, Rishi stops for lunch. Afterwards, he plays a few games of Ping-Pong with the crew. It's important to eat and relax when you have to work hard.

You are probably wondering when Rishi has time for school. Well, his classes are on the set, too. Rishi puts in 3$\frac{1}{2}$ hours a day with a private **tutor**. On busy days, the time gets broken up into 20-minute lessons.

After his movie scenes and schoolwork are over, the day ends at last. Everyone goes home. But there will be more makeup and more lines to remember tomorrow. That's the life of an actor.

Think About It

What do you think is the most difficult part of an actor's day? What is the most interesting?

Name _____ Date _____

Check Your **Understanding**

Fill in the letter with the best answer for each question.

1. After he gets up and gets dressed, Rishi
- Ⓐ studies his lines for the movie.
- Ⓑ calls his tutor.
- Ⓒ is dropped off at his trailer.
- Ⓓ begins to act in a scene in the movie.

2. Before he sits down for makeup, Rishi
- Ⓐ has lunch.
- Ⓑ calls his mom.
- Ⓒ changes his clothes.
- Ⓓ talks to his tutor.

3. After makeup is complete, Rishi
- Ⓐ reports to the set.
- Ⓑ plays Ping-Pong with the crew.
- Ⓒ changes his clothes.
- Ⓓ has lunch.

4. What is the main idea of "An Actor's Day"?
- Ⓐ It's important to eat and relax if you're an actor.
- Ⓑ Young actors study on the set.
- Ⓒ Acting is all fun and games.
- Ⓓ Acting takes long hours of work.

5. What is the most important thing an actor must do before filming a scene?
- Ⓐ attend classes on the set
- Ⓑ get up early
- Ⓒ eat and relax
- Ⓓ study his or her lines

Vocabulary

Find each vocabulary word in the selection. The words and sentences around it will help you figure out its meaning.

Fill in the letter with the best definition of the underlined word.

1. It's <u>rough</u> to get up early in the morning.
- Ⓐ easy
- Ⓒ hard
- Ⓑ healthy
- Ⓓ a law

2. First, Rishi changes into his <u>wardrobe</u>.
- Ⓐ acting costume
- Ⓑ locker
- Ⓒ set or stage
- Ⓓ closet

3. Afterwards, Rishi <u>reports</u> to the set.
- Ⓐ drives to
- Ⓑ checks in
- Ⓒ walks around
- Ⓓ telephones

4. A movie is being <u>shot</u> today.
- Ⓐ filmed
- Ⓑ listened to
- Ⓒ seen
- Ⓓ opened

5. Rishi studies with his own <u>tutor</u>.
- Ⓐ person who plays the flute
- Ⓑ person who directs a movie
- Ⓒ teacher who gives private lessons
- Ⓓ person in the army

Hi-Lo Nonfiction Passages for Struggling Readers: Grades 4–5 • Scholastic Inc.

Name _____ Date _____

Word Work

A **suffix** is an ending that changes the meaning of a base word. Knowing the meaning of a suffix helps you figure out the meaning of the whole word. The suffix **-or** means "a person who." The suffix **-ly** means "in a certain way."

act<u>or</u>   someone who acts

wise<u>ly</u>   in a wise way

Write a word that fits the definition by adding the suffix *-or* or *-ly* to the base word.

1. in a quick way   quick_____

2. someone who sails   sail_____

3. someone who invents things invent_____

4. in a loud manner   loud_____

5. someone who directs a movie direct_____

Each word on the left contains a base word and a suffix. Complete the definition by writing the correct form of the base word.

6. instructor   someone who _____

7. quietly   in a _____ way

8. conductor   someone who _____

9. proudly   in a _____ manner

10. collector   someone who _____

Write Now

In the story "An Actor's Day," you learned what an actor does all day. Rishi's schedule of activities looked like this:

morning	• ride to the set • change clothes for movie wardrobe • go to makeup chair for makeup • report to the set for acting
noon	• lunch • Ping-Pong
afternoon	• more acting • meet with tutor • go home

• Plan to write a schedule for a day of fun. Perhaps it is a day at an amusement park, at a museum, or at the beach. Brainstorm the activities for the day.

• Write your schedule of activities. Make a chart like the one above. List interesting things to do in the morning, at noon, and in the afternoon.

UNKNOWN!

by Theresa Froberg

In the 1500s, Europeans believed that there was a large landmass near Asia. But no one could reach it. They called it "unknown southern land."

Dutch navigators were the first to reach Australia. When their ships **arrived** in 1606, they explored the north, west, and south **coasts**. They found **uninviting** dry lands where

Set Your Purpose

What do you know about Australia?

nothing grew. The people there had no gold or jewels. The Dutch had no reason to stay. Soon after, the English landed. They didn't stay either.

About 100 years later, an Englishman, James Cook, landed on the east coast. He found **fertile**, green lands. Cook brought the good news back to England.

Captain James Cook

No one explored the interior of Australia until the 1830s. Some found salt, while others found gold. One man walked across from east to west. Two others walked from the south to the north. All of them added to our knowledge of an earlier "unknown" land.

Think About It

Is there any land that is "unknown" today?

Name _____   Date _____

Check Your **Understanding**

Fill in the letter with the best answer for each question.

1. The first Europeans to reach Australia were the
- Ⓐ Spanish.
- Ⓒ Dutch.
- Ⓑ English.
- Ⓓ French.

2. The first people from Europe to reach Australia found
- Ⓐ green lands full of plants.
- Ⓑ dry lands where nothing grew.
- Ⓒ people who were rich in jewels.
- Ⓓ people who were rich in gold.

3. What part of Australia was first explored in the 1830s?
- Ⓐ the east coast
- Ⓑ the south and west coast
- Ⓒ the north coast
- Ⓓ the interior

4. Which of the following do you think is true?
- Ⓐ The first European settlers probably lived on the west coast.
- Ⓑ The first European settlers probably lived on the east coast.
- Ⓒ The first European settlers probably lived on the north coast.
- Ⓓ The first European settlers probably lived on the south coast.

Vocabulary

Find each vocabulary word in the selection. The words and sentences around it will help you figure out its meaning.

Fill in the letter with the best definition of the underlined word.

1. The Dutch <u>arrived</u> in Australia before the English.
- Ⓐ destroyed
- Ⓒ fought
- Ⓑ got to
- Ⓓ left

2. The north, south, and west <u>coasts</u> of Australia were dry.
- Ⓐ lands next to the sea
- Ⓑ mountains
- Ⓒ lands in the middle of a country
- Ⓓ rivers

3. The east coast looked like an <u>inviting</u> place to settle.
- Ⓐ pleasant
- Ⓒ nervous
- Ⓑ terrible
- Ⓓ dry

4. One coast was green and <u>fertile</u>.
- Ⓐ poor for growing things
- Ⓑ good for climbing
- Ⓒ good for growing things
- Ⓓ poor for climbing

Name _____ Date _____

Word Work

A **prefix** is a word part that is added to the beginning of a based word. Knowing the meaning of a prefix helps you figure out the meaning of the whole word.

The prefix **un-** means "not."

> **un**known   =   not known

The prefix **re-** means "again."

> **re**visit   =   visit again

Read the definitions below. Add the prefix *un-* or *re-* to the base word to make a new word that fits the definition. Write the word.

1. not happy _____

2. write again _____

3. do again _____

4. not explored _____

5. not true _____

6. think again _____

Fill in the letter with the correct definition of the word in dark type.

7. reread
- Ⓐ read again
- Ⓑ not read
- Ⓒ read well
- Ⓓ read poorly

8. unsafe
- Ⓐ be safe
- Ⓑ not safe
- Ⓒ not save
- Ⓓ save again

9. reflow
- Ⓐ flow out
- Ⓑ not flow
- Ⓒ flow again
- Ⓓ flow quickly

10. unsteady
- Ⓐ steady again
- Ⓑ stay again
- Ⓒ not stay
- Ⓓ not steady

Write Now

In the article "Unknown" you learned about Australia and some of its early history.

When	Who	What
1500s	Europeans	knew there was land south of Asia
1606	Dutch	explored Australia's north, west, and south coasts

- Plan to write a timeline. First, copy the chart and complete it with information from the article.

- Create your timeline, using your chart to help you. Put the facts and dates in time order.

Hi-Lo Nonfiction Passages for Struggling Readers: Grades 4–5 • Scholastic Inc.

185

Jackie Robinson:
AMERICAN HERO

adapted by Eva Ramos

There was a time in the United States when African-American people could not go to the same schools as white people. They could not drink from the same water fountains. They were also not **allowed** to play major league baseball.

Set Your Purpose

Who was Jackie Robinson? Why is he an American hero? Read this biography to find out.

Two special men changed that. One was an African-American baseball player named Jackie Robinson. The other was a white baseball club owner named Branch Rickey. As a team, these two men worked together to make sure African-Americans had the same chances as others to play baseball.

Jackie was good enough to play ball in the majors, but until 1947 he could play only in the African-American league.

That year, Branch Rickey asked Jackie to play for his big-league team, the Brooklyn Dodgers. He **warned** Jackie that he would have to be brave and keep a stiff upper lip. Fans and other players would call him names. He couldn't get mad. Jackie said that he'd try.

In his first year, Jackie was the **Rookie** of the Year. After his career ended in 1956, he was **elected** to the Baseball Hall of Fame.

Think About It

Were you surprised to learn that African Americans did not play big-league ball before 1947? How would you describe Jackie Robinson and Branch Rickey?

More African-American Firsts

- Bill Cosby was one of the first African Americans to win an Emmy award. It was for the 1964 TV adventure series *I Spy*.

- In 1992, Mae Jemison became the first African-American woman **astronaut** in space. She was in the crew of the space shuttle *Endeavour*.

Jackie Robinson and Branch Rickey recall their days with the Brooklyn Dodgers.

Name _____ Date _____

Check Your **Understanding**

Fill in the letter with the best answer for each question.

1. Which event happened first?

Ⓐ Jackie Robinson was elected to the Baseball Hall of Fame.

Ⓑ Jackie Robinson played in an African-American baseball league.

Ⓒ Jackie Robinson joined the Brooklyn Dodgers.

Ⓓ Jackie Robinson became the Rookie of the Year.

2. What happened after Jackie Robinson's baseball career ended in 1956?

Ⓐ He was elected to the Baseball Hall of Fame.

Ⓑ He was chosen as Rookie of the Year.

Ⓒ He won an Emmy award for a television appearance.

Ⓓ He met a man named Branch Rickey.

3. What is the main idea of the first paragraph?

Ⓐ Americans drink from water fountains.

Ⓑ In the past, African Americans were not treated equally.

Ⓒ All Americans like school.

Ⓓ Long ago, baseball players were all white.

4. Which event happened last?

Ⓐ African Americans could not play major league ball.

Ⓑ Bill Cosby won an Emmy award.

Ⓒ Jackie Robinson teamed up with Branch Rickey.

Ⓓ Mae Jamison became the first African-American woman in space.

5. What conclusion can you draw from the article?

Ⓐ Jackie Robinson was the first African-American Rookie of the Year.

Ⓑ Bill Cosby was an astronaut.

Ⓒ Jackie Robinson grew up in New York.

Ⓓ Baseball is a popular sport.

Vocabulary

Find each vocabulary word in the selection. The words and sentences around it will help you figure out its meaning.

Fill in the letter with the best definition of the underlined word.

1. He wasn't <u>allowed</u> to play major league ball.

Ⓐ about   Ⓒ asked

Ⓑ permitted   Ⓓ believed

2. Rickey <u>warned</u> Jackie that fans would call him names.

Ⓐ told of coming danger   Ⓒ tried hard

Ⓑ fought   Ⓓ ended a talk

3. Jackie was named <u>Rookie</u> of the Year.

Ⓐ player   Ⓒ pitcher

Ⓑ newcomer   Ⓓ batter

4. In 1956, he was <u>elected</u> to the Baseball Hall of Fame.

Ⓐ forgotten   Ⓒ called names

Ⓑ asked to leave   Ⓓ chosen by votes

5. Mae Jemison was the first African-American woman <u>astronaut</u> in space.

Ⓐ athlete   Ⓒ space traveler

Ⓑ stage performer   Ⓓ spy

Name _____ Date _____

Word Work

An **idiom** is a group of words used in a way that has a special meaning. This special meaning is different from the usual meaning of those words.

Write the letter of the definition that matches the idiom in the left column.

Idioms	Definitions
___ **1.** beat around	**A.** in trouble
___ **2.** in hot water	**B.** sick or unwell
___ **3.** under the weather	**C.** agree
___ **4** drives me up a wall	**D.** not get right to the point
___ **5.** see eye to eye	**E.** annoys me

Read each sentence. The idiom is underlined. Find the meaning of the idiom below. Write the meaning.

brag   in a joyful mood   teased
sad   give up

6. I had never hit a home run, and I was <u>down in the dumps</u>. _____

7. Players on the other team <u>picked on</u> me.

_____

8. Some of them liked to <u>talk big</u> about their home runs. _____

9. I was ready to <u>throw in the towel</u>.

_____

10. In my next game, I hit a home run and was <u>walking on air</u>. _____

Write Now

Look at this chart. It shows the order of some events in Jackie Robinson's life.

- Plan to write a brief biography of your favorite athlete. First, make a chart like the one shown on the right to list events, in order, for your biography.

- Write your biography. Use your chart to help you write events in order.

| Jackie met Branch Rickey of the Brooklyn Dodgers. |
| Jackie played for the Dodgers. |
| After his first year, Jackie was voted Rookie of the Year. |

Hi-Lo Nonfiction Passages for Struggling Readers: Grades 4-5 • Scholastic Inc.

189

What a Catch!

by Pat Chandler

The year is 1942. The place is the baseball field at Hayes High School in Westfield, Alabama. It was practice time, and a boy named Ray was talking to the coach.

"Whoever is in the outfield is really good!" Ray said to the coach. "He's gotten every ball so far."

"That's Willie Mays," **noted** the coach, "the little kid from elementary school. He told me he 'listens to the bat.' When he hears the bat go CRACK as it hits the ball, he 'guesses' just where it's going to go. Without even looking, he runs to that place—and most of the time the ball lands where he expected."

"Can we sign him up for our team? The kid hasn't missed one yet!"

Set Your Purpose

What's the secret of being a good outfielder? Willie Mays knew that secret. Read this article to find out about Willie.

The coach laughed. "He's only 11 years old. Let's wait, OK?"

Eight years later, at 19, Mays **signed** with the New York Giants and soon became a star. And one **magical** day, in the World Series of 1954, Mays made what fans still call "The Catch," possibly the greatest catch ever made in the history of baseball.

It was the first game of the series. The score was tied. A leading hitter on the **opposite** team hit a towering fly ball. Mays was off and running at the crack of the bat. With his head down, he raced straight to the wall and reached it just in time to see the ball flying high over his head. In one huge leap, he grabbed the ball out of the air, **whirled** around, fired it home, and stopped the scoring run at the plate.

The Giants went on to win the game, and more important, Willie Mays showed the world what an amazing player he was.

Think About It

What was so special about "The Catch" made by Willie Mays? Why do you think people still remember it?

Name _____   Date _____

Check Your Understanding

Fill in the letter with the best answer for each question.

1. In the World Series game, what did Mays do after he heard the crack of the bat?
- (A) He ran to the stands.
- (C) He raced to the wall.
- (B) He threw the ball.
- (D) He stepped up to bat.

2. After Mays saw the ball flying over his head, what did he do?
- (A) He jumped up and caught the ball.
- (B) He raced to the wall.
- (C) He ran to home plate.
- (D) He threw the ball.

3. After Mays made "The Catch," what did he do?
- (A) He ran to the wall.
- (B) He signed with the New York Giants.
- (C) He threw the ball to home plate.
- (D) He joined another team.

4. Who did Mays practice with when he was 11 years old?
- (A) the Little League
- (B) his brothers and sisters
- (C) high school players
- (D) his classmates

5. What was Mays's "secret"?
- (A) He loved the game.
- (B) He listened to the ball hitting the bat.
- (C) He watched the ball.
- (D) He always ran toward the wall.

Vocabulary

Find each vocabulary word in the selection. The words and sentences around it will help you figure out its meaning.

Fill in the letter with the best definition of the underlined word.

1. "That's Willie Mays," <u>noted</u> the coach.
- (A) mentioned
- (C) wondered
- (B) laughed
- (D) wrote

2. Willie <u>signed</u> with the New York Giants.
- (A) was hired with a contract
- (B) traveled with the other players
- (C) became friends with
- (D) approved of by others

3. The day that Willie made "The Catch" was a <u>magical</u> day.
- (A) scary
- (C) wonderful
- (B) difficult
- (D) strange

4. The players on the <u>opposite</u> team could not believe he caught the ball.
- (A) the one they were playing against
- (B) the one they were cheering for
- (C) the one they were most like
- (D) the one in another league

5. After Mays caught the ball, he <u>whirled</u> around and fired it.
- (A) walked quickly
- (C) jumped high
- (B) spun
- (D) looked

Name _____ Date _____

Word Work

Some words have more than one meaning. You can often figure out the meaning of a word by looking at how the word is used in a sentence.

1. row *(noun)* – a line
We sat in the *row* behind our parents.

2. row *(verb)* – to paddle
Let's *row* the boat to the island.

Decide if the underlined word in each sentence has the meaning A or B. Fill in the letter with the correct answer.

1. The <u>coach</u> talked to Mays.
Ⓐ to teach or help
Ⓑ a person who helps or teaches

2. Mays should <u>coach</u> other players.
Ⓐ to teach or help
Ⓑ a person who helps or teaches

3. He ran at the <u>crack</u> of the bat.
Ⓐ a loud sound
Ⓑ to break or split something

4. Did he <u>crack</u> the bat when he hit the ball?
Ⓐ a loud sound
Ⓑ to break or split something

5. Mays tried to <u>play</u> the best baseball possible.
Ⓐ a story acted out
Ⓑ participate in the game

6. We wrote a <u>play</u> about Mays's life.
Ⓐ a story acted out
Ⓑ participate in the game

7. I ate a <u>plate</u> of beans at the ball game.
Ⓐ a dish
Ⓑ the last base in baseball to be touched to score a run

8. People loved to <u>watch</u> Mays in action.
Ⓐ something to tell time with
Ⓑ to look at

9. The <u>crowd</u> always cheered him on.
Ⓐ a large group of people
Ⓑ to push or shove

10. Fans lined up in <u>rows</u> to get his autograph.
Ⓐ lines
Ⓑ paddles a boat

Write Now

Did you ever see an athlete do something amazing? In "What a Catch!" you read about the amazing catch made by Willie Mays. The chart lists what happened in order.

- Plan to write a description of an amazing sports play. Pretend you are a radio announcer describing the play as it happens. First, brainstorm ideas by making a chart like the one shown.

- Write your description. Use your chart to make sure the steps are in order.

Steps Mays Followed to Make "The Catch"

1. Batter hits a long fly ball. Mays hears the sound.

2. Mays races back to wall.

3. Mays sees the ball flying overhead.

4. Mays leaps up and catches the ball.

5. Mays fires the ball home to keep the run from scoring.

Hi-Lo Nonfiction Passages for Struggling Readers: Grades 4–5 • Scholastic Inc.

193

Something Fishy

by Sean McCarthy

Set Your Purpose

Who is Eugenie Clark? What did she discover? Read this article to find out.

Fish, fish, and more fish is all that Eugenie Clark seemed to have in mind. Animals that swim, dip, dive, and splash fascinated her.

Eugenie Clark grew up in New York City. You might think there wouldn't be many fish in a big city. But Clark found them. She frequently visited an **aquarium**, where she saw fish of all sizes, shapes, and colors. At home, she also kept small fish as pets. Like a good scientist, she carefully **studied** her pets and took notes about their habits.

When Clark went to college, she followed her interest: fish, fish, and more fish! After college, she went all over the world to learn more about them. During that time, Clark made new friends— sharks! To learn more about sharks, she often swam with them. That's why people called her "the shark lady."

Once, while she was diving, Clark made a surprising **discovery**. She noticed that sharks would refuse to go near a fish called the Moses sole. Why? This small, flat fish gives off a **poison** that keeps sharks away. It works just like bug spray works to keep bugs away. Clark's amazing discovery might someday prevent shark attacks on people.

Eugenie Clark and other people like her have discovered many interesting facts about life **underwater**. Would you like to be a scientist who spends time with fish, fish, and more fish?

Think About It

What did Eugenie Clark discover? How could her discovery be used to help people?

Name_____ Date_____

Check Your Understanding

Fill in the letter with the best answer for each question.

1. When did Eugenie Clark first become interested in studying fish?
   Ⓐ after she swam with sharks
   Ⓑ when she was a child living in New York City
   Ⓒ as a student in college
   Ⓓ after she graduated from college

2. What did Eugenie Clark do after she graduated from college?
   Ⓐ She stayed in New York City.
   Ⓑ She traveled around the globe to find out more about fish.
   Ⓒ She took notes about her own pet fish.
   Ⓓ She studied the fish at a New York City aquarium.

3. The best word to describe Eugenie Clark is
   Ⓐ determined.   Ⓒ timid.
   Ⓑ foolish.   Ⓓ amusing.

4. What conclusions can you draw about scientists from the selection?
   Ⓐ They usually don't get along with people and prefer to work with fish.
   Ⓑ They observe and keep careful records about what they see.
   Ⓒ They never make any new discoveries.
   Ⓓ They have a lot of free time.

5. What did Eugenie Clark discover about the Moses sole that surprised her?
   Ⓐ The Moses sole is not good to eat.
   Ⓑ The Moses sole is a small fish that attacks large sharks.
   Ⓒ The Moses sole produces something that keeps sharks away.
   Ⓓ The Moses sole can be chased away with bug spray.

Vocabulary

Find each vocabulary word in the selection. The words and sentences around it will help you figure out its meaning.

Fill in the letter with the best definition of the underlined word.

1. Eugenie Clark visited an <u>aquarium</u>, where she saw all kinds of fish.
   Ⓐ pet store
   Ⓑ place people go to look at fish
   Ⓒ laboratory where discoveries are made
   Ⓓ school where people get a college degree

2. She <u>studied</u> her pets and took notes about them.
   Ⓐ worried about   Ⓒ learned about
   Ⓑ took good care of   Ⓓ remembered

3. Eugenie Clark made a surprising <u>discovery</u>.
   Ⓐ kind of fish   Ⓒ experiment
   Ⓑ new observation   Ⓓ unhappy event

4. The Moses sole gives off a <u>poison</u> that keeps away sharks.
   Ⓐ anything with a pleasant smell
   Ⓑ smell that attracts killer sharks
   Ⓒ warning sound
   Ⓓ something that can kill or harm

5. Eugenie Clark discovered many interesting facts about life <u>underwater</u>.
   Ⓐ in a submarine   Ⓒ beneath the sea
   Ⓑ in very small holes   Ⓓ on top of the ocean

Hi-Lo Nonfiction Passages for Struggling Readers: Grades 4–5 • Scholastic Inc.

Name _____   Date _____

Word Work

The endings **-ed** and **-ing** can be added to many verbs. Many one-syllable verbs that end with an *e* will drop the *e* when *-ed* or *-ing* is added.

| splash | splashed | splashing |
| dive | dived | diving |

Add the suffix -ed to each verb. Write the new word.

1. seem _____

2. learn _____

3. like _____

4. join _____

5. dance _____

Read each sentence. Add the suffix -ed or -ing to the word in dark type.

6. visit   Clark frequently
_____
the aquarium.

7. refuse   The sharks
_____ to go
near the Moses sole.

8. surprise Clark's discovery was
_____.

9. learn   We have been
_____ more
about sharks.

10. discover We are _____
many interesting facts.

Write Now

"Something Fishy" is about Eugenie Clark. This chart shows events in her life.

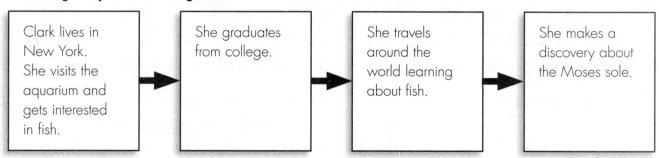

Clark lives in New York. She visits the aquarium and gets interested in fish. → She graduates from college. → She travels around the world learning about fish. → She makes a discovery about the Moses sole.

- Imagine that you are a famous underwater scientist like Eugenie Clark. Plan to write about the events that led up to a famous discovery that you made. Create a sequence chart like the one shown here. Write the important events in your rise to fame in order in the boxes.

- Use your sequence chart to write your story. Make the sequence of events clear by using signal words. Some examples are *first, then, next,* and *finally.*

Keep the Great Lakes GREAT!

adapted by Cecily Robinson

Set Your Purpose

Scan this article and predict what it is about.

What would you see if you stood on the moon and looked down at Earth? How about a wolf and a mitten?

It sounds impossible, but it's not exactly.

From the moon, you could see the wolf-head shape of Lake Superior, one of the five Great Lakes. You could also see the mitten shape of the land **bordered** by Lakes Michigan, Erie, and Huron.

The Great Lakes are huge lakes on the border of the United States and Canada. They provide drinking water for more than 25 million people. However, the Great Lakes have pollution problems.

Read the timeline to understand the history of these problems.

1890s Cities are built around the lakes. People and **factories** dump trash and waste into the water.

1900s The Great Lakes are polluted. Many people get sick from drinking the water.

1930s People **notice** fewer fish in the lakes. Pollution is killing the fish.

1940s Farmers near the lakes use chemicals to **boost** crop growth. More chemicals get into the lakes.

1960s In 1969, a river leading to Lake Erie is so polluted with trash and oil that it catches on fire.

1970s New laws **force** cities to stop dumping trash into the lakes.

1980s The lakes look cleaner. Scientists worry about chemicals that have settled on the bottom of the lake. These chemicals can stay in the mud for more than 100 years.

1990s The United States and Canada work together to clean up the lakes. They plan to scoop out the polluted mud.

What will happen next? Hopefully, people will continue to clean up the Great Lakes. It will take time and money. It will take lots of work from people who care. But it can be done. The Great Lakes can once again become great lakes for all of us to enjoy.

Think About It

Do you think the author chose a good title for this selection? Why or why not?

Name _____   Date _____

Check Your Understanding

Fill in the letter with the best answer for each question.

1. Which of these events happened first?

Ⓐ Factories begin to dump trash and waste in the lake.

Ⓑ The United States and Canada make a plan to clean the lakes.

Ⓒ Chemicals from farms get into the lake.

Ⓓ People get sick from drinking water from the lakes.

2. What happened after new laws forced cities to stop dumping trash into the lakes?

Ⓐ New smaller lakes were polluted.

Ⓑ Factories moved away from the lakes.

Ⓒ Another Great Lake was built.

Ⓓ The Great Lakes looked cleaner.

3. Why were there fewer fish in the 1930s?

Ⓐ Pollution was killing them.

Ⓑ People were eating too many fish.

Ⓒ The fish eggs can't hatch in the lake.

Ⓓ People were catching too many fish.

4. Canada and the United States will work together because

Ⓐ the Great Lakes have no fish.

Ⓑ both countries border the Great Lakes.

Ⓒ they want to build factories.

Ⓓ chemicals remain in the mud.

5. The author of the selection wrote this to

Ⓐ describe the view of Earth from the moon.

Ⓑ explain the history of pollution in the Great Lakes.

Ⓒ teach people about pollution laws.

Ⓓ get people to visit the Great Lakes.

Vocabulary

> Find each vocabulary word in the selection. The words and sentences around it will help you figure out its meaning.

Fill in the letter with the best definition of the underlined word.

1. A mitten-shaped piece of land is <u>bordered</u> by Lakes Michigan, Erie, and Huron.

Ⓐ looked down on   Ⓒ forgotten

Ⓑ ruined   Ⓓ surrounded

2. People <u>notice</u> fewer fish in the lakes.

Ⓐ throw   Ⓒ see

Ⓑ eat   Ⓓ burn

3. People and <u>factories</u> dump trash and waste into the water.

Ⓐ businesses that make the goods we buy

Ⓑ people who don't like lakes

Ⓒ places where too many people live

Ⓓ hospitals

4. Farmers near the lakes use chemicals to <u>boost</u> crop growth.

Ⓐ harm   Ⓒ stop

Ⓑ clean   Ⓓ help

5. New laws <u>force</u> cities to stop dumping trash into the lakes.

Ⓐ have an idea

Ⓑ make someone do something

Ⓒ worry about something

Ⓓ work together

Hi-Lo Nonfiction Passages for Struggling Readers: Grades 4–5 • Scholastic Inc.

Name_____ **Date**_____

Word Work

Antonyms are words that have opposite meanings. For example, *up* and *down* are antonyms.

Read each sentence. Fill in the letter of the antonym of the word in dark type.

1. The Great Lakes are **huge**.
   Ⓐ big   Ⓒ tiny
   Ⓑ wide   Ⓓ beautiful

2. The water is **deep**.
   Ⓐ cold   Ⓒ shallow
   Ⓑ warm   Ⓓ dangerous

3. The lake water was **polluted**.
   Ⓐ clean   Ⓒ smelly
   Ⓑ dirty   Ⓓ wet

4. There were **fewer** fish in the lakes.
   Ⓐ little   Ⓒ gold
   Ⓑ some   Ⓓ more

5. Chemicals stay in the mud for a **long** time.
   Ⓐ tall   Ⓒ big
   Ⓑ short   Ⓓ thin

A **possessive noun** shows ownership.

To make a singular noun possessive, add **'s**. To make a plural noun possessive, add an apostrophe after the final (**s'**).

belonging to the dog ⟶ the dog's
belonging to the dog ⟶ the dogs'

Read each pair of sentences. Write the correct possessive noun that completes the second sentence.

6. The trash comes from the city. It is the _____ trash.

7. The chemicals belong to the farmers. They are the _____ chemicals.

8. The laws are from this country. They are this _____ laws.

9. The idea is from the scientists. It is the _____ idea.

10. The tools belong to the workers. They are the _____ tools.

Write Now

The timeline in "Keep the Great Lakes Great" shows how pollution started in the Great Lakes. It also shows what is being done to fix the problem.

- Plan to write a petition form for keeping the Great Lakes clean. A petition is a letter many people sign. First, make a list of reasons why people should care about the Great Lakes. Use information from the article.

- Write your petition with a paragraph explaining why people should sign it. Use your list to help you.

We should care about the Great Lakes because:
1._____
2._____
3._____

Comparing & Contrasting

❖ When reading a story or an article, it's helpful to think about how things are alike and how they are different.

- As you read, ask yourself: **"What is the same about these things?"** and **"How are they different?"**

- When you think about how things are alike, you **compare** them.

- When you think about how things are different, you **contrast** them.

❖ Read this paragraph. Look for the answers to these **compare/contrast** questions.

- How are foxes and cats alike?
- How are they different?

Contrast

These sentences tell how foxes and cats are different: *Foxes belong to the dog family and cats to the cat family.*

Compare

These sentences tell how foxes and cats are alike: *They hunt alike, can retract their claws, and have similar eyes.*

Foxes and Cats

Foxes are members of the dog family. Cats are members of the cat family. Dogs and cats aren't usually alike, are they? However, foxes and cats are alike in some ways. Foxes hunt like cats. They sneak up on their prey and pounce on it, just as cats do. Unlike dogs, cats can pull in, or retract, their claws. Foxes can retract their claws part way. Foxes and cats also have similar eyes. Their pupils become big and round at night, so they see well in dim light.

❖ You could chart how things are alike and different like this:

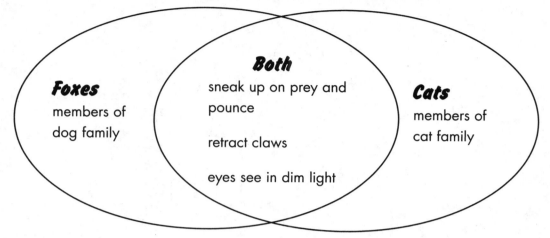

Foxes
members of
dog family

Both
sneak up on prey and
pounce

retract claws

eyes see in dim light

Cats
members of
cat family

Your Turn

❖ Read this passage. **Compare** and **contrast** the saw-whet owl and the great horned owl. Make a chart like the one above.

Birds of a Different Feather

There are 12 kinds of owls in North America. They're all alike in many ways. They all have huge, fixed eyes in the front of their heads. Their feathers have soft edges, so they hardly make any noise when they fly. All owls are meat-eaters.

The saw-whet owl is the smallest owl. It measures only 7 inches and weighs 3 ounces. Its wingspan is about 17 inches.

One of the largest owls at up to 2 feet is the great horned owl. It weighs between 2 ½ and 3 pounds. A great horned owl's wings can stretch 5 feet from tip to tip.

If you hear a long series of toots or whistles at night, you may be hearing a saw-whet owl. If you hear deep, low hoots, it's probably a great horned owl.

Waves for You

by Martina Hanson

Set Your Purpose

Where can you play in the waves when the ocean is far away? Read this article to find out.

Here's the problem: You love to play in the waves, but you don't live near the sea. You also don't like jellyfish or sharks! Maybe you hate getting knocked over when the ocean is **rough**.

What can you do? You can go to a wave pool! Wave pools look like **normal** swimming pools, but they're not.

Special machines make waves that can be turned on and off. Sometimes the waves are gentle.

Then you can swim or **float**. At other times, the waves are big and **wild**!

Some wave pools even have beaches or slides. Find one near you—and have fun!

Think About It

Would you rather swim at a wave pool or in the ocean? Why?

Name _____ Date _____

Check Your Understanding

Fill in the letter with the best answer for each question.

1. Wave pools look like other swimming pools but they
   Ⓐ are far away.
   Ⓑ have beaches.
   Ⓒ have waves that can be turned on and off.

2. How are wave pools different from the ocean?
   Ⓐ They do not have jellyfish.
   Ⓑ They can have big waves.
   Ⓒ They have sharks.

3. The waves in a wave pool are made by
   Ⓐ the sea.
   Ⓑ machines.
   Ⓒ swimmers.

4. The author thinks that wave pools are
   Ⓐ a fun place to go.
   Ⓑ not safe.
   Ⓒ full of sharks.

Vocabulary

Find each vocabulary word in the selection. The words and sentences around it will help you figure out its meaning.

Fill in the letter with the best definition of the underlined word.

1. Some waves are big and <u>rough</u>.
   Ⓐ fancy
   Ⓑ not gentle
   Ⓒ yellow

2. Do you like to <u>float</u> in the pool?
   Ⓐ rest on top of the water
   Ⓑ sail a boat
   Ⓒ dig in the sand

3. There are no waves in <u>normal</u> swimming pools.
   Ⓐ deep
   Ⓑ special
   Ⓒ regular

4. I don't like it when the waves are <u>wild</u>.
   Ⓐ big and scary
   Ⓑ very cold
   Ⓒ salty

Hi-Lo Nonfiction Passages for Struggling Readers Grades 4–5 • Scholastic Inc.

Name _____ **Date** _____

Word Work

The letter **a** stands for the **long-a** sound in *cake*.

Look at the pictures. Fill in the letter with the picture whose name has the long-a sound.

1. Ⓐ   Ⓑ Ⓒ
2. Ⓐ Ⓑ Ⓒ
3. Ⓐ Ⓑ 5 Ⓒ
4. Ⓐ Ⓑ Ⓒ
5. Ⓐ Ⓑ Ⓒ 9

Read the words below. Write the word that completes each sentence.

lake   shade   take   wave   face

6. I wish I could go swimming in a _____ pool.

7. It's more fun than swimming in a _____.

8. Do you mind it when your _____ gets wet?

9. If it gets hot, we can sit in the _____ of the tree.

10. I'll ask Mom if she'll _____ us there soon.

Write Now

In the article "Waves for You," you read about ways that wave pools and oceans are the same and different. One way is shown in the diagram at right. Would you rather swim in the ocean or in a wave pool?

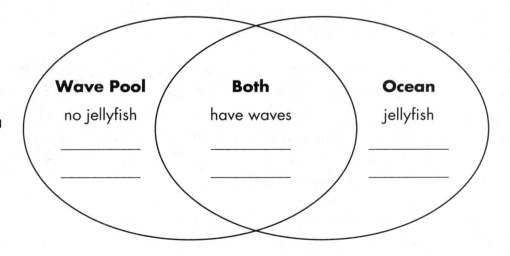

Wave Pool — no jellyfish
Both — have waves
Ocean — jellyfish

- Plan to write a paragraph about which you like better. First, copy the diagram and then finish filling it in.

- Write your paragraph. Use the ideas in the diagram to help you. Then draw a picture of yourself swimming or playing in a wave pool or the ocean.

Kid Inventors

by Carole Osterink

Set Your Purpose

What's your favorite toy? How do you think it was first invented? Read to find out what two kids invented.

Toys and games are fun, but inventing them is serious **business**. Big toy companies have adults who do nothing but think up new toys. Sometimes they even work in **locked** rooms so no one can steal their ideas!

But not every new toy is invented that way. Some of the best inventions are made by kids.

Thirteen-year-old Casey Golden loved to play golf. He invented a way to make the game more fun. He invented a new golf tee. It is called the Biotee®. Most golf tees are made from wood, but Casey's tee is made out of **recycled** paper. It does not harm the environment. Casey started his own **company** to make his new tee. He's already had orders for millions of them.

Jessica Peach invented a toy when she was only eight. Jessica likes to jump rope. She jumps alone and she jumps with friends. To jump alone, you need a short rope. With friends, you need a long rope. So Jessica invented an adjustable

jump rope. The length of Jessica's jump rope can be **modified**. It can be made long to jump with friends. Or it can be made short to jump alone. When you are done jumping, you can even turn the jump rope into a belt. Now Jessica has a business to sell her jump ropes.

Do you have a great idea for a new invention? Give your idea a try. It may become the next Biotee or latest jump rope!

Think About It

Why would toy companies want to keep their new toy ideas a secret?

Name _____ **Date** _____

Check Your Understanding

Fill in the letter with the best answer for each question.

1. How is the Biotee different from most golf tees?
  Ⓐ It is made out of recycled paper, not wood.
  Ⓑ The inventor loved to play golf.
  Ⓒ Casey had orders for millions of Biotees.
  Ⓓ The inventor started his own company.

2. How are Casey Golden and Jessica Peach alike?
  Ⓐ Both invented something before the age of ten.
  Ⓑ Both work for a big toy company.
  Ⓒ Both invented toys that didn't harm the environment.
  Ⓓ Both started their own companies to make and sell their inventions.

3. All inventions are created
  Ⓐ by accident.
  Ⓑ after hours of hard work.
  Ⓒ in little locked rooms.
  Ⓓ with creative thinking.

4. In big toy companies, inventing toys is serious business because
  Ⓐ toys are hard to find and expensive.
  Ⓑ the more toys a company sells, the more money it makes.
  Ⓒ not many companies make them.
  Ⓓ the best toys are invented by kids.

5. Before Jessica invented the Adjustable Jump Rope, she had to
  Ⓐ use two different ropes to jump alone or with friends.
  Ⓑ stop jumping rope with her friends.
  Ⓒ stop jumping rope alone.
  Ⓓ borrow belts from her friends.

Vocabulary

Find each vocabulary word in the selection. The words and sentences around it will help you figure out its meaning.

Fill in the letter with the best definition of the underlined word.

1. Toys and games are fun, but inventing them is a serious <u>business</u>.
  Ⓐ sport   Ⓒ hobby
  Ⓑ job   Ⓓ class

2. Sometimes, inventors work in <u>locked</u> rooms so no one can steal their ideas.
  Ⓐ closed with a key   Ⓒ walled
  Ⓑ open with a key   Ⓓ joined

3. The Biotee is made of <u>recycled</u> paper.
  Ⓐ red   Ⓒ used
  Ⓑ new   Ⓓ biked

4. Casey started his own <u>company</u> to make his new tee.
  Ⓐ store in a shopping center
  Ⓑ small shop at a fair
  Ⓒ group of people living in one place
  Ⓓ group of people formed to do work

5. The length of Jessica Peach's Adjustable Jump Rope can be <u>modified</u>.
  Ⓐ jumped   Ⓒ washed
  Ⓑ changed   Ⓓ carried

210

Name _____ Date _____

Word Work

The suffixes **-ed** and **-ing** can be added to verbs.

walk   The children are *walking* to school.

They *walked* to school yesterday, too.

Add the suffixes -ed and -ing to each verb. Write the new words.

1. invent _____ _____

2. lock _____ _____

3. happen _____ _____

4. play _____ _____

5. work _____ _____

Read each sentence. Add the suffix -ed or -ing to the word in dark type.

6. **invent**   Some kids are _____ new toys.

7. **start**   Some of them are _____ their own companies.

8. **enjoy**   Jessica _____ jumping rope with her friends.

9. **need**   She _____ a shorter rope to jump alone.

10. **jump**   When Jessica is done _____, she can turn her jump rope into a belt.

Write Now

In "Kid Inventors," you read about how the Biotee® and the Adjustable Jump Rope were invented.

- Plan to create a poster for your own invention. Think of a problem that your invention might solve. Make a chart like the one at the right to organize your ideas.

- Create a poster for your invention. Explain what your invention is. Draw a diagram of it and explain how it works.

Biotee®	Adjustable Jump Rope
Problem: Wooden tees made by cutting down trees	**Problem:** Need two ropes for jumping alone and jumping with others
Solution: Tees made from recycled paper	**Solution:** A rope that adjusts to two sizes

Hi-Lo Nonfiction Passages for Struggling Readers: Grades 4-5 • Scholastic Inc.

211

Home, Sweet Home!

by Yolanda Canols

Set Your Purpose

How do ants and termites build their homes? Read this article to find out.

Here are underground tunnels, air-conditioned castles, and mud skyscrapers. Is this the work of smart, hardworking builders? Yes. Is this the work of men and women? No! It's the work of ants and termites.

Believe it or not, tiny insects build the most amazing homes. Insects build these homes to protect themselves and their families. Some dirt and hard work is all these little guys need!

ANTS

Ants build the most unusual homes. These homes are underground mazes of tunnels and rooms. There are **chambers** for eggs. There are separate rooms for baby ants. There are places to store food. And there are **snoozing** rooms. That's where ants sleep away the winter.

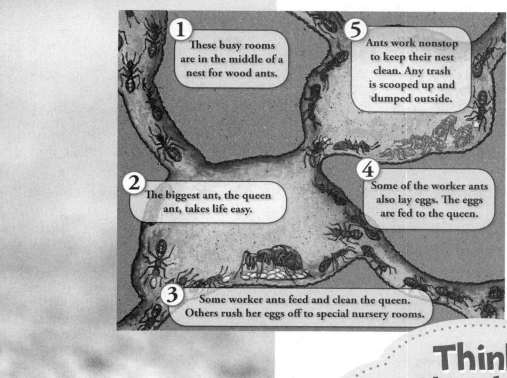

1. These busy rooms are in the middle of a nest for wood ants.

5. Ants work nonstop to keep their nest clean. Any trash is scooped up and dumped outside.

2. The biggest ant, the queen ant, takes life easy.

4. Some of the worker ants also lay eggs. The eggs are fed to the queen.

3. Some worker ants feed and clean the queen. Others rush her eggs off to special nursery rooms.

Think About It

How are ant homes and termite homes alike? How are they different?

Ants are always fixing and changing their homes. New tunnels are built. Walls are **repaired**. New chambers are dug out. Old chambers are closed. No wonder ants sleep all winter! They work hard.

TERMITES

A termite castle is an **excellent** example of how clever insects can be. There are tiny holes on the surface of the castle. But termites don't fit through them. These holes are not entrances. And they're not exits. They're part of the castle's air-conditioning system! Even termites like to stay cool.

Some termite mounds are shaped like mushrooms. Some are shaped like barrels. Others are as tall as giraffes. These are termite skyscrapers! Imagine if humans could build a skyscraper out of dirt and spit, with only their hands as tools. That would be similar to what termites do!

With mud, made of soil mixed with their spit, termites build homes with very strong, thick walls. Farmers sometimes have to clear termite nests from their fields. Some termite towers are so strong, the only way to **shatter** them is to blow them up with dynamite!

Name _____ Date _____

Check Your Understanding

Fill in the letter with the best answer for each question.

1. Which statement is true for ant homes and termite homes?
- Ⓐ There are snoozing rooms where they sleep away the winter.
- Ⓑ They are simple and uncomplicated.
- Ⓒ They are the work of smart, hardworking builders.
- Ⓓ There are tiny holes on the surface.

2. Which statement shows how termite homes are different from ant homes?
- Ⓐ They are built to protect themselves and their families.
- Ⓑ They have holes on the surface to keep the inhabitants cool.
- Ⓒ They are built with some dirt and hard work.
- Ⓓ They are complicated.

3. Which statement shows how termite homes are stronger than ant homes?
- Ⓐ They are shaped like mushrooms.
- Ⓑ They are as tall as giraffes.
- Ⓒ They are like skyscrapers built out of dirt and spit.
- Ⓓ Farmers have to blow them up to clear the nests from their land.

4. From this story, you can guess that ants spend a lot of time
- Ⓐ building and fixing their homes.
- Ⓑ riding around on giraffes.
- Ⓒ fighting over food.
- Ⓓ in air-conditioned skyscrapers.

5. The author of this story probably wanted to
- Ⓐ show you how to build a castle.
- Ⓑ teach you about ant and termite homes.
- Ⓒ teach you about giraffes.
- Ⓓ entertain you with a made-up story about an ant family.

Vocabulary

Find each vocabulary word in the selection. The words and sentences around it will help you figure out its meaning.

Fill in the letter with the best definition of the underlined word.

1. There are special <u>chambers</u> for the eggs.
- Ⓐ dirt
- Ⓑ mazes
- Ⓒ rooms
- Ⓓ ants

2. Ants sleep in <u>snoozing</u> rooms in winter.
- Ⓐ fighting
- Ⓑ sleeping
- Ⓒ borrowing
- Ⓓ building

3. Broken walls are <u>repaired</u>.
- Ⓐ left alone
- Ⓑ looked at
- Ⓒ climbed
- Ⓓ fixed

4. A termite castle is an <u>excellent</u> example of insect engineering.
- Ⓐ very good
- Ⓑ boring
- Ⓒ terrible
- Ⓓ unfair

5. The only way to <u>shatter</u> termite homes is to blow them up.
- Ⓐ lift up
- Ⓑ glue or fasten together
- Ⓒ break apart
- Ⓓ give as a gift

214

Name _____   Date _____

Word Work

> A **compound word** is made of two shorter words. Combining the meaning of the two shorter words often explains the meaning of the compound word.
>
> **weekend** = **end** of the **week**

Make compound words by combining each word on the left with a word on the right. Write the compound words.

1. sky   ground   _____

2. hard   selves   _____

3. under   working   _____

4. some   scraper   _____

5. them   times   _____

Read the definitions below. Join two words from each definition to make a compound word that fits the definition. Look at the sample.

SAMPLE   definition: a **house** for a **bird**
          compound word: **birdhouse**

6. a ball of snow   _____

7. a book with a
   story in it   _____

8. the light from a star   _____

9. a pole for a flag   _____

10. a fighter who puts
    out a fire   _____

Write Now

In the selection "Home, Sweet Home," you read about the interesting homes that ants and termites build. Look at the list of ant-nest parts shown.

- Plan to write about another kind of home. It can be an animal home or your own home. First, make a diagram or picture of the home you plan to write about. Label its parts. You may want to use the list shown for ideas.

- Write one or two sentences to go with your diagram. Tell what animal or person lives in the home and what materials are used to build the home.

Ant Nest Parts
Tunnels
Egg room
Room for babies
Food-storage room
Sleeping room

Hi-Lo Nonfiction Passages for Struggling Readers: Grades 4-5 • Scholastic Inc.

215

PET PALS

by Carole Osterink

Goldfish, hamsters, parrots, and even pigs—about half of all families in the United States have a pet! If there are ten homes on your street, pets probably live in five of them. What pets live in your **neighborhood**?

Pets come in all sizes and shapes. They can have soft fur, colorful feathers, or smooth skin. They can have four legs, two legs, or none at all! The most popular pets are four-legged and furry. They're cats and dogs, of course! Which furry friend do you **prefer**?

Set Your Purpose

Some people are dog lovers, while others like cats more. Read this article to find out why.

Most cats are happy to stay **indoors** and nap. If you leave them food and water, they don't mind staying alone. They're **extremely** clean so they don't need baths. And they're usually peaceful and quiet.

Dogs need food, water, and baths. They also need to be taken for walks—sometimes late at night! Dogs get lonely so you can't leave them alone for long. Some people think all that noisy barking is just too annoying!

One thing's certain about both dogs and cats. If you take care of them and love them, they'll love you in return. Isn't that the most important thing?

Think About It

Which kind of pet would you rather have? Why?

Name _____ Date _____

Check Your Understanding

Fill in the letter with the best answer for each question.

1. The most popular pets are
   Ⓐ pigs and parrots.
   Ⓑ gerbils and goldfish.
   Ⓒ cats and dogs.
   Ⓓ snakes and goldfish.

2. Dogs and cats both have
   Ⓐ feathers.
   Ⓑ four legs.
   Ⓒ smooth skin.
   Ⓓ two legs.

3. What is the same about cats and dogs?
   Ⓐ They have to be taken on walks.
   Ⓑ They need food and water.
   Ⓒ They chase cars.
   Ⓓ They are usually peaceful and quiet.

4. According to the article, which statement is true?
   Ⓐ Everyone has pets.
   Ⓑ Dogs are less popular than parrots.
   Ⓒ Everyone likes cats more than dogs.
   Ⓓ Hamsters are less popular than cats.

Vocabulary

Find each vocabulary word in the selection. The words and sentences around it will help you figure out its meaning.

Fill in the letter with the best definition of the underlined word.

1. I've seen three cats in my <u>neighborhood</u>.
   Ⓐ grocery store
   Ⓑ classroom
   Ⓒ part of town
   Ⓓ mom's car

2. Some people like cats, but I <u>prefer</u> dogs.
   Ⓐ sing to
   Ⓑ like better
   Ⓒ learn about
   Ⓓ act like

3. Most cats like to stay <u>indoors</u> and nap.
   Ⓐ at the pet store
   Ⓑ in a car
   Ⓒ on the street
   Ⓓ inside the house

4. Puppies and kittens are <u>extremely</u> playful.
   Ⓐ very
   Ⓑ not at all
   Ⓒ a little
   Ⓓ never

Hi-Lo Nonfiction Passages for Struggling Readers: Grades 4–5 • Scholastic Inc.

Name _____ **Date** _____

Word Work

A **contraction** is a short way of writing two words as one. In a contraction, one or more letters are left out. An apostrophe (') takes the place of the missing letters.

you're	=	you are
she'd	=	she would

Write the two words that each contraction stands for.

1. you'll _____

2. he's _____

3. we're _____

4. you've _____

5. I'm _____

Read the sentences. Circle each contraction and write the two words that form it.

6. Look over there! Aren't those your dogs?

_____

7. They're running away from your parents.

_____

8. Don't worry, they'll catch the dogs.

_____

9. My parents won't let me have a dog.

_____

10. I'd tell them that dogs are great pets.

_____

Write Now

In the article "Pet Pals," you read about cats and dogs—the most popular pets. You learned that cats and dogs are alike in some ways and different in other ways.

- Do you think dogs or cats make better pets? Plan to write a short speech to convince someone to agree with you. Copy and complete a Venn diagram like the one shown.

- Write your speech. Use the information you wrote in the diagram to help you. Practice reading it. Then, read your speech to your classmates.

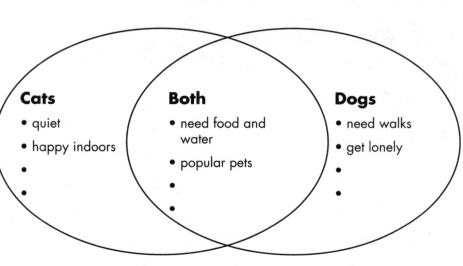

Cats
- quiet
- happy indoors
-
-

Both
- need food and water
- popular pets
-
-

Dogs
- need walks
- get lonely
-
-

INSECTS THAT GO FOR THE GOLD!

adapted by Laura Johnson

Set Your Purpose

Some insects can do amazing things. Read this article to find out about some real winners.

Imagine if insects held their own Olympic games! Which ones might win gold medals?

In the fastest-flying race, the dragonfly could win the gold. Dragonflies can **flutter** their four strong wings almost 2,000 times in one minute! Have you ever seen a dragonfly zoom through the air? It looks and sounds like a tiny airplane!

What about a running race? Many insects are fast runners. But it would be hard for any insect to **compete** against the cockroach. This insect has six long, skinny legs. They help the cockroach dash across the ground.

Which do you think is the loudest insect? The male cicada [sih KAY duh] might win that contest. His song can be heard more than a mile away! He is hoping to **impress** a female cicada. The cicada's song also helps to tell the time of year. It **announces** the end of summer.

In the weight-lifting event, cheer for the beetle. The rhinoceros beetle is really strong. It can hold up to 850 times its own weight. That's the same as a person carrying about 75 cars!

Think About It

Do you know any other amazing things that insects can do?

Name _____ Date _____

Check Your **Understanding**

Fill in the letter with the best answer for each question.

1. Compared to other insects, dragonflies
  Ⓐ have longer legs.
  Ⓑ are stronger.
  Ⓒ can run faster.
  Ⓓ can fly faster.

2. Compared to cockroaches, beetles
  Ⓐ have louder calls.
  Ⓑ have more legs.
  Ⓒ can carry more weight.
  Ⓓ can carry less weight.

3. According to the article, the cicada is
  Ⓐ not an insect.
  Ⓑ most like a beetle.
  Ⓒ the loudest insect.
  Ⓓ always female.

4. How is a dragonfly like an airplane?
  Ⓐ They have wings and are noisy flyers.
  Ⓑ They are about the same size.
  Ⓒ They both carry people.
  Ⓓ They are both insects.

Vocabulary

Find each vocabulary word in the selection. The words and sentences around it will help you figure out its meaning.

Fill in the letter with the best definition of the underlined word.

1. Dragonflies <u>flutter</u> their wings about 30 times a second.
  Ⓐ take off and put on
  Ⓑ wave back and forth
  Ⓒ change the color of
  Ⓓ fly without using

2. It's hard for any insect to <u>compete</u> against the cockroach.
  Ⓐ take part in a contest
  Ⓑ cheer for a team
  Ⓒ pretend to be
  Ⓓ finish

3. The male cicada wants to <u>impress</u> a female with his voice.
  Ⓐ trick
  Ⓑ bring food to
  Ⓒ make unhappy
  Ⓓ affect the feelings of

4. A cicada's song <u>announces</u> the end of summer.
  Ⓐ calls out
  Ⓑ makes up
  Ⓒ pretends it is
  Ⓓ explains

Hi-Lo Nonfiction Passages for Struggling Readers Grades 4–5 • Scholastic Inc.

Name _____ **Date** _____

Word Work

A **suffix** is a word part that is added to the end of a base word. Knowing the meaning of a suffix helps you figure out the meaning of the whole word.

When added to a describing word, the suffix **-er** means "more." Use the suffix *-er* when you are comparing two things.

I am strong, but you are much strong<u>er</u>.

The suffix **-est** means "most." Use the suffix *-est* when you compare more than two things.

The cockroach is the fast<u>est</u> insect of all.

Write a word that fits the definition by adding the suffix **-er** or **-est** to the base word. Write the new word.

1. more smart _____

2. most hard _____

3. most low _____

4. more dark _____

5. most quiet _____

Write Now

In "Insects That Go for the Gold!" you read about some amazing insects. Imagine that there really was an Insect Olympics and you were a TV reporter.

- Plan to write a news report about one race in the contest. Make a chart like this one to plan your report.

- Write the news report. Use your imagination to describe a flying or running race, or a singing or weight-lifting contest. Tell how the insects felt when they won.

Write the correct form of the words in parentheses to complete each sentence.

6. Which do you think is the _____ insect of all? (*slower, slowest*)

7. A dragonfly is _____ than an airplane. (*smaller, smallest*)

8. The cicada is _____ than the beetle. (*louder, loudest*)

9. That was the _____ anthill I ever saw! (*taller, tallest*)

10. July is the _____ month of the year. (*warmer, warmest*)

Dragonfly	• fastest flying • four wings • looks and sounds like a tiny airplane
Cockroach	
Cicada	
Beetle	

223

What a GOOD Dad!

by Jamal Massoud

Set Your Purpose

How are seahorses and penguins alike? Read this article and find out!

Here's a **riddle**. What animal father takes very good care of its **young**? If your answer is the male seahorse, you are right. If your answer is the male emperor penguin, you are right, too.

The male seahorse has a pouch on its belly. The female lays her eggs in this pocket. Then she swims away. The male seahorse swims around with the eggs in his pouch. When the eggs hatch, hundreds of babies emerge from the pouch.

A similar story describes the birth of emperor penguins. In the Antarctic, where emperor penguins live, the female climbs onto the ice. She lays one egg on the ice. Then, like the female seahorse, she has done her job, and she swims away.

Like the male seahorse, the male emperor penguin **protects** his unborn young. He does this by rolling the egg onto his feet. He uses the lower part of his fat, warm belly to cover the egg. Then, with the egg on his feet, he joins a group of other males. For two months, they crowd together to keep their eggs and themselves warm. During this time, they don't eat.

After two months, a baby penguin, or chick, hatches. The male penguin feeds the chick with a milky **liquid** that comes from his throat. Soon, the female penguin **appears**. She takes over the care of the baby while the male returns to the sea to hunt for food for his family. After six months, the chick is ready to live on its own.

Think About It

How are penguins and seahorses alike?

Name _____ Date _____

Check Your Understanding

Fill in the letter with the best answer for each question.

1. In what way is a male seahorse like a male emperor penguin?
  Ⓐ They both live in the Antarctic.
  Ⓑ They both take care of their unborn babies.
  Ⓒ They are both called chicks.
  Ⓓ They both have fat, warm bellies.

2. How is a female seahorse like a female emperor penguin?
  Ⓐ They both have pouches on their bellies.
  Ⓑ They both take care of their newborn babies.
  Ⓒ They both eat more than the males.
  Ⓓ They both lay eggs and then swim away.

3. How is the birth of seahorses different from the birth of penguins?
  Ⓐ Seahorses are born on ice.
  Ⓑ Seahorses are born in a pouch.
  Ⓒ Seahorses are protected by their fathers at birth.
  Ⓓ Seahorses don't eat anything for months.

4. Which of these events happens first?
  Ⓐ A female seahorse lays her eggs in the male's pouch.
  Ⓑ Hundreds of babies emerge from the male's pouch.
  Ⓒ The male seahorse swims around with eggs in his pouch.
  Ⓓ Hundreds of seahorse eggs hatch.

5. What is the main idea of the second paragraph?
  Ⓐ A male seahorse has a pouch on its belly.
  Ⓑ Male seahorses protect their unborn children.
  Ⓒ Female seahorses lay hundreds of eggs.
  Ⓓ Male seahorses don't eat while they have eggs in their pouch.

Vocabulary

Find each vocabulary word in the selection. The words and sentences around it will help you figure out its meaning.

Fill in the letter with the best definition of the underlined word.

1. Did you know the answer to the riddle?
  Ⓐ animal with no feet
  Ⓑ empty space
  Ⓒ instrument with four strings
  Ⓓ puzzling problem or question

2. What animal father takes very good care of its young?
  Ⓐ enemies   Ⓒ children
  Ⓑ home   Ⓓ fruits or vegetables

3. The male emperor penguin protects his unborn young.
  Ⓐ keeps safe   Ⓒ laughs at
  Ⓑ throws   Ⓓ eats

4. The male penguin feeds the chick with a milky liquid that comes from his throat.
  Ⓐ acorn   Ⓒ long pole or stick
  Ⓑ hat   Ⓓ wet substance that is not solid

5. Soon, the female penguin appears.
  Ⓐ attacks   Ⓒ swims away
  Ⓑ shows up   Ⓓ eats

Hi-Lo Nonfiction Passages for Struggling Readers Grades 4-5 • Scholastic Inc.

Name _____ **Date** _____

Word Work

> **Antonyms** are words that have opposite meanings. For example, *hot* and *cold* are antonyms.

Write the word from below that means the opposite of the word in dark type.

alone   wrong   upper   harms   thin

1. Sunscreen **protects** your skin from the sun. Too much sunlight _____ your skin.

2. Use sunscreen **together** with clothing. Sunscreen _____ may not be enough protection.

3. Don't wear **thick** clothing that will make you hot. Wear _____, light clothes instead.

4. Cover your legs on the **lower** part of your body. Cover your arms on the _____ body as well.

5. Being careful is the **right** way to have fun in the sun. To be careless is _____.

> The endings **-ed** and **-ing** can be added to many verbs without changing the spelling of the base word.
>
> **protect   protected   protecting**
>
> Many one-syllable verbs that end with an *e* will drop the *e* when the *-ed* or *-ing* is added.
>
> **name   named   naming**

Read each sentence. Add the suffix -ed or -ing to the word in dark type.

6. visit   Last week, our class _____ the aquarium.

7. guide   Someone at the aquarium _____ us around.

8. live   We saw a seahorse _____ in the water.

9. float   A seahorse moves by _____ because it cannot swim well.

10. like   Our class _____ learning about the seahorse.

Write Now

In "What a Good Dad!" you read about ways that seahorses and penguins are alike and different. Look at the Venn diagram below.

- Plan to write a paragraph about how two plants or animals are alike in some ways and different in other ways. First, make a diagram, like the one shown, to compare your two plants or animals.

- Write a paragraph that compares and contrasts the two plants or animals you have chosen. Use the ideas on your diagram. Use words that compare, such as *alike*, *unlike*, *similar*, and *different*.

Seahorse
- Female lays hundreds of eggs.
- Male swims with eggs in pouch.
- Hundreds of babies emerge from pouch.

Both
- Mother lays eggs.
- Mother swims away.
- Father takes care of unborn babies.

Emperor Penguin
- Female lays one egg on ice.
- Male rolls egg onto feet.
- Male joins other male penguins to keep warm.
- Male does not eat for two months.

227

GLOBE HOPPING

by Frank Bean

Set Your Purpose

Do you know how to play hopscotch? Read this article to find out how children play hopscotch in three other countries.

Children around the world play hopscotch. Each country has its own **variation** of the game. The game has different names and different rules. However, in every version, children draw a **pattern** on the ground. Then they hop or jump from **section** to section on that pattern. The patterns may be outlined in chalk or paint, or they can be scratched with a stick in dirt or sand.

Let's "hopscotch" around the **globe** to learn where and how children play the game.

FRANCE

In France, children play *escargot*, the word for snail. As you might guess, the pattern is a snail shape filled with numbers. Players hop on one foot, in and out of the **spiral**, twice. The player then gets to write his or her initials in a square, called a "house." On the next round, the player can rest there, but other players have to hop over it. At the end, the player with the most "houses" wins.

NIGERIA

Nigerian children play *ta galagala*. Their hopscotch has eight circles. A player throws a stone into the first circle. The player hops over the first circle, and hops and jumps to the end of the pattern. Then the player claps, jumps around, and hops and jumps back to the beginning.

BOLIVIA

La thunkuña is the name for hopscotch in Bolivia. Here, children draw a ladder pattern. Each square in the pattern has a word in it. The last two squares have the Spanish words for *heaven* and *Earth*. Players take turns throwing markers into a square. They hop over the square, and hop and jump their way to Earth. They repeat this until they have gone through the whole pattern without making a mistake. The first one to do this wins.

Think About It

Which other hopscotch is most like the hopscotch game that you know? Which one is different?

Name _____ Date _____

Check Your **Understanding**

Fill in the letter with the best answer for each question.

1. How is hopscotch the same wherever it is played?

Ⓐ Children always use chalk to draw the hopscotch board.

Ⓑ Children hop in and out of a spiral shape.

Ⓒ Children draw a ladder pattern.

Ⓓ Children hop or jump on a design they draw on the ground.

2. How is hopscotch alike in France, Nigeria, and Bolivia?

Ⓐ Children hop their way through this design only once.

Ⓑ Children hop over sections with markers or initials.

Ⓒ Children hop in and out of a spiral shape.

Ⓓ Children hop and clap when they reach the end.

3. How is hopscotch different in France and Bolivia?

Ⓐ One uses a spiral design, and the other uses a design of eight circles.

Ⓑ One is drawn in sand, and one is painted.

Ⓒ One uses a spiral design, and one uses a ladder design.

Ⓓ In one, children clap and jump, and in the other, children just hop.

4. In which country do children write their initials in "houses"?

Ⓐ France   Ⓒ Bolivia

Ⓑ Nigeria   Ⓓ all three countries

5. What conclusion can you draw?

Ⓐ Children all over the world enjoy playing games.

Ⓑ Children do not like games.

Ⓒ Hopscotch was invented in France.

Ⓓ Most children dislike hopscotch.

Vocabulary

Find each vocabulary word in the selection. The words and sentences around it will help you figure out its meaning.

Fill in the letter with the best definition of the underlined word.

1. Each country has its own <u>variation</u> of hopscotch.

Ⓐ opinion

Ⓑ different form of something

Ⓒ name

Ⓓ feeling

2. Children draw a <u>pattern</u> on the ground.

Ⓐ sound   Ⓒ design

Ⓑ written rules Ⓓ open space

3. They hop and jump from one <u>section</u> to another.

Ⓐ part   Ⓒ rule

Ⓑ marker Ⓓ scratch marks

4. Children around the <u>globe</u> play hopscotch.

Ⓐ hopscotch shape Ⓒ game marker

Ⓑ pile of dirt   Ⓓ world

5. In France, children hop in and out of a snail-shaped <u>spiral</u>.

Ⓐ curved design Ⓒ color

Ⓑ shell   Ⓓ building

Hi-Lo Nonfiction Passages for Struggling Readers: Grades 4-5 • Scholastic Inc.

Name _____ Date _____

Word Work

> **Antonyms** are words that have opposite meanings. For example, *lost* and *found* are antonyms.

Read the sentences and the words below. Write the word that means the opposite of the word in dark type.

catch   different   last   lose   out

1. The rules are not the **same**. The rules are _____.

2. I will **throw** the ball. You will _____ the ball.

3. I was not the **first** in line. I was the _____ in line.

4. I hope I **win** the game. I don't want to _____.

5. I put the chalk **in** the box. You took the chalk _____ of the box.

> Most nouns are made **plural** by adding **-s** or **-es**. If a noun ends in *y*, we usually change the *y* to *i* and add -*es*.
>
> **pattern** ⟶ **patterns**
>
> **country** ⟶ **countries**

Write the plural of each word.

6. initial   _____

7. house   _____

8. player   _____

9. game   _____

10. candy   _____

Write Now

In "Globe Hopping," you read about hopscotch in several different countries and learned how the games were alike and different. Look at the Venn diagram shown. It compares hopscotch in Nigeria to hopscotch in Bolivia. How are the two games alike? How are they different?

- Create your own Venn diagram to compare and contrast two versions of a game. You might compare card games, board games, outdoor games, or sports. Use headings that will help you figure out what is the same and what is different about the games.

- Use your Venn diagram to help you write a paragraph comparing and contrasting two games.

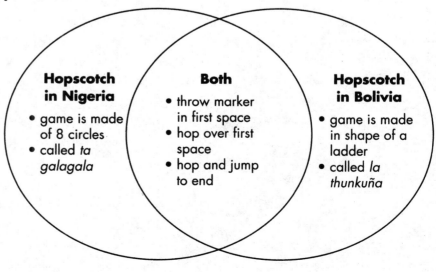

Hopscotch in Nigeria
- game is made of 8 circles
- called *ta galagala*

Both
- throw marker in first space
- hop over first space
- hop and jump to end

Hopscotch in Bolivia
- game is made in shape of a ladder
- called *la thunkuña*

Mr. Naismith's Game

by Erna Steck

Set Your Purpose

What do you know about basketball? Read this article to find out how this game started and how it has changed.

Winter in Springfield, Massachusetts, could make a penguin shiver. Snow and wind keep people inside. Days can seem very long.

That's as true today as it was in 1891 when James Naismith lived there.

Naismith was a gym teacher. His students were bored with the same indoor exercises. They wanted excitement.

So Naismith **invented** a game.

First, he found two peach baskets and nailed them to the balconies at opposite ends of the gymnasium.

Next, he made some rules—thirteen in all.

Then, he **divided** students into two teams. Each team had nine players who wore long pants and long-sleeved jerseys. The idea of the game was to **toss** an old soccer ball into the baskets. The team that **scored** the most baskets won. They called the game Basket Ball!

Naismith's game was a hit. His students loved playing, and so did others who heard about it. Soon people in other states were playing. As the game grew, rules changed. Equipment changed, too. But the idea was the same; put the ball in the basket.

In those early days, basketball was a rough sport. Excited fans often **interfered** with the game, and rowdy fans threw objects onto the court. Players pushed each other and got into fights. For a while, referees carried weapons to maintain control of the game!

Today, basketball has changed. Players wear shorts and sleeveless jerseys. The basket is a metal hoop with a net. The basketball is bouncy and round. Players and fans behave themselves most of the time.

Some things haven't changed, though. Basketball is still exciting and fun. People still love to play. And, of course, the idea of the game is the same; put the ball in the basket!

Think About It

How has basketball changed since it was invented?

Name _____   Date _____

Check Your Understanding

Fill in the letter with the best answer for each question.

1. Peach baskets were first used in basketball; today, baskets are made of
  (A) wire hoops with nails.
  (B) peach hoops.
  (C) soccer hoops.
  (D) metal hoops with nets.

2. Which of these has not changed in the game of basketball?
  (A) the idea of the game
  (B) the players' uniforms
  (C) the way that fans behave
  (D) the rules

3. Compared to basketball games today, basketball games long ago were
  (A) quiet and boring.
  (B) played outdoors.
  (C) very rough and violent.
  (D) long and tiring.

4. Naismith invented basketball because
  (A) he wanted to be a professional basketball player.
  (B) he wanted to be rich and famous.
  (C) every other sport had already been invented.
  (D) his students wanted to play something new and exciting.

5. Which of these is a fact?
  (A) James Naismith invented basketball in 1891.
  (B) Basketball is an exciting and fun game to play.
  (C) Fans who throw objects onto the court should be punished.
  (D) The best players always follow the rules.

Vocabulary

Find each vocabulary word in the selection. The words and sentences around it will help you figure out its meaning.

Fill in the letter with the best definition of the underlined word.

1. Naismith <u>invented</u> a game.
  (A) refused to play
  (B) forgot
  (C) made up
  (D) worried about

2. He <u>divided</u> students into two teams.
  (A) split into groups
  (B) yelled at loudly
  (C) taught skills to
  (D) was mean to

3. The idea of the game was to <u>toss</u> a ball into the baskets.
  (A) wish
  (B) knock over
  (C) remember
  (D) throw

4. The team that <u>scored</u> the most baskets won.
  (A) named
  (B) had an idea
  (C) made points in a game
  (D) heard about

5. Excited fans often <u>interfered</u> with the game.
  (A) got angry
  (B) got in the way
  (C) received a gift
  (D) served food

Name _____ Date _____

Word Work

Most nouns are made **plural** by adding **-s** or **-es**. If a noun ends in *y*, we usually change the *y* to *i* and add *-es*.

Write the plural of each word.

1. teacher _____

2. student _____

3. balcony _____

4. object _____

5. factory _____

Read each sentence and the words below. Write the correct plural form of the word that best completes each sentence.

exercise   player   community
basket   trophy

6. Before each game, the team does _____ to warm up.

7. The _____ practice passing the ball to each other.

8. Each of the _____ has its own basketball league.

9. I scored seven _____ in our last game!

10. Both teams got _____ after the game.

Write Now

In the selection "Mr. Naismith's Game," you read about the game of basketball. Now, compare basketball to another sport you enjoy. Look at the chart. It will help you get started.

- Plan to write a short essay comparing basketball to another sport. Begin with a topic sentence that states your main idea. For example, "Basketball is more fun to play than baseball."

- Write your short essay. Your chart can help you add details that support your main idea.

Basketball
Players are divided into two teams.
It is a popular game.
Players toss the ball in a basket to score points.

Hi-Lo Nonfiction Passages for Struggling Readers: Grades 4–5 • Scholastic Inc.

235

Summarizing

❖ When you read, it's a good idea to stop now and then to **summarize** the important points.

- As you read, ask yourself: **"What is the selection about?"**

- The answer tells you the **topic.** This can be a word, a phrase, or a sentence.

- Ask yourself: **"What are the most important points?"** Restate these in your own words.

- Keep the summary short. Include only the important points.

❖ Read this paragraph. Think about the topic and the main points the author is making about the topic. How can you **summarize** the paragraph?

Topic
The second sentence states the **topic:** *the Dog Museum of America.*

Main Points
These sentences make important points about the topic.

A Museum for Dog Lovers

Are you a dog lover? <u>Then you'd love the Dog Museum of America in St. Louis, Missouri.</u> Visitors are greeted by a giant merry-go-round figure of a mastiff known as Queen. <u>The museum has oil paintings and statues of dogs. It has videotapes where you can learn about more than 80 kinds of dog.</u> Best of all—this is one museum where dogs are welcome guests!

❖ You could **summarize** this paragraph like this:

> The Dog Museum of America is in Saint Louis, Missouri. The museum has paintings and statues of dogs and videotapes about different breeds of dog.

Your Turn

❖ Read this passage. Look for the most important points to **summarize**. Then write your summary.

There's a Museum for That?

Somewhere there's a museum for just about anything you can name. Pick a topic, any topic. There's bound to be a museum for it. Here are just a few of the stranger ones.

The Museum of Dirt in Boston has collections of—dirt! Its walls are lined with vials of dirt from interesting places and from famous people.

At the Children's Garbage Museum and Education Center in Stratford, Connecticut, you can watch trash being recycled.

The Museum of Bathroom Tissue in Madison, Wisconsin, features more than 3,000 rolls of tissue. One of its more valuable rolls came from Elvis Presley's home, Graceland.

The Great Wall of China

by Nancy Crowley

Set Your Purpose

Read this article to learn about one of the most amazing things ever built—the Great Wall of China.

What's the biggest wall you've ever seen? Is it 30 feet tall? Is it thousands of miles long? Does it show up in some pictures from space? Probably not. There's only one wall that big. It's the Great Wall of China.

Think About It

Do you think that a wall like the Great Wall could still protect China from its enemies? Why or why not?

Two thousand years ago, China had many enemies. The emperor thought a strong wall would keep China **secure**. He had people **mend** old walls. He had them build new ones out of stone and mud. Then they **connected** all the walls. It was 3,000 miles long!

For the next 1,000 years, other emperors **extended** the wall. Finally, it stretched for 4,500 miles. Much of it still stands today.

Name _____ Date _____

Check Your Understanding

Fill in the letter with the best answer for each question.

1. Which event happened first?

Ⓐ Astronauts saw the Great Wall from space.

Ⓑ People mended old walls.

Ⓒ The emperor decided to build the wall.

2. Which event happened last?

Ⓐ Old walls and new walls were connected.

Ⓑ Other emperors extended the wall.

Ⓒ China had many enemies.

3. The building of the Great Wall began

Ⓐ about 2,000 years ago.

Ⓑ two years ago.

Ⓒ about 20 years ago.

4. Which statement is a fact?

Ⓐ The Great Wall was 4,500 miles long.

Ⓑ Building the Great Wall was a bad idea.

Ⓒ The Great Wall was a Chinese folktale.

Vocabulary

Find each vocabulary word in the selection. The words and sentences around it will help you figure out its meaning.

Fill in the letter with the best definition of the underlined word.

1. The strong wall kept China <u>secure</u>.

Ⓐ safe

Ⓑ old

Ⓒ modern

2. People had to <u>mend</u> the old, broken walls.

Ⓐ tear down

Ⓑ fix

Ⓒ climb over

3. The old walls were <u>connected</u> to the new walls.

Ⓐ moved

Ⓑ mailed

Ⓒ joined

4. Later, other emperors <u>extended</u> the Great Wall.

Ⓐ tore down

Ⓑ made longer

Ⓒ didn't like

Name _____ **Date** _____

Word Work

| The letters **a_e** stand for the **long-a** sound in *space*. |
| The letters **i_e** stand for the **long-i** sound in *mile*. |
| The letters **o_e** stand for the **long-o** sound in *stone*. |

Read the word. Fill in the letter with the picture whose name has the same long vowel sound.

1. lace   Ⓐ   Ⓑ

2. size   Ⓐ   Ⓑ **5**

3. rope   Ⓐ   Ⓑ

4. tide   Ⓐ   Ⓑ

5. date   Ⓐ   Ⓑ

6. home   Ⓐ   Ⓑ

Read the words below. Write the word that completes each sentence.

safe   miles   stones   gates

7. The Great Wall is thousands of _____ long.

8. It was built to keep China _____ from enemies.

9. People could travel through _____ in the wall.

10. The Great Wall was built out of _____ and mud.

Write Now

In the article "The Great Wall of China," you read about why the wall was built. Imagine that you are the emperor of China.

• Plan to write a speech explaining why building the wall is a good idea. Copy the web shown here. Use facts from the article and your imagination. Add your ideas to the web.

• Write your speech. Use the ideas on your web.

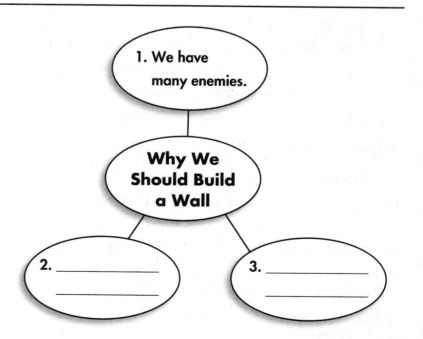

1. We have many enemies.

Why We Should Build a Wall

2. _____

3. _____

SAGUAROS of the SOUTHWEST

by Ann Ripton

Set Your Purpose

Would you know a saguaro when you see one? Read this article to learn more about this gentle giant of the Southwest.

The Native Americans of Arizona have a friend in the saguaro (sah GWAR oh) plant. This type of plant is a **cactus**. Cactus plants grow in the desert.

Spotting a saguaro cactus is not hard. These cactuses grow to 60 feet. That's very tall! Their branches **curve** upward. Birds and small animals often build nests in holes in the saguaro. An old saguaro can have so many nests it is almost like an animal apartment house.

Not much rain falls in the desert. When it does rain, the roots of the saguaros soak up all the water they can. They store the water in their branches. The desert gets most of its rain in the late spring. That is when the saguaros bloom. Their huge flowers are white. Birds, bats, and insects drink the nectar from them. They also spread **pollen** from flower to flower.

Soon after the saguaro flowers, the fruit begins to grow. It is purple and shaped like an egg. It **ripens** slowly. Then it falls to the ground and splits open. The fruit is the same color as the inside of a watermelon. It has black seeds like a watermelon, too. Bats and birds and insects suck on the fruit. Some of them also eat the seeds.

The Native Americans gather the fruit also. They love its taste. They make it into jams, jellies, and a thick **syrup**.

Native Americans have lived with the giant saguaros for centuries and honor them for what they provide. And all people love the beauty the saguaros bring to the desert.

Think About It

How does the saguaro cactus help the people and animals of the Arizona desert?

Name_____   Date_____

Check Your **Understanding**

Fill in the letter with the best answer for each question.

1. How is the saguaro useful to animals of the desert?

Ⓐ It gives them a place to nest and food to eat.
Ⓑ It keeps them warm.
Ⓒ It makes the desert cooler.
Ⓓ It makes more rain fall in the desert.

2. How does the saguaro get enough water to survive?

Ⓐ Its branches collect dew.
Ⓑ Its roots suck up rainwater. The water is stored in the branches.
Ⓒ The plant's upward-curving branches reach for rain.
Ⓓ Huge pools of water surround the plant after a rain.

3. How is the saguaro flower useful?

Ⓐ The flower is very large and white.
Ⓑ The flower has a lovely smell.
Ⓒ The flower produces nectar to feed birds, bats, and insects.
Ⓓ The flower blooms in the spring.

4. How is the saguaro fruit useful?

Ⓐ The fruit is purplish in color.
Ⓑ The fruit is pink with black seeds.
Ⓒ The fruit supplies food for desert creatures and humans.
Ⓓ The fruit splits when it hits the ground.

5. How is a saguaro cactus like an apartment house?

Ⓐ It has an elevator.
Ⓑ It has many homes in it.
Ⓒ It is found in a city.
Ⓓ It is made of bricks.

Vocabulary

Find each vocabulary word in the selection. The words and sentences around it will help you figure out its meaning.

Fill in the letter with the best definition of the underlined word.

1. The saguaro is a <u>cactus</u> that stores water in its branches.

Ⓐ type of desert sand
Ⓑ animal who lives in the desert
Ⓒ kind of desert plant
Ⓓ person who lives in the desert

2. The branches of the saguaro <u>curve</u> gently.

Ⓐ bend   Ⓒ break
Ⓑ grow   Ⓓ rot

3. Birds, bats, and insects spread <u>pollen</u> from flower to flower.

Ⓐ desert sand   Ⓒ small bugs in a plant
Ⓑ raindrops   Ⓓ tiny yellow grains in a flower

4. When the fruit <u>ripens</u>, we can eat it.

Ⓐ gets hard and sour
Ⓑ gets mushy and old
Ⓒ becomes soft and ready to eat
Ⓓ turns brown and rots

5. We made a <u>syrup</u> from the juices.

Ⓐ sour drink   Ⓒ lumpy paste
Ⓑ thin soup   Ⓓ thick, sweet liquid

Hi-Lo Nonfiction Passages for Struggling Readers Grades 4–5 • Scholastic Inc.

Name _____   Date _____

Word Work

A **possessive noun** shows ownership. To make a singular noun possessive, add **'s**. To make a plural noun possessive, add an apostrophe after the s (**s'**). Add 's to plural nouns that do not end in s.

cat ⟶ cat's
cats ⟶ cats'

Match the word on the left with its correct possessive form on the right.

____ **1.** deserts   **A.** desert's

____ **2.** desert   **B.** flowers'

____ **3.** fruits   **C.** fruit's

____ **4.** fruit   **D.** fruits'

____ **5.** flowers   **E.** deserts'

Read each pair of sentences. Write the correct possessive noun that completes the second sentence.

6. This nest belongs to a mouse. It is the
_____ nest.

7. These fruits belong to the saguaros. They are the _____ fruits.

8. That sand belongs to the desert. It is the _____ sand.

9. Those shadows belong to the bats. They are the _____ shadows.

10. The saguaro is the state plant of Arizona. It is _____ state plant.

Write Now

In the selection "Saguaros of the Southwest," you learned about a kind of cactus that helps many animals and humans in the deserts of Arizona.

• Plan to write a poem from the saguaro's point of view. Use the pronoun *I*, as if you were the cactus. Describe what it is like to be a cactus in the desert. Explain how you are useful. Use a chart like the one below to organize your ideas.

What It's Like to Be a Saguaro	
What I see, hear, and feel in the desert	How I am useful and good

• Write your poem. Remember to write as if the plant were really talking. (Your poem does not need to rhyme.) Use your chart to help you.

Go, Dog, Go!

by Carole Osterink

Set Your Purpose

Read the title of this article. What do you think the article might be about? Read to find out.

Dogs play sports. Some dogs play catch. Some go swimming. In Alaska, dogs are famous for **competing** in sled races with their owners. But dogs don't have to play human sports. Dogs have their very own sports to play.

Dog shows are a **type** of dog sport. During dog shows, dogs compete to win prizes. They can win at **different** kinds of contests. In one contest, called Dog Agility, dogs run an obstacle course.

An obstacle is something that gets in your way. The obstacles in Dog Agility are just like things found in real life. Dogs must walk over a swinging bridge. They must **weave** around

Think About It

Was your prediction about the article correct? Why do you think the selection is called "Go, Dog, Go!"?

poles. They must jump over fences and crawl through tunnels. **Handlers** run alongside their dogs. They teach their dogs how to get past each obstacle. Dogs are scored on how well and how quickly they run the course.

Dog Agility is an exciting sport. It's exciting for the dogs and their handlers. It is certainly fun to watch. It's also the fastest-growing dog sport in the country.

Dogs enjoy sports, just as humans do. They enjoy learning. They like working to become really good at their sport. They like winning. They even like performing for their fans.

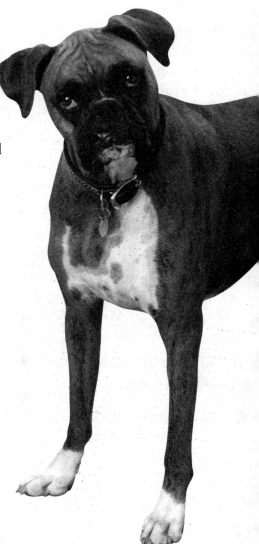

Name_____ Date_____

Check Your **Understanding**

Fill in the letter with the best answer for each question.

1. Another good name for this article would be
Ⓐ Dogs Run Wild.
Ⓑ Dog Agility: A New Exciting Sport.
Ⓒ Dogs Are Great.
Ⓓ Dogs Who Are Sports Stars.

2. In Dog Agility, dogs
Ⓐ jump over streams.
Ⓑ run obstacle courses.
Ⓒ run through the woods.
Ⓓ play catch and swim.

3. Dog sports are
Ⓐ fun for dogs, but boring to watch.
Ⓑ too difficult for most dogs.
Ⓒ exciting for dogs and people.
Ⓓ fun to watch, but boring for dogs.

4. What do the people who handle the dogs do?
Ⓐ They teach their dogs how to get past each obstacle.
Ⓑ They toss balls to their dogs.
Ⓒ They give each dog a score.
Ⓓ They feed their dogs between obstacles.

5. Which of the following states an opinion?
Ⓐ Dog shows are a type of dog sport.
Ⓑ Dog sports are more exciting than human sports.
Ⓒ Obstacle courses have bridges, poles, fences, and tunnels.
Ⓓ Dogs are scored on how well they run the course.

Vocabulary

Find each vocabulary word in the selection. The words and sentences around it will help you figure out its meaning.

Fill in the letter with the best definition of the underlined word.

1. In Alaska, dogs are famous for <u>competing</u> in sled races.
Ⓐ completing
Ⓑ playing to win
Ⓒ watching a game
Ⓓ being strong

2. Dog shows are a <u>type</u> of dog sport.
Ⓐ kind or sort
Ⓑ letter or key
Ⓒ display
Ⓓ movie

3. At dog shows, dogs can win at <u>different</u> kinds of contests.
Ⓐ more fun
Ⓑ harder
Ⓒ not the same
Ⓓ similar

4. Dogs must jump over fences and <u>weave</u> around poles.
Ⓐ move slowly
Ⓑ walk straight into
Ⓒ tie strings together
Ⓓ move from side to side to get through

5. Dog Agility is an exciting sport for dogs and their <u>handlers</u>.
Ⓐ people who do odd jobs
Ⓑ people who buy dogs
Ⓒ people who sell dogs
Ⓓ people who train their dogs

Hi-Lo Nonfiction Passages for Struggling Readers: Grades 4–5 • Scholastic Inc.

Name _____ **Date** _____

Word Work

A **compound word** is made of two shorter words. To understand a compound word, separate it into the two shorter words and think about the meaning of those words.

some + thing = something

Make compound words by combining each word on the left with a word on the right. Write the compound word that best completes the sentence.

foot	park
touch	one
dog	down
every	house
ball	ball

1. In one movie, a dog became a _____ player.

2. He caught the ball and ran for a _____.

3. The crowd in the _____ was amazed.

4. When the game was over, _____ wanted to pat the dog.

5. The dog hid in his _____.

Many one-syllable verbs that end with an *e* will drop the e when **-ed** or **-ing** is added.

live   lived   living

Read each sentence. Add the suffix *-ed* or *-ing* to the word in dark type.

6. score   Dogs are _____ on how well they run the course.

7. excite   Being in the agility trials is _____ for all the dogs.

8. like   All the dogs _____ running the agility course.

9. imagine   We never _____ dogs had their own sports.

10. weave   The dogs were _____ in and out of the poles.

Write Now

Use the information in "Go, Dog, Go!" to picture the obstacle course in your mind. If you could design your own, what would it look like?

• Plan to write a description of a dog running an obstacle course. First, design an obstacle course on paper. Decide what kinds of obstacles you want in your course. Then decide what order they should be in. Use a diagram like the one shown here to arrange your obstacles.

• Write a paragraph describing an obstacle race. It may help you to imagine yourself as a sports announcer as you write.

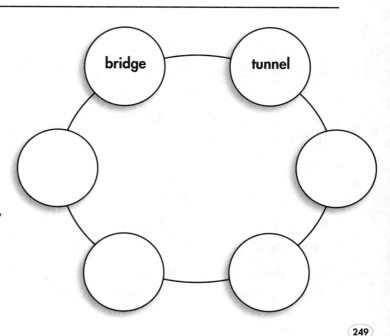

SURPRISE!
10,000 for Dinner

by Stephanie Lesser

Set Your Purpose

How much do you know about dolphins? Read this article to find out some interesting facts about these playful creatures.

A ship was sailing in a part of the ocean called the Persian Gulf. Suddenly, people on the ship saw a strange sight. It looked like a huge reef. (A reef is like an **island** made out of coral.) But there wasn't any reef on their maps.

As the ship sailed closer, the reef moved! Then the people on the ship saw that it wasn't a reef at all. It was **dolphins**! 10,000 dolphins! They had gathered for a dolphin dinner party. It was one of the largest collections of dolphins ever seen at one time.

Dolphins **travel** in groups called pods. A dolphin pod will often join another pod to catch and eat fish. Often pods get together about the same time each day to eat. A pod will catch and eat fish for about an hour.

Want to know more about dolphins? Here's Dolly Dolphin to explain.

Every part of a dolphin's body does a special job.

I open my blowhole to **breathe** in air. I'm a mammal, you know. I close my blowhole when I dive underwater.

I may have small ears, but I hear much better than humans do.

My flippers help me steer. They go left, right, up, and down!

My dorsal, or back, fin keeps me from tipping over. Some people think this fin makes me look like a shark.

Think About It

Did you learn anything new about dolphins?

My tail is very strong. When I move it up and down—whoosh— I **speed** through water.

Name _____ Date _____

Check Your **Understanding**

Fill in the letter with the best answer for each question.

1. What is another good title for this article?
Ⓐ Calypso and a Strange Sight
Ⓑ Playing with Dolphins
Ⓒ The Dolphin Dinner Party
Ⓓ The Sailing Ship

2. Which sentence is the best summary of everything Dolly Dolphin says?
Ⓐ A dolphin is built to move quickly and easily through water.
Ⓑ A dolphin uses its flippers for steering.
Ⓒ Dolphins are often mistaken for sharks.
Ⓓ A dolphin's tail is very strong.

3. A dolphin pod is
Ⓐ a place where dolphins sleep.
Ⓑ a group of dolphins that travel together.
Ⓒ a pool where dolphins swim.
Ⓓ dolphins that eat at the same time of the day.

4. Which of these sentences states a fact?
Ⓐ People who see dolphins are lucky.
Ⓑ Dolphins are playful and sweet.
Ⓒ Dolphins use their flippers to steer.
Ⓓ Animals with small ears look funny.

5. From what Dolly Dolphin says about her blowhole, you can conclude that
Ⓐ dolphins can breathe underwater.
Ⓑ dolphins hold their breath underwater.
Ⓒ dolphins don't hear as well as humans do.
Ⓓ dolphins are very poor swimmers.

Vocabulary

Find each vocabulary word in the selection. The words and sentences around it will help you figure out its meaning.

Fill in the letter with the best definition of the underlined word.

1. A coral reef is like an underlined{island}.
Ⓐ land surrounded by water
Ⓑ a party
Ⓒ a ship
Ⓓ a cold place

2. Dolphins underline{travel} in groups called pods.
Ⓐ go places   Ⓒ dinner
Ⓑ talk loudly   Ⓓ have a party

3. It was one of the largest collections of underline{dolphins} ever seen at one time.
Ⓐ animals that live on land
Ⓑ animals that live in ponds
Ⓒ animals that live in the ocean
Ⓓ animals that live in rain forests

4. A dolphin opens its blowhole to underline{breathe} in air.
Ⓐ chew loudly   Ⓒ watch from a distance
Ⓑ open up   Ⓓ bring air into the body

5. A dolphin's tail can make it underline{speed} through the water.
Ⓐ stay still   Ⓒ move very fast
Ⓑ tip over   Ⓓ sink to the bottom

Name_____ **Date**_____

Word Work

A **noun** names a person, place, or thing. A **plural noun** names more than one person, place, or thing. To make the plural of most nouns, add **-s**. Add **-es** if the noun ends with s, ss, x, sh, ch, or tch.

Examples:

map	maps
box	boxes
wish	wishes

Write the plural of each word.

1. pod _____
2. creature _____
3. dish _____
4. class _____
5. watch _____

Read each sentence. Write the correct plural form of the word in dark type.

6. **dolphin** It was neat to see _____ swimming at the beach.

7. **whistle** Dolphins speak to each other with squeaks and _____.

8. **fox** Dolphins are as clever as _____.

9. **blowhole** Dolphins breathe in air through their _____.

10. **ear** Dolphins have small _____ but they hear very well.

Write Now

In "Surprise! 10,000 for Dinner," you learned how dolphins travel, how they eat, and how their bodies are built. Look at the chart.

How dolphins travel	How dolphins eat	How dolphins' bodies are built
In pods	Pods get together with other pods. A pod catches and eats fish for about an hour.	Strong tail—for speed Dorsal fin—for balance Flippers—for steering Blowhole—to breathe air Ears—small but powerful

• Plan to describe a different animal. Make a chart like the one above. List the features that make this animal special. Describe or explain each feature.

• Write your description. Use the information in your chart. If you wish, draw a picture of the animal and label its special features.

A Tasty Time

by Barbara M. Linde

Where can you take a bite out of a giant chocolate dinosaur? Where can you munch on a **huge** peanut butter sandwich? Where can you eat buckets of ice cream? Where? At a food festival, that's where!

All kinds of communities hold food festivals. They often celebrate foods made from local crops. People come from all over to eat the good food. They also enter cooking contests.

Set Your Purpose

Do you like to try new foods? Read this article to find out about some places where trying new foods is the thing to do.

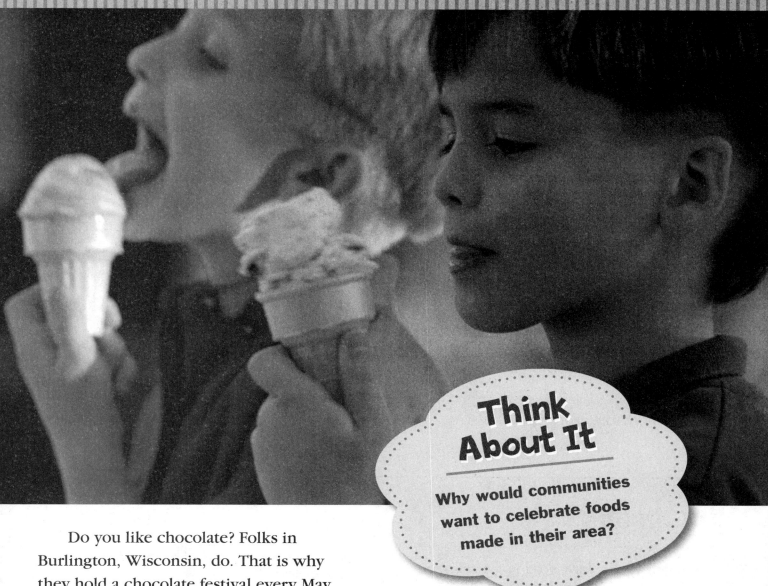

Think About It

Why would communities want to celebrate foods made in their area?

Do you like chocolate? Folks in Burlington, Wisconsin, do. That is why they hold a chocolate festival every May. People make giant chocolate **castles** and dinosaurs. On the last day of the festival, they get big hammers. They break the chocolate. Then everybody can eat it. If you don't want to eat a lot, you can enjoy the parade. Or you can visit the petting zoo or watch the clowns.

Have you had enough chocolate? Then visit the home of the world's largest peanut butter sandwich. It was made at the Georgia Peanut Festival in Georgia. It was almost 13 feet long and 13 feet wide! You can watch the parade while you eat. Before you leave, you can also buy a book of peanut **recipes**. They are written by kids just like you.

If you want a cool treat, go to Lancaster, Pennsylvania. Every July they hold an ice cream festival. There is even a contest for kids. Kids **stack** as much ice cream onto their cones as they can. The one with the most **scoops** wins free ice cream for a whole year!

Are you hungry yet? Find a food festival near you. Just follow your nose to all those yummy smells!

Name _____ Date _____

Check Your Understanding

Fill in the letter with the best answer for each question.

1. Most people go to food festivals to
   - Ⓐ try new foods.
   - Ⓑ tease the cooks.
   - Ⓒ draw pictures.
   - Ⓓ buy clothes.

2. The chocolate festival and the peanut festival both have
   - Ⓐ clowns.
   - Ⓑ animals.
   - Ⓒ parades.
   - Ⓓ contests.

3. Only the peanut festival has a
   - Ⓐ circus.
   - Ⓑ cooking contest.
   - Ⓒ recipe book written by kids.
   - Ⓓ giant dinosaur and a castle.

4. The winner of the ice cream scoop contest gets
   - Ⓐ a ribbon.
   - Ⓑ a trophy.
   - Ⓒ ice cream cones for his or her friends.
   - Ⓓ free ice cream for a whole year.

5. Each of the festivals is
   - Ⓐ expensive.
   - Ⓑ open to the public.
   - Ⓒ in July.
   - Ⓓ in Pennsylvania.

Vocabulary

Find each vocabulary word in the selection. The words and sentences around it will help you figure out its meaning.

Fill in the letter with the best definition of the underlined word.

1. Where can you find a huge sandwich?
   - Ⓐ very hard
   - Ⓑ very cold
   - Ⓒ very large
   - Ⓓ very sticky

2. The giant castles and dinosaurs were made of chocolate.
   - Ⓐ small wagons with two wheels
   - Ⓑ animals that live in the jungle
   - Ⓒ sweet-smelling flowers
   - Ⓓ very large buildings

3. Every year, they sell a book of peanut recipes.
   - Ⓐ stories and jokes
   - Ⓑ paper dolls
   - Ⓒ instructions for making food
   - Ⓓ places that have festivals

4. We had to stack scoops of ice cream to win.
   - Ⓐ pile up
   - Ⓑ cook
   - Ⓒ put in a row
   - Ⓓ wrap in paper

5. The boy or girl with the most scoops wins.
   - Ⓐ chunks of chocolate
   - Ⓑ a big, deep spoonful of food
   - Ⓒ food eaten with a fork
   - Ⓓ bits of broken ice cream cone

Name _____   Date _____

Word Work

> The letters **oo** can stand for the sound you hear in *book*. They can also stand for the sound you hear in *boots*.
>
> **b**oo**k**   **b**oo**ts**

Read each word in dark print. Fill in the letter of the word that has the same vowel sound.

1. cook
Ⓐ book   Ⓑ boots

2. food
Ⓐ book   Ⓑ boots

3. scoops
Ⓐ book   Ⓑ boots

4. wood
Ⓐ book   Ⓑ boots

5. foot
Ⓐ book   Ⓑ boots

Fill in the letter of the word that has the same sound as the underlined word.

6. The peanut ice cream tastes <u>good</u>.
Ⓐ cook   Ⓒ stool
Ⓑ moon   Ⓓ broom

7. Did you pet the <u>goose</u> at the chocolate festival?
Ⓐ book   Ⓒ tooth
Ⓑ hoof   Ⓓ took

8. I <u>stood</u> on a bench to see the peanut festival parade.
Ⓐ broom   Ⓒ goof
Ⓑ foot   Ⓓ pool

9. How may <u>scoops</u> of ice cream did you stack?
Ⓐ brook   Ⓒ shook
Ⓑ hood   Ⓓ boots

10. What recipe did you <u>cook</u> for the contest?
Ⓐ soon   Ⓒ tooth
Ⓑ noon   Ⓓ look

Write Now

In "A Tasty Time," you learned about food festivals and the fun things people can do at them. Think about how you might advertise or tell people about an upcoming festival.

- Plan to make a flyer, or ad, for a food festival. What food would you like to celebrate? What activities would you like to have at the festival? When and where would you hold the festival? Use a word web like the one shown to help you organize your ideas.

- Create a flyer for a food festival. Make sure to tell people the name of the festival and when and where it will be held. Describe some of the activities. Illustrate your flyer.

OCEANS
in Motion

adapted by Elsa Schmidt

Set Your Purpose

Scan this article and predict what it is about. Then read to find out why the author chose this title.

What's wet and covers three-fourths of the Earth's surface? It's the water that makes up the Earth's four oceans. These oceans are the Pacific, the Atlantic, the Indian, and the Arctic. The Pacific Ocean is the largest and deepest. The Arctic is the smallest and **shallowest**.

Waves

Stand on a beach sometime and watch the ocean. You will see that it is never still. The ocean is in **constant** motion. Wind blows across the surface of the water. This makes waves. Ocean waves **vary** in height. A light wind causes little ripples. In a hurricane, winds can whip up huge, dangerous waves more than 45 feet high.

Currents and Tides

Ocean currents are masses of water that move from shore to shore. Like waves, currents are caused by the wind. Ocean currents can be warm or cold. Near land, warm ocean currents make the air warmer. Cold ocean currents make the air colder.

At high tide, the ocean covers much of the beach. At low tide, you can walk on sand that had earlier been covered by ocean water. Tides are caused by the pull of gravity as the moon revolves around Earth.

More Than a Giant Pool

The ocean is the source of many different things people need. Ocean water **contains** salt, a basic cooking need. Ocean fishing provides many people with work and food.

The ocean is also a fun place to visit. Children who live near the ocean often like to swim in the waves, hunt for shells, and play in the sand.

The ocean may look like a giant pool of water. But it's much more than that.

Think About It

Do you think the author chose a good title for this selection? Why or why not?

Name _____ Date _____

Check Your Understanding

Fill in the letter with the best answer for each question.

1. Which is the best summary of the first paragraph?
- (A) Four oceans cover three-fourths of Earth's surface.
- (B) Water is wet.
- (C) The Pacific Ocean is the largest ocean.
- (D) The Arctic Ocean is the smallest.

2. Which is the best summary of "Waves"?
- (A) The ocean can be dangerous.
- (B) Blowing wind causes ocean waves.
- (C) Ocean waves vary in height.
- (D) Ripples are very small waves.

3. Another good title for "Oceans in Motion" would be
- (A) Water on the Move.
- (B) Ocean Fishing.
- (C) What Makes Oceans Pretty.
- (D) What Makes Oceans Noisy.

4. What happens when the hurricane winds blow across the water?
- (A) High waves form.
- (B) Small ripples form.
- (C) Air on land gets hot.
- (D) Ocean waters fall.

5. From the information in the selection, you can figure out that
- (A) the Indian Ocean is bigger than the Atlantic Ocean.
- (B) oceans provide many of the things people need.
- (C) it is always colder near the ocean.
- (D) everyone loves to swim.

Vocabulary

Find each vocabulary word in the selection. The words and sentences around it will help you figure out its meaning.

Fill in the letter with the best definition of the underlined word.

1. The Arctic is the smallest and <u>shallowest</u> ocean.
- (A) least deep
- (B) deepest
- (C) most dry
- (D) farthest away

2. The ocean is in <u>constant</u> motion.
- (A) very quiet and still
- (B) sometimes wild
- (C) always remembering
- (D) never stopping

3. Ocean waves <u>vary</u> in height.
- (A) always stay the same
- (B) are different
- (C) crash loudly
- (D) move quickly

4. The moon <u>revolves</u> around Earth.
- (A) rises and falls
- (B) warms and lights
- (C) breaks apart
- (D) moves in a circle around

5. Ocean water <u>contains</u> salt.
- (A) cleans
- (B) swims
- (C) holds
- (D) visits

Hi-Lo Nonfiction Passages for Struggling Readers Grades 4–5 • Scholastic Inc.

Name_____ Date_____

Word Work

> **Antonyms** are words that have the opposite meanings. For example, *hot* and *cold* are antonyms.

Read the sentences and the words below. Write the word that means the opposite of the word in dark type.

cool   falling   smallest   tiny   hotter

1. The Pacific is the **largest** ocean. The Arctic is the _____.

2. In the summer, the water is **warm**. In winter, the water is _____.

3. Currents can make the air **colder**. They can also make the air _____.

4. The number of fish in the oceans isn't **rising**. It is _____.

5. Hurricanes cause **huge** waves. Light winds cause _____ ripples.

> A **suffix** is an ending that changes the meaning of a base word. Knowing the meaning of a suffix helps you figure out the meaning of the whole word. The suffix **-er** means "more." The suffix **-est** means "most."
>
> **smaller**   more small
> **smallest**   most small

Write a word that fits the definition by adding the suffix -er or -est to the base word.

6. most hard   **hard**_____
7. most light   **light**_____
8. more cold   **cold**_____
9. most deep   **deep**_____
10. more near   **near**_____

Write Now

In "Oceans in Motion," you learned that the wind keeps Earth's oceans in motion. Look at the chart to see some other details about the ocean.

- Plan to write a poem about the ocean. First, add more facts from the article to the chart. Make check marks next to the facts you want to use in your poem.

- Write your poem about the ocean. Use the ideas you checked. You can make your poem rhyme or not—it's up to you.

> **Ocean Facts**
> **1.** Ocean currents can be warm or cold.
> **2.** At high tide, the ocean covers much of the beach.

Hi-Lo Nonfiction Passages for Struggling Readers: Grades 4–5 • Scholastic Inc.

261

A STICKY, SWEET DISASTER

by Margaret Ryan

BOSTON, MASSACHUSETTS — Some people said they heard a groaning sound as they walked by the tank. One woman said she heard loud knocking. It was as if someone were inside the huge tank trying to escape.

There wasn't anyone inside the tank, but there was molasses. In fact, there was more than one million gallons of molasses!

The molasses belonged to the Purity Distilling Company. It was **stored** in a large tank near the boat docks in Boston. The 50-foot-high tank was made of large iron plates that were held together with rivets, or metal bolts.

Molasses

is a thick syrup made from raw sugar. People use it to sweeten cereal, cakes, and cookies.

Set Your Purpose

Can you imagine a river of molasses? Read this newspaper article to find out about an unusual disaster.

The molasses flood destroyed houses.

At about noon on Wednesday, January 15, 1919, the pressure inside the tank became too great. One by one, the rivets popped, and the tank caved in. More than one million gallons of warm molasses poured out. The river of molasses moved with **tremendous** force.

The Great Molasses Flood of 1919 caused much damage in Boston.

Waves of molasses, from 15 to 35 feet high, swept the streets. Nothing in its path could escape. The molasses **flood** destroyed houses. It **demolished** cars. It caused a section of the city's elevated train tracks to collapse. Sadly, the Great Molasses Flood of 1919 also claimed 21 lives and injured 150 people.

The city of Boston was left with the stickiest mess in history.

Plain water wouldn't wash the molasses away. The city had to use saltwater from the harbor. It took six months before all traces of the molasses disappeared. But people said a sweet smell **lingered** in the air for much longer.

Some say that on a hot summer day in Boston the whiff of sweet molasses still perfumes the air!

Think About It

What happened in the Great Molasses Flood?

Name _____ **Date** _____

Check Your **Understanding**

Fill in the letter with the best answer for each question.

1. Which sentence is the best summary of this selection?

Ⓐ People heard strange noises when they passed by the molasses tank.

Ⓑ In 1919, a huge tank of molasses split open and flooded the streets of Boston.

Ⓒ The waves of molasses were 15 to 35 feet high!

Ⓓ More than one million gallons of molasses poured out of the tank.

2. Which sentence summarizes the damage done by the molasses flood?

Ⓐ A river of molasses poured down the streets.

Ⓑ People washed the sticky molasses off the streets, houses, and cars.

Ⓒ Cars, houses, and train tracks were destroyed, and 21 people died.

Ⓓ The molasses tank burst because the pressure inside became too great.

3. What did city workers discover about molasses during the cleanup?

Ⓐ It easily washes with plain water.

Ⓑ When warm, molasses spreads rapidly.

Ⓒ Saltwater washed away the molasses better than plain water.

Ⓓ There was no way to wash it away.

4. What was the author's purpose in writing this selection?

Ⓐ to entertain the reader with a funny story

Ⓑ to teach the reader about molasses

Ⓒ to inform the reader about a strange historical event

Ⓓ to warn the reader about a disaster

5. In which book would you probably find this selection?

Ⓐ *Early American History*

Ⓑ *Cooking With Molasses*

Ⓒ *Cleaning Our City Streets*

Ⓓ *Strange Accidents and Disasters*

Vocabulary

Find each vocabulary word in the selection. The words and sentences around it will help you figure out its meaning.

Fill in the letter with the best definition of the underlined word.

1. Molasses was <u>stored</u> near the boat docks.

Ⓐ held together   Ⓒ heard about

Ⓑ placed and kept in   Ⓓ forgotten for a short time

2. The river of molasses moved with <u>tremendous</u> force.

Ⓐ very small   Ⓒ very great

Ⓑ very cold   Ⓓ very weak

3. The molasses <u>flood</u> caused a lot of damage.

Ⓐ stickiness caused by melted sugar   Ⓒ sweet smell

Ⓑ large flow of water or other liquid over dry land   Ⓓ heavy rain

4. The flood of molasses damaged houses and <u>demolished</u> cars.

Ⓐ repaired quickly   Ⓒ destroyed

Ⓑ washed off   Ⓓ had a sweet smell

5. The sweet smell of molasses <u>lingered</u> in the air for months.

Ⓐ stayed behind   Ⓒ tasted

Ⓑ described   Ⓓ stood in a line

Name _____   Date _____

Word Work

Most nouns are made plural by adding **-s** or **-es**. If a noun ends in *y*, we usually change the *y* to *i* and add *-es*.

bike ⟶ **bikes**

baby ⟶ **babies**

Write the plural of each word.

1. cookie _____

2. gallon _____

3. city _____

4. wave _____

5. pony _____

Synonyms are words that have similar meanings. For example, *little* and *small* are synonyms.

Read the sentences and the words below. Write the word that means almost the same as the word in dark type.

discovered   dunked   smell   took   sign

6. I walked into the house and got a **whiff** of something yummy. _____

7. My nose detected a **trace** of molasses. _____

8. I **found** warm cookies in the kitchen. _____

9. I **claimed** a few for myself. _____

10. I **dipped** the cookies in a glass of milk. _____

Write Now

In a "A Sticky, Sweet Disaster," you read about the Great Molasses Flood, an event that really happened. In newspapers, you can read cartoons about events that happen in real life. Look at the chart to see some facts about the flood.

• Plan to write your own clever caption for a cartoon about "A Sticky, Sweet Disaster." Add some more interesting details about the flood to your chart. Think about pictures you could draw and captions you could write.

• Draw your cartoon and write your caption. Use language in a clever way to describe what is happening in your cartoon.

Great Molasses Flood

1. One million gallons of molasses poured onto the streets.

2. The flood destroyed houses.

What's a Chunnel?

adapted by Luther Owens

Set Your Purpose

How do you build a tunnel under a large body of water? Read this article to find out.

Here's a riddle: What is underwater, about 31 miles long, and cost 15 billion dollars to build? It's the Chunnel!

The Chunnel is under a part of the Atlantic Ocean called the English Channel. The English Channel is a body of water that **separates** England and France. Before the Chunnel opened in 1994, the only way to cross this water was to take a boat or a plane. Now there is another way.
A high-speed train system carries not only people, but their cars, too!

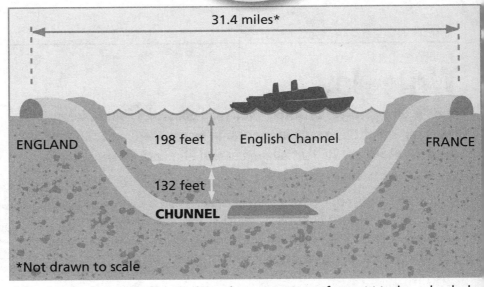

31.4 miles*

ENGLAND   198 feet   English Channel   FRANCE

132 feet

CHUNNEL

*Not drawn to scale

The Chunnel is 330 feet below the water's surface. Workers built the Chunnel where England and France are the closest together.

These workers are standing in front of the mole—the large piece of equipment that digs tunnels with its teeth.

The word *Chunnel* is a mix of two words: *channel* and *tunnel*. The Chunnel **links** England to other countries in Europe and makes moving people and goods a quick and easy **task**.

People had been trying to figure out a way to tunnel underneath the English Channel for almost 200 years. In 1986, work finally began.

The Chunnel is really three tunnels. Two tunnels are for traveling. One is an **emergency** escape tunnel. To build the tunnels, workers used special drilling machines called moles. The moles have hard steel teeth to **crunch** up rocks and dirt. These huge machines helped remove about 200 million pounds of rock!

In all, it took seven years to build the Chunnel. Ten thousand workers helped to make the tunnels. Workers dug from both England and France, and they met in the middle.

Finally, eight years and 15 billion dollars later, travelers don't have to swim, sail, or fly across the English Channel anymore. They can "Chunnel" their way through.

Think About It

What is the Chunnel? Why was it built?

Name _____ **Date** _____

Check Your **Understanding**

Fill in the letter with the best answer for each question.

1. Choose the best summary of the selection.
- Ⓐ Moving people from place to place is not always easy.
- Ⓑ The Chunnel makes it easy to travel from England to France.
- Ⓒ People have emergencies in the Chunnel.
- Ⓓ People can travel to France by boat.

2. Which statement best summarizes the work that was involved in building the Chunnel?
- Ⓐ The Chunnel cost 15 billion dollars.
- Ⓑ The Chunnel connects England with France.
- Ⓒ Work began in 1986.
- Ⓓ Workers broke up and removed 200 million pounds of rock.

3. What problem did the Chunnel solve?
- Ⓐ It made the movement of people and goods quicker and easier.
- Ⓑ It put cars on a high-speed train.
- Ⓒ It cost 15 billion dollars and took seven years.
- Ⓓ It kept ten thousand workers busy.

4. Why do you think the author wrote this selection?
- Ⓐ to entertain us
- Ⓑ to sell us tickets on the Chunnel train
- Ⓒ to teach us about the Chunnel
- Ⓓ to encourage us to build tunnels at home

5. An article about the Chunnel might be found in a magazine about
- Ⓐ traveling between England and Europe.
- Ⓑ strange stories from England and France.
- Ⓒ real people who live in England or Europe.
- Ⓓ current events in England or Europe.

Vocabulary

Find each vocabulary word in the selection. The words and sentences around it will help you figure out its meaning.

Fill in the letter with the best definition of the underlined word.

1. The English Channel <u>separates</u> England and France.
- Ⓐ mixes
- Ⓑ makes it different
- Ⓒ divides
- Ⓓ goes away

2. The Chunnel <u>links</u> England to other countries in Europe.
- Ⓐ starts a war
- Ⓑ connects
- Ⓒ has a party
- Ⓓ destroys

3. The Chunnel makes moving people and goods a quick and easy <u>task</u>.
- Ⓐ body of water
- Ⓑ type of tunnel
- Ⓒ country
- Ⓓ job

4. One of the three tunnels is an <u>emergency</u> escape tunnel.
- Ⓐ extra
- Ⓑ relating to travel
- Ⓒ relating to danger
- Ⓓ exciting

5. The moles have hard steel teeth to <u>crunch</u> up rocks and dirt.
- Ⓐ crush or grind
- Ⓑ find
- Ⓒ help or aid
- Ⓓ build

Hi-Lo Nonfiction Passages for Struggling Readers Grades 4-5 • Scholastic Inc.

Name _____ Date _____

Word Work

> The letter combinations **ch**, **th**, and **sh** each stand for a special sound that is different than the sounds of the two letters pronounced separately.
>
> **<u>ch</u>eese   ma<u>th</u>   fi<u>sh</u>**

Read the definitions. Complete the word by adding the letters *ch, th,* or *sh.* Write the entire word.

1. to crush or grind   crun_____

2. from England   Engli_____

3. number equal to ten hundreds   _____ousand

4. to shake when cold   _____iver

5. one more   ano_____er

Each sentence below has an incomplete word. Add *ch, th,* or *sh* to complete the word. Write the entire word.

6. We took the train through the _____**unnel**.

7. It was faster than sailing to France on a _____**ip**.

8. We traveled _____**rough** the tunnel in less than an hour.

9. A **bun**_____ of people rode on the train with us.

10. Some people took their cars, and **o**_____**er** people didn't.

Write Now

In this article, you read that French workers dug from France and English workers dug from England and that they met in the middle.

- Plan to write a short conversation between two of the workers. Look at the sample on the right. Imagine what they might have said when they met.

- Write your conversation between the two workers.

> **French worker:** Wow! This will be an exciting project!
>
> **English worker:** Yes, it will make a better way to travel.
>
> **French worker:** _____
> _____
>
> **English worker:** _____
> _____

Hi-Lo Nonfiction Passages for Struggling Readers: Grades 4–5 • Scholastic Inc.

269

CHAMPIONS
of the Games

by Barb Kelly

Do you enjoy table tennis? Do you ever play chess with a friend? Do you wonder sometimes how champs reach the top? If so, you need to meet two top players in the world of **competitive** games. Li Ai plays table tennis. Judit Polgar plays chess. These young women play with skill and intelligence.

Set Your Purpose

Can young people reach the top in the world of professional games? Read this article to find out.

Li Ai loves table tennis. She began playing when she was seven. She was living in China then. From the start, she had good training from her mother. Li Ai's mother is an experienced table-tennis player herself. She **coached** the U.S. National Table Tennis Team. She taught Li Ai how to play this exciting game. Li Ai speaks today of the **physical** and mental power required in this game.

When Li Ai was ten, she and her family moved to the United States. She began her competitive career then. At age 12, she was the national champion in her division. At age 16, she was a member of the U.S. National Team. She was **ranked** second among all women players in the United States. Today she is a force in the world of women's table tennis.

Judit Polgar started playing chess at age five in her hometown in Hungary. By the time she was ten, she had competed in tournaments all over the world.

At age 15, Judit took the chess world by storm. She became the youngest chess grandmaster ever! How did she do it? She beat three players who were already grandmasters. That's how you become a grandmaster.

There are only about 350 chess grandmasters in the world today. Judit is the fourth female to join the ranks! She is proud to be a grandmaster and continues to be active in her competitive life. She plays in **various** chess tournaments around the world.

Think About It

How can you tell that both of these young women are top players?

Name _____   Date _____

Check Your **Understanding**

Fill in the letter with the best answer for each question.

1. Which sentence summarizes the way Li Ai feels about table tennis?

    Ⓐ It is a tough game to play.

    Ⓑ It is a game that requires fitness of mind and body.

    Ⓒ It is a game that is popular all over the world.

    Ⓓ It is a game that girls enjoy playing.

2. Which sentence summarizes why Judit Polgar surprised the chess world?

    Ⓐ She started playing chess when she was only five.

    Ⓑ She has played in chess tournaments all over the world.

    Ⓒ She is a native of Hungary.

    Ⓓ She became a grandmaster at the age of 15.

3. How are Li Ai and Judit Polgar similar?

    Ⓐ They both live in the U.S.

    Ⓑ They were both coached by their mothers.

    Ⓒ They are both top players in their games.

    Ⓓ They are both grandmasters.

4. Which event came first in Li Ai's life?

    Ⓐ She moved to the United States.

    Ⓑ She began playing table tennis.

    Ⓒ She was the national champion in her division.

    Ⓓ She was a member of the U.S. National Team.

5. From the article, you can infer that

    Ⓐ some top players start training at an early age.

    Ⓑ chess is more difficult than table tennis.

    Ⓒ table tennis is more difficult than chess.

    Ⓓ Li Ai and Judit are good friends.

Vocabulary

Find each vocabulary word in the selection. The words and sentences around it will help you figure out its meaning.

Fill in the letter with the best definition of the underlined word.

1. They are the top players in the world of <u>competitive</u> games.

    Ⓐ where players try to win

    Ⓑ where everyone wins

    Ⓒ where everyone loses

    Ⓓ played by teams

2. She <u>coached</u> a table-tennis team.

    Ⓐ fought and won   Ⓒ taught and trained

    Ⓑ beat   Ⓓ joined

3. She speaks of the <u>physical</u> power needed to play table tennis.

    Ⓐ of the body   Ⓒ of the brain

    Ⓑ of the mind   Ⓓ of the heart

4. She was <u>ranked</u> second among her players.

    Ⓐ placed in a list as   Ⓒ approved of

    Ⓑ rejected by the   Ⓓ lost out to team as

5. She plays in <u>various</u> tournaments around the country.

    Ⓐ the same   Ⓒ a few

    Ⓑ many   Ⓓ different

Name _____ **Date** _____

Word Work

> **Synonyms** are words that have similar meanings. For example, *little* and *small* are synonyms.

> A **possessive noun** shows ownership. To make a singular noun possessive, add **'s**. To make a plural noun possessive, add an apostrophe after the (**s'**). Add **'s** to plural nouns that do not end in *s*.
>
> table ⟶ table's
>
> girls ⟶ girls'
>
> women ⟶ women's

Read the sentences and the words below. Write the word that means almost the same as the word in dark type.

likes   education   defeat   started   talks

1. Li Ai **enjoys** table tennis.   _____

2. From the start, she had good **training**.   _____

3. Li Ai **speaks** of the mental power needed.   _____

4. Her career **began** at age ten.   _____

5. You must **beat** three grandmasters to become one yourself.   _____

Match the word on the left with its correct possessive form on the right. Write the letter.

_____ **6.** player   **A.** mother's

_____ **7.** players   **B.** players'

_____ **8.** mother   **C.** player's

_____ **9.** game   **D.** games'

_____ **10.** games   **E.** game's

Write Now

In the selection "Champions of the Games," you read about two young players who excel at certain games. How might they have trained to become the top players in their games?

Name of the sport	Skills it requires	How to train for it
Table tennis	Physical power Mental power	Eat right, sleep right Practice every day

- Plan to write an article that gives advice on how to train for a particular game or sport. Organize your ideas in a chart like the one shown.

- Write an article that gives useful advice to those who want to be good at your chosen sport. Use your chart to help you.

Drawing Conclusions

❖ When reading a story, you can use details and ideas in the story and what you already know to make judgments about what you have read.

  • As you read, look for details and ideas that can help you form a new idea.

  • Ask yourself: **"What do I already know about something like this!"**

  • Use the story details and what you already know to **draw a conclusion.**

❖ Read this selection. What **conclusion** can you draw about what ride the writer is on?

Hair-Raising Fun

Story Clues
These sentences give clues to the ride the writer is on.

I take a deep breath as I get ready for the ride. <u>This ride on wooden tracks will rattle, clank, and bump its way up and down those gigantic hills!</u> Can I change my mind? Too late! <u>The safety harness feels snug against my body.</u> I hope it's tight enough! <u>The car chugs up the first hill. It creaks and rumbles as it climbs to the top.</u> I close my eyes and hold on tight. <u>Then we begin to hurtle down the hill. The car screeches as it bangs from side to side! I hope we don't fly right off the track!</u> I listen to myself scream on each stomach-turning dip. Two minutes seem like forever. My terrified heart is pounding as the ride finally stops. That was fun—I'm ready to go again!

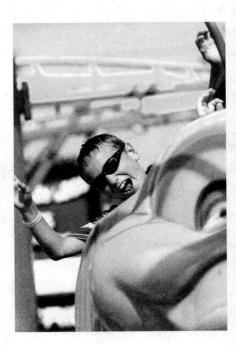

❖ You could chart the information you learned to draw a **conclusion** like this:

Clues		What I Already Know		My Conclusion
This ride on wooden tracks will rattle, clank, and bump its way up and down those gigantic hills! The safety harness feels snug against my body. The car chugs up the first hill. It creaks and rumbles as it climbs to the top. Then we begin to hurtle down the hill.	+	Some roller coasters go on wooden tracks. Roller coasters go up and down hills.	=	The writer is on a roller-coaster ride.

Your Turn

❖ Read this selection. **Draw conclusions** about Mars. Make a chart like the one above.

Mars—A New View

On July 4, 1997, the *Pathfinder* spacecraft landed on the red soil of Mars. It carried Sojourner, a small robot car, or rover. Sojourner's job was to explore and send back to Earth close-up photos of Mars. Sojourner did not explore on its own. Controllers on Earth sent signals telling it where to go. However, signals between Earth and Mars take 11 minutes to travel through space. In that time, Sojourner could have fallen over a cliff or crashed into a rock. To help prevent such accidents, the rover moved very slowly—just two feet per minute. There is no water on the surface of Mars. However, to everyone's surprise, Sojourner's photos showed water flow channels. There were also signs of a huge flood. It was a new view of Mars.

Set Your Purpose

Who was Sacajawea? Read this article to learn about this brave woman.

Her Name Was SACAJAWEA

by Martina Hanson

Sacajawea guided the Lewis and Clark expedition.

In 1803, President Thomas Jefferson sent two men to explore part of the West. Their names were Lewis and Clark. There were no maps and they needed a **guide**. They **hired** a fur trader and his wife. Her name was Sacajawea (sah cuh juh WEE uh).

Sacajawea grew up in the Shoshone (shoh SHOH nee) tribe. She knew how to hunt and fish. She knew every inch of the land.

Sacajawea showed the men the best way to go. She found food when there was none. They walked through deep snow and **paddled** on rough waters. The journey was dangerous.

The trip was successful. Sacajawea is remembered as a **brave** woman who helped explore the West.

Think About It

Do you think it was unusual for a woman to go on such a dangerous journey? Why or why not?

Name _____ Date _____

Check Your Understanding

Fill in the letter with the best answer for each question.

1. From the article you can figure out that
   Ⓐ Sacajawea was Native American.
   Ⓑ Lewis and Clark were Native American.
   Ⓒ President Jefferson was Native American.

2. If there were no maps, there also were probably no
   Ⓐ oceans.
   Ⓑ rivers.
   Ⓒ roads.

3. If Sacajawea had not gone on the journey, it might not have been
   Ⓐ dangerous.
   Ⓑ successful.
   Ⓒ fun.

4. Which statement do you think is true?
   Ⓐ Lewis and Clark were thankful to Sacajawea.
   Ⓑ Lewis and Clark were annoyed at Sacajawea.
   Ⓒ Sacajawea was a very old woman.

Vocabulary

> Find each vocabulary word in the selection. The words and sentences around it will help you figure out its meaning.

Fill in the letter with the best definition of the underlined word.

1. Sacajawea was a <u>guide</u> on Lewis and Clark's journey.
   Ⓐ leader
   Ⓑ student
   Ⓒ driver

2. They <u>hired</u> a fur trader and his wife.
   Ⓐ gave a job to
   Ⓑ asked help from
   Ⓒ wrote a letter to

3. Sacajawea and the men <u>paddled</u> on rough waters.
   Ⓐ took baths
   Ⓑ walked
   Ⓒ rowed a boat

4. Sacajawea was a very <u>brave</u> woman.
   Ⓐ old
   Ⓑ fearless
   Ⓒ young

Name_____   Date_____

Word Work

> The letters **ee** stand for the **long-e** sound in *feet*.
>
> The letters **ea** stand for the **long-e** sound in *seal*.

Read the words. Circle the word with the long-*e* sound.

1. bread   meat

2. dream   great

3. sweet   head

4. heat   thread

5. heavy   teeth

Read the words below. Write the word that completes each sentence.

deep   reach   lead   seen   streams

6. The explorers wanted to _____ the ocean.

7. They had never _____ these lands before.

8. The guide helped _____ them on their journey.

9. She helped them cross rivers and _____.

10. She helped them walk through _____ snow.

Write Now

In the story "Her Name was Sacajawea," you read about a brave woman. This chart shows some of the things she did. Do you know someone who is brave?

- Plan to write a paragraph about someone who you think is brave. You can list some brave things that he or she has done on a chart like the one shown.

- Write your paragraph. Use the ideas on your chart. Draw a picture to go with your paragraph.

> **Sacajawea**
> 1. She hunted and fished.
> 2. She went on a dangerous journey.
> 3. She found food.
> 4. She showed the best way to go.

Who Invented Arthur?

by Pat Chandler

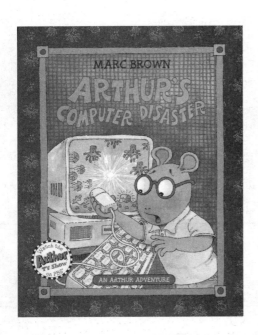

Maybe you know Arthur. He and his friends are in many storybooks. They are on TV, too! Do you know any Arthur stories—like the one in which he plays the Deep, Dark Sea game on the **computer** when he isn't supposed to? He learns that he should listen to his mom. The name of this story is *Arthur's Computer Disaster*.

Set Your Purpose

Who creates the characters you read about in storybooks? Read this article to find out about who created Arthur, the funny, friendly anteater.

That is just one Arthur story. He and his friends have lots of other adventures. Who could think of such a cute character and such funny stories? Marc Brown is the **storyteller** who invented Arthur. He writes all the Arthur books. He makes wonderful **drawings** for his books.

How did he learn to tell such good stories? How did he learn to draw funny animals like Arthur? As a kid, Marc Brown liked to tell stories. His friend did, too. Often, one would tell a story while the other listened. Then the other one would tell a story. This was good practice for Marc. He learned how to tell good stories.

Years later, Marc went to art school. He learned many ways to create pictures. **Afterward**, he got married and had children of his own. Marc read his stories to his kids. He showed them his pictures. His kids **taught** him what kids like and don't like in a book.

Kids are important to Marc Brown. He wants to create good stories for them. He is always looking for ideas. He wants to make the best stories he can.

Think About It

Did Marc Brown get good practice by telling stories to his friend and to his kids? Why?

Name_____ Date_____

Check Your Understanding

Fill in the letter with the best answer for each question.

1. As a kid, Marc Brown probably liked to
- Ⓐ read books.
- Ⓑ study music.
- Ⓒ play sports.
- Ⓓ do chores.

2. Marc makes wonderful drawings because
- Ⓐ he invented Arthur.
- Ⓑ he wants to create good stories for adults.
- Ⓒ he uses a computer.
- Ⓓ he went to art school.

3. One possible reason that Marc is a good storyteller is that
- Ⓐ he has been telling and listening to stories since he was a kid.
- Ⓑ the Arthur books have made him very popular.
- Ⓒ he went to art school.
- Ⓓ he likes scary stories.

4. The author of this article wants to
- Ⓐ tell better stories about Arthur.
- Ⓑ tell us about the creator of Arthur stories.
- Ⓒ stop Marc Brown from telling more stories.
- Ⓓ draw better pictures of Arthur.

5. One reason children love Marc Brown's stories is that he
- Ⓐ draws the pictures before writing the story.
- Ⓑ has kids who tell him how to make his stories better.
- Ⓒ has traveled a lot.
- Ⓓ he writes his stories on a computer.

Vocabulary

Find each vocabulary word in the selection. The words and sentences around it will help you figure out its meaning.

Fill in the letter with the best definition of the underlined word.

1. Arthur plays a game on a <u>computer</u>.
- Ⓐ house
- Ⓑ machine
- Ⓒ car
- Ⓓ person

2. Marc is a good <u>storyteller</u>.
- Ⓐ someone on TV
- Ⓑ someone who paints
- Ⓒ someone who teaches
- Ⓓ someone who tells stories

3. Marc makes the <u>drawings</u> for his books.
- Ⓐ pages
- Ⓑ colors
- Ⓒ pictures
- Ⓓ covers

4. <u>Afterward</u>, Marc draws the pictures.
- Ⓐ before
- Ⓑ while
- Ⓒ later
- Ⓓ at no time

5. Marc's kids <u>taught</u> him what kids like.
- Ⓐ showed
- Ⓑ carried
- Ⓒ teased
- Ⓓ asked

Hi-Lo Nonfiction Passages for Struggling Readers: Grades 4–5 • Scholastic Inc.

Name _____ Date _____

Word Work

| Synonyms are words that have similar meanings. For example, *little* and *small* are synonyms. | Antonyms are words that have the opposite meanings. For example, *hot* and *cold* are antonyms. |

Read the sentences and the words below. Write the word that means almost the same as the word in dark type.

hard   terrific   enjoyed   fast   usually

1. Arthur **liked** playing games on his computer.

_____

2. He was very **quick** at thinking of the answers.

_____

3. He **often** won the game.

_____

4. Arthur's friend gave him a **tough** game.

_____

5. Arthur thought it was a **great** game.

_____

Read the sentences and the words below. Write the word that means the opposite of the word in dark type.

started   same   on   bright   right

6. The computer was **off**. Arthur turned it _____.

7. He saw a **different** picture. It was not the _____ one.

8. He thought the picture was too **dark**. He made it _____.

9. Then the computer **stopped**. No matter how hard he tried, it could not be _____.

10. Something was **wrong** with the computer. Something was not _____.

Write Now

In the selection "Who Invented Arthur?" you learned about a story character named Arthur and the man who created him. What if you could create your own character?

Where will the story take place?	at home	at school	at the mall
What does your character find?	a secret room in the house	something new on the playground	a strange group of people
What does your character do?	crawls inside it	tries to figure out what it might be	listens to them make their plans

• Plan to write a story about your own character. First, make a chart like the one shown above to help you organize your ideas.

• Write a brief summary of your story. When you have more time, write the complete story.

The Yak

adapted by Pat Cusick

Set Your Purpose

What is a yak? Where does it live? Read this article to find out about a very interesting animal.

The Himalaya Mountains in India are the highest in the world. You can probably guess that it is hard to live in these rocky, **lofty** peaks covered with snow and ice. Only the toughest animals can survive in this faraway land. And the yak is one tough animal. It seems as if the yak and the Himalaya Mountains were made for each other.

Keeping Warm

The yak has a thick, **shaggy** coat. Some say the big and bulky yak looks like a walking mop! But the yak doesn't mind. In this land, it's better to have a shaggy coat than a thin one! The yak's coat is a blanket of warmth that keeps off the wind and the snow.

Turn Back, Yak!

When the winds howl down from the mountain peaks, this tough animal simply turns its back on the **gusty** weather. It waits for the winds to calm down and the snow to go.

Let It Snow!

Everything freezes in the Himalayas. This can make it hard to find drinking water. Does this bother the yak? Are you kidding? Yaks are tough. When they get thirsty, they simply eat the snow!

Keeping Warm

Food is scarce where the yak lives, so yaks might go for days without eating. But under the snow, plants called lichens grow. The yak uses its powerful hooves to scratch through the deep snow and find these tasty green and red plants.

The Yak Helps Out

People in the Himalayas face many problems and **hardships**. The yak helps out. This animal pulls heavy loads for people. It supplies them with milk, cheese, butter, meat, wool, and warm skins. A yak's fur can even be **spun** into rope. Now that is a tough animal!

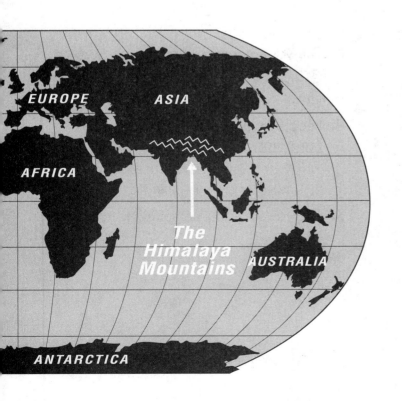

EUROPE

ASIA

AFRICA

The Himalaya Mountains

AUSTRALIA

ANTARCTICA

Think About It

If you lived in the Himalaya Mountains, why would it be nice to own a yak?

Name _____   Date _____

Check Your Understanding

Fill in the letter with the best answer for each question.

1. You can conclude that people in the Himalaya Mountains
   - Ⓐ hardly ever see a yak.
   - Ⓑ are afraid of the yak.
   - Ⓒ try not to go near a yak.
   - Ⓓ depend on the yak to survive.

2. The yak survives in the cold weather because
   - Ⓐ it gets exercise by climbing the rocks.
   - Ⓑ it stays inside the tents of the people.
   - Ⓒ it has a thick, shaggy coat.
   - Ⓓ it eats cheese and butter.

3. The yak eats snow when it is thirsty because
   - Ⓐ yaks like the taste of snow.
   - Ⓑ water is hard to find in the freezing cold.
   - Ⓒ snow is cleaner than water.
   - Ⓓ snow is very good for the health of a yak.

4. The peaks of the Himalaya Mountains are
   - Ⓐ sunny and warm.
   - Ⓑ wet and rainy.
   - Ⓒ cold and snowy.
   - Ⓓ gloomy and wet.

5. Which sentence is the best summary of this selection?
   - Ⓐ The yak is large and has a heavy coat.
   - Ⓑ The yak eats lichens under the snow.
   - Ⓒ The yak is able to survive in the harsh Himalaya Mountains.
   - Ⓓ The yak is able to carry heavy loads.

Vocabulary

Find each vocabulary word in the selection. The words and sentences around it will help you figure out its meaning.

Fill in the letter with the best definition of the underlined word.

1. Mountains in the area have <u>lofty</u> peaks.
   - Ⓐ very beautiful   Ⓒ very cold
   - Ⓑ very high   Ⓓ very dark

2. The yak has a <u>shaggy</u> coat.
   - Ⓐ thick and hairy
   - Ⓑ short and stubby
   - Ⓒ wet and slick
   - Ⓓ smooth and shiny

3. The yak's coat is warm in <u>gusty</u> weather.
   - Ⓐ brave   Ⓒ nice
   - Ⓑ hot   Ⓓ windy

4. People in the Himalayas face many <u>hardships</u>.
   - Ⓐ joys   Ⓒ discussions
   - Ⓑ kinds of work   Ⓓ difficulties

5. The yak's fur can be <u>spun</u> into rope.
   - Ⓐ tangled   Ⓒ mixed
   - Ⓑ melted   Ⓓ twisted

Name _____ Date _____

Word Work

Synonyms are words that have similar meanings. For example, *little* and *small* are synonyms.	Antonyms are words that have opposite meanings. For example, *hot* and *cold* are antonyms.

Read the sentences and the words below. Write the word that means almost the same as the word in dark type.

grip   large   drag   difficult   powerful

1. The yak looks **big** and clumsy.   _____

2. Its short legs are **strong**.   _____

3. The yak can **pull** heavy
loads for people.   _____

4. Its hooves can **hold**
the slippery rock.   _____

5. The animal doesn't care
that life is **hard**
where it lives.   _____

Read the sentences and the words below. Write the word that means the opposite of the word in dark type.

strong   thick   shaggy   cold   tall

6. My pet yak is not **short**. It is _____.

7. Her coat is not **thin**. It is very _____.

8. Her coat is not **smooth**, either.
It is _____.

9. She is not a **weak** animal. This yak
is _____.

10. The climate here is not **warm**. It is very
_____.

Write Now

This chart lists information from "The Yak." The first column lists some things about the weather in the Himalayas. The second column lists what a yak does to deal with the weather.

• Pretend that you are a yak. Plan to write a postcard to a yak friend telling how you spent the
day. First, brainstorm ideas by copying the chart
shown. Then complete it with information from the
selection.

• Write your postcard. Explain what you did during
the day. Make sure you mention what the weather
conditions were. Remember to write as if you were
a yak. Make up a name for yourself and sign your
postcard.

Mountain Weather	What a Yak Does
howling wind	stands and waits for the storm to end
frozen water	
deep snow	

A STORY IN STONE

adapted by Pat Cusick

Set Your Purpose

There are many ways to tell a story. Read this article about one story that is carved in stone.

Do you know the story of Crazy Horse? He was a Sioux (pronounced SUE) **warrior**. He and his people lived in what is now the state of South Dakota. This state is famous for its beautiful mountains, known as the Black Hills.

One day, when Crazy Horse was a young man, United States soldiers came. They **ordered** the Sioux Indians to leave the Black Hills. Crazy Horse and his people refused. They wouldn't go. This was their land. They would fight to keep it.

The soldiers and Native Americans went to war with each other. Crazy Horse led his braves in the fight. He fought with all his heart. The Sioux **defeated** the soldiers and kept their land. It was a great **victory** for Crazy Horse and the Sioux people. Crazy Horse became a hero. Today, the Sioux tell his story over and over.

The Sioux decided to honor Crazy Horse. Artists are carving his portrait on the side of a mountain in South Dakota. His face is finished now. It is 87 feet tall, as tall as a 9-story building!

It will take the artists many years to finish the huge carving. When the giant artwork is **completed**, it will show Crazy Horse riding his horse. People can learn about this Native American hero. His story will be written in stone.

Chief Crazy Horse (1845–1877)

Think About It

Why did the Sioux want to carve the figure of Crazy Horse into the mountain?

Name_____ Date_____

Check Your **Understanding**

Fill in the letter with the best answer for each question.

1. You can conclude from this article that
- Ⓐ few people care about Crazy Horse.
- Ⓑ the Sioux are proud of Crazy Horse.
- Ⓒ many artists helped carve the face of Crazy Horse on the side of a tree.
- Ⓓ there are many books about Crazy Horse.

2. You can conclude from this article that
- Ⓐ the final carving of Crazy Horse will be huge.
- Ⓑ the carving of Crazy Horse will never be completed.
- Ⓒ the carving of Crazy Horse will not fit on the mountain.
- Ⓓ the face of the carving is too far away to see clearly.

3. The main idea of the third paragraph is that
- Ⓐ there have been wars between U.S. soldiers and the Sioux.
- Ⓑ Crazy Horse was a Sioux Indian.
- Ⓒ Crazy Horse won a great battle and became a hero.
- Ⓓ the Sioux still tell the story of Crazy Horse.

4. Which word best describes Crazy Horse?
- Ⓐ crazy   Ⓒ quiet
- Ⓑ brave   Ⓓ tired

5. Which event happened first?
- Ⓐ The Sioux decided to honor Crazy Horse.
- Ⓑ Crazy Horse's story is written in stone.
- Ⓒ Crazy Horse and his braves defeated the U.S. soldiers.
- Ⓓ U. S. soldiers ordered the Sioux to leave the Black Hills.

Vocabulary

> Find each vocabulary word in the selection. The words and sentences around it will help you figure out its meaning.

Fill in the letter with the best definition of the underlined word.

1. Crazy Horse was a <u>warrior</u>.
- Ⓐ baby   Ⓒ good athlete
- Ⓑ son   Ⓓ person who fights

2. The soldiers <u>ordered</u> the Sioux to go to a reservation.
- Ⓐ offered   Ⓒ demanded that
- Ⓑ voted   Ⓓ wanted

3. The Sioux <u>defeated</u> the soldiers.
- Ⓐ beat   Ⓒ frightened
- Ⓑ fought   Ⓓ led

4. It was a great <u>victory</u> for Crazy Horse and his people.
- Ⓐ loss   Ⓒ sad time
- Ⓑ big win   Ⓓ match

5. Someday, the carving of Crazy Horse will be <u>completed</u>.
- Ⓐ carved   Ⓒ finished
- Ⓑ admired   Ⓓ forgotten

Name _____ Date _____

Word Work

A **contraction** is two words joined to make one. One or more letters have been left out. The apostrophe (') shows where the letters were left out.

could + not = couldn't

Fill in the letter of the contraction formed by the two words in dark type.

1. was not
- Ⓐ weren't
- Ⓒ won't
- Ⓑ wasn't
- Ⓓ wouldn't

2. have not
- Ⓐ hadn't
- Ⓒ weren't
- Ⓑ hasn't
- Ⓓ haven't

3. will not
- Ⓐ can't
- Ⓒ weren't
- Ⓑ won't
- Ⓓ wasn't

4. had not
- Ⓐ hadn't
- Ⓒ doesn't
- Ⓑ haven't
- Ⓓ hasn't

5. has not
- Ⓐ haven't
- Ⓒ hasn't
- Ⓑ won't
- Ⓓ hadn't

Read each sentence. Write the contraction that can be formed by the two underlined words.

6. They <u>are not</u> coming with us on the bus. _____

7. We <u>have not</u> seen the face of Crazy Horse. _____

8. It <u>is not</u> far from here. _____

9. We <u>were not</u> late for dinner. _____

10. We <u>could not</u> wait to start up the mountain! _____

Write Now

This chart shows information from "A Story in Stone."

Where it is located	What it is
Black Hills, South Dakota	face of Crazy Horse, a Native American hero, carved into the mountain 87 feet high

- Plan to write a postcard. Pretend you are on vacation and you have gone to see the face of Crazy Horse. What would it feel like to look at this huge face on the side of a mountain?

- Write your postcard to a friend. Tell your friend where you have gone and what you have seen. Use the information on the chart and from the article. Make sure to tell your friend how it felt to look up at the giant stone face!

A Gorilla Saves the Day

adapted by Helena Agnew

Set Your Purpose

Suppose you were badly hurt, and the only one around to help was a great big gorilla. Read this article to find out what might happen.

Binti Jua with her baby, Koola.

What's your idea of a hero? Is it a big hairy ape? You may not think of an ape as a hero, but for one three-year-old boy and his family, a hairy gorilla named Binti Jua (BIN-tee JOO-wah) is the hero they will never forget.

In 1996, the little boy and his family visited the Brookfield Zoo in Illinois. The boy climbed on a **rail** to watch Binti, who was taking care of her baby daughter, Koola. Binti had been raised by human zoo workers. They had used stuffed animals to teach her how to be a good mom. So Binti did not fear or dislike humans.

Binti carries the injured three-year-old boy to a door the zoo workers used to enter the gorilla's home.

All at once, the boy slipped and fell almost 18 feet into the gorilla's home. He lay on the ground without moving. The boy's parents became **frantic**. They rushed around and shouted for help. They did not know what to do, but Binti did.

A crowd had gathered. These people were surprised by what happened next.

Binti went to the boy and gently picked him up. She rocked him in her arms while her own baby was **clinging** to her back. Binti kept other gorillas away. Then she carried the boy to a door that zoo workers used to enter the gorilla's home. She laid him on the ground near the door. Zoo workers were waiting to **whisk** the boy to safety.

The boy was hurt, but he **recovered**. Now he is safe and healthy, thanks to a hero named Binti.

Think About It

Were you surprised by what Binti did? Why or why not?

Name _____   Date _____

Check Your Understanding

Fill in the letter with the best answer for each question.

1. Why do you think Binti helped the little boy?
   - Ⓐ She wanted him to play with Koola.
   - Ⓑ All gorillas love children.
   - Ⓒ She was raised by humans and was afraid of them.
   - Ⓓ She liked humans and was a good mom.

2. The crowd was surprised because they
   - Ⓐ thought they would get hurt.
   - Ⓑ knew the gorillas would harm the boy.
   - Ⓒ didn't know what Binti would do.
   - Ⓓ couldn't see the boy.

3. Binti kept the other gorillas away because they
   - Ⓐ didn't see the boy.
   - Ⓑ might hurt the boy.
   - Ⓒ would have kept the boy.
   - Ⓓ would have helped the boy.

4. Which of these events happened first?
   - Ⓐ Binti gently picked up the three-year-old boy and rocked him in her arms.
   - Ⓑ Zoo workers used stuffed animals to teach Binti how to be a good mom.
   - Ⓒ A three-year-old boy fell.
   - Ⓓ Binti kept other gorillas away.

5. What happened after the boy fell?
   - Ⓐ The boy cried.
   - Ⓑ Binti picked him up.
   - Ⓒ The boy played with Koola.
   - Ⓓ Zoo workers picked up the boy.

Vocabulary

Find each vocabulary word in the selection. The words and sentences around it will help you figure out its meaning.

Fill in the letter with the best definition of the underlined word.

1. The boy climbed on a <u>rail</u> to watch Binti.
   - Ⓐ train
   - Ⓑ roll
   - Ⓒ fence
   - Ⓓ tree

2. The boy's parents became <u>frantic</u>.
   - Ⓐ gentle and caring
   - Ⓑ rich and famous
   - Ⓒ funny and foolish
   - Ⓓ very worried and upset

3. The gorilla's baby was <u>clinging</u> to her back.
   - Ⓐ hopping on
   - Ⓑ climbing up
   - Ⓒ holding on
   - Ⓓ crawling

4. Zoo workers were waiting to <u>whisk</u> the boy to safety.
   - Ⓐ drop
   - Ⓑ quickly take away
   - Ⓒ dislike
   - Ⓓ refuse to bring

5. The boy was hurt in the fall, but he <u>recovered</u>.
   - Ⓐ rushed around
   - Ⓑ laughed
   - Ⓒ got better
   - Ⓓ climbed

Name _____ **Date** _____

Word Work

> A **prefix** comes at the beginning of a word and changes the meaning of the word. The prefixes **dis-** and **un-** mean "not." The prefix **re-** means "again" or "back."
>
> <u>dis</u>like   **to not like something**
>
> <u>un</u>safe   **not safe**
>
> <u>re</u>pay   **to pay back**

Fill in the letter with the correct definition of the word in dark type.

1. disagree

   Ⓐ not agree   Ⓒ one who agrees

   Ⓑ agree again   Ⓓ agree a lot

2. unable

   Ⓐ able again   Ⓒ not able

   Ⓑ more able   Ⓓ newly able

3. displeased

   Ⓐ not pleased   Ⓒ more pleased

   Ⓑ pleased again   Ⓓ always pleased

4. refill

   Ⓐ not filled   Ⓒ fill in advance

   Ⓑ fill again   Ⓓ fill wrongly

5. unsure

   Ⓐ most sure   Ⓒ very sure

   Ⓑ always sure   Ⓓ not sure

Read the definitions below. Add the prefix *dis-*, *un-*, or *re-* to the base word to make a new word that fits the definition.

6. open again   _____ **open**

7. not usual   _____ **usual**

8. not appear   _____ **appear**

9. think again   _____ **think**

10. not certain   _____ **certain**

Write Now

Look at the flowchart. It shows the order of events in "A Gorilla Saves the Day."

| **1.** The boy climbs on the rail to watch Binti. | → | **2.** The boy falls into the gorilla area. | → | **3.** Binti gently picks up the boy and rocks him. | → | **4.** Binti puts the boy on the ground near the door. | → | **5.** Zoo workers take the boy to safety. |

- Plan to write a story about an interesting or exciting moment in your own life. For example, you could write about a trip you took. Make a flowchart like the one shown above. Think of the order of events in your story. Put the events in order in your chart.

- Write your personal story. Use your flowchart to help you put events in the correct order. Add details and action words to make the events come to life.

BUNNICULA

adapted by Pat Chandler

Set Your Purpose

How does a writer think of a good story? Read this interview to find out.

James Howe's **mystery** books will tickle your funnybone. They will also make your teeth **chatter** in fear! His book *Bunnicula* is about a cute little rabbit who is really a vampire. He sucks juice from innocent vegetables! It is an enjoyable book that readers will have fun with. James Howe spoke to an interviewer about his book.

Interviewer: How did you get the idea for *Bunnicula*?

James Howe: I really don't remember. I had watched a lot of vampire movies. They always **struck** me as funny as well as scary. I probably just asked myself what the funniest vampire I could imagine would be. A rabbit popped into my head.

Interviewer: Did you always know that you wanted to be a writer?

James Howe: I never wanted to be a writer. To me, writing was just something I did for fun. I wanted to be an actor. It was not until I was working on my third book that I thought about what fun it was to write. Then I **decided** that I would like to do it full-time.

Interviewer: Is writing still a lot of fun for you?

James Howe: Yes and no. It is harder to have fun with it. When I started out, I did not know what I was doing, so that made it a lot easier. Now I have to work harder to keep it **fresh** and fun for myself.

Interviewer: So, what do you do to keep it fun?

James Howe: Sometimes I read for a while. Reading gets my mind thinking about different things. It often gets me going in a new direction.

Think About It

What does James Howe do to keep writing fun? How do these things help?

Name_____ Date_____

Check Your Understanding

Fill in the letter with the best answer for each question.

1. You can conclude that, as a child, James Howe probably
   Ⓐ played a lot of baseball.
   Ⓑ wrote a lot of letters.
   Ⓒ saw a lot of movies.
   Ⓓ did a lot of garden work.

2. The story *Bunnicula* most likely takes place in
   Ⓐ a space ship.
   Ⓑ a vegetable garden.
   Ⓒ a forest.
   Ⓓ a classroom.

3. In the story *Bunnicula*, James Howe probably makes fun of
   Ⓐ vampires.   Ⓒ editors.
   Ⓑ authors.   Ⓓ children.

4. One reason *Bunnicula* is a great story is because it is
   Ⓐ scary but confusing.   Ⓒ funny but long.
   Ⓑ easy but cute.   Ⓓ scary but funny.

5. James Howe became a writer because
   Ⓐ it was hard to find acting work.
   Ⓑ someone asked him to write a book.
   Ⓒ he realized he enjoyed writing.
   Ⓓ his teachers told him he was a good writer.

Vocabulary

Find each vocabulary word in the selection. The words and sentences around it will help you figure out its meaning.

Fill in the letter with the best definition of the underlined word.

1. James Howe writes <u>mystery</u> books.
   Ⓐ suspenseful   Ⓒ romance
   Ⓑ school   Ⓓ picture

2. His latest book will make your teeth <u>chatter</u>.
   Ⓐ knock together   Ⓒ fall out
   Ⓑ hurt   Ⓓ babble

3. Vampire movies always <u>struck</u> James Howe as funny as well as scary.
   Ⓐ bored
   Ⓑ was incorrect
   Ⓒ didn't make sense
   Ⓓ hit one's mind or feelings

4. James <u>decided</u> to become a writer.
   Ⓐ hated   Ⓒ chose
   Ⓑ wanted   Ⓓ refused

5. James tries to keep writing <u>fresh</u> and fun.
   Ⓐ dull   Ⓒ confusing
   Ⓑ new   Ⓓ tasty

Name _____   Date _____

Word Work

An **idiom** is a group of words used in a way that has a special meaning. This meaning is different from the usual meaning of those words.

Synonyms are words that have similar meanings. For example, *little* and *small* are synonyms.

Write the letter of the definition that matches the idiom in dark type.

Read the sentences and the words below. Write the word that means almost the same as the word in dark type.

Idioms   ### Definitions

_____ **1. do away with**   **A.** got rid of

_____ **2. run across**   **B.** tell the truth

_____ **3. throw a fit**   **C.** meet

_____ **4. come clean**   **D.** got an idea

_____ **5. popped into my head** **E.** get angry

enjoyable   frighten   watch   desire   cute

6. I liked to **see** vampire movies. _____

7. Those movies **scare** me a lot. _____

8. The **pretty** little rabbit is really a vampire! _____

9. I want to write a vampire story that is **fun**. _____

10. He did not **want** to be a writer at first. _____

Write Now

In the interview you just read, you learned about *Bunnicula* by James Howe. It tells of a rabbit who is really a vampire. Do you have some good story ideas?

Animal	What it does secretly
a squirrel	throws flowers at people's bedroom windows
a whale	teaches lobsters to dance and sing

- Plan to write a summary of a story idea. Think of a story about a wild creature that secretly does something funny. The chart above will help you brainstorm for good ideas.

- Summarize your story idea in a short paragraph. When you have time, you can write the actual story.

The Arctic:
Closer Than You Think

adapted by Kurt Metz

Set Your Purpose

How does the Arctic affect our everyday life? How do we affect life in the Arctic? Read this article to find out.

The next time you get caught in a rainstorm, you might have the icy Arctic to thank. It may sound strange, but it's true. This **region** at the top of the world affects us all. And we affect it!

The Arctic may seem like a **foreign** land. But scientists say Arctic weather has an impact on weather all over the world. This is how: Cold, dry air forms over the Arctic, and then wind currents shift this cold air to the south. When this cold air hits warm, wet air, storms form. These storms are part of weather patterns that travel around the globe.

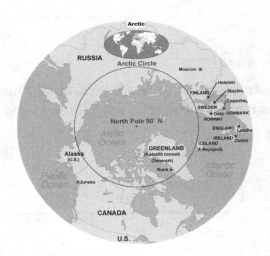

Scientists draw an imaginary circle to show the Arctic region. It includes the Arctic Ocean and parts of three continents.

An Unwanted Gift

The Arctic might bring rainstorms to our part of the world. But what we bring to the Arctic can be much worse. Wind and water carry chemicals from factories in the United States and other countries to the Arctic. There the frigid Arctic environment **functions** like a freezer. Chemicals last for a long time in the atmosphere around the North Pole. These chemicals get into the food supply. The animals and people of the Arctic region can get sick from drinking **polluted** water. They can get ill from eating polluted food.

Science at the North Pole

Because so much pollution ends up in the Arctic, scientists say it's a good place to study the environment. They **examine** the icy ocean. They study the nearby land. They test the Arctic air. That gives them an idea of how much pollution the world is creating. It tells them about the health of the whole planet.

This scientist is using special equipment to test the Arctic water.

Think About It

How is the Arctic affected by factories and cities far away?

Name _____ Date _____

Check Your **Understanding**

Fill in the letter with the best answer for each question.

1. What conclusion can you draw about weather from the selection?
Ⓐ Weather moves in patterns that scientists can trace.
Ⓑ Weather makes interesting patterns in the sky.
Ⓒ Only the Arctic has weather patterns.
Ⓓ All Arctic weather is stormy.

2. What conclusion can you draw about the Arctic region?
Ⓐ It's too cold for people to live there.
Ⓑ People there don't own freezers.
Ⓒ The animals of the Arctic have all died.
Ⓓ The Arctic is polluted.

3. Why is the Arctic a good place for scientists to study air and water pollution?
Ⓐ The Arctic has nice, clean air and water.
Ⓑ Pollution from all over the world collects in the Arctic.
Ⓒ No one bothers the scientists in the Arctic.
Ⓓ The Arctic Ocean is at the North Pole.

4. Look at the map. Which of these is not part of the Arctic region?
Ⓐ Asia   Ⓒ Africa
Ⓑ North America   Ⓓ Europe

5. The author of this selection wants people to
Ⓐ stop working in factories.
Ⓑ know how pollution gets to the Arctic.
Ⓒ become scientists and study the Arctic.
Ⓓ move to the Arctic.

Vocabulary

Find each vocabulary word in the selection. The words and sentences around it will help you figure out its meaning.

Fill in the letter with the best definition of the underlined word.

1. The Arctic <u>region</u> is at the top of the world.
Ⓐ test   Ⓒ explanation
Ⓑ area   Ⓓ weather

2. The Arctic may seem like a <u>foreign</u> land.
Ⓐ full of fur   Ⓒ cold and snowy
Ⓑ too long in time   Ⓓ very distant

3. The frigid Arctic environment <u>functions</u> like a freezer.
Ⓐ moves   Ⓒ opens
Ⓑ acts   Ⓓ closes

4. You can get sick from drinking <u>polluted</u> water.
Ⓐ hot   Ⓒ dirty
Ⓑ icy   Ⓓ sweet

5. Scientists <u>examine</u> the environment.
Ⓐ study   Ⓒ create
Ⓑ harm   Ⓓ drink

Hi-Lo Nonfiction Passages for Struggling Readers Grades 4–5 • Scholastic Inc.

Name _____ Date _____

Word Work

> **Synonyms** are words that have similar meanings. For example, *little* and *small* are synonyms.

Fill in the letter of the synonym of the word in dark type.

1. A **cold** wind blew across the water.
  Ⓐ hot   Ⓒ true
  Ⓑ wonderful   Ⓓ chilly

2. Some **animals** have fur to keep them warm.
  Ⓐ creatures   Ⓒ rocks
  Ⓑ plants   Ⓓ wheels

3. Scientists will examine the icy water for **signs** of pollution.
  Ⓐ cubes   Ⓒ sicknesses
  Ⓑ examples   Ⓓ tastes

4. Pollution **creates** problems for people around the world.
  Ⓐ makes   Ⓒ paints
  Ⓑ melts   Ⓓ breaks

5. The **whole** island was actually a floating block of ice.
  Ⓐ gloomy   Ⓒ entire
  Ⓑ last   Ⓓ other

> The letters **ar** stand for the sound you hear in the word *car*. The letters **air** stand for the sound you hear in *hair*.
>
>   c<u>ar</u>   h<u>air</u>

Read the definitions. Complete the word by adding the letters *ar* or *air*. Write the word.

6. two of something   p_____

7. a cold region near the North Pole   _____ctic

8. a section or area   p_____t

9. a flight of steps   st_____s

10. something to sit on   ch_____

Write Now

The web at right shows some facts and details from "The Arctic: Closer Than You Think."

- Plan to write a cartoon about the Arctic. Look at the information in the web shown. Polar bears, seals, and arctic foxes are animals that live in the Arctic. You may want to draw these animals in your cartoon. What might those animals say about life in the Arctic or the scientists who study the Arctic?

- Write and draw your cartoon about the Arctic. You can write a caption or you can write speech bubbles for the animals or people in your picture.

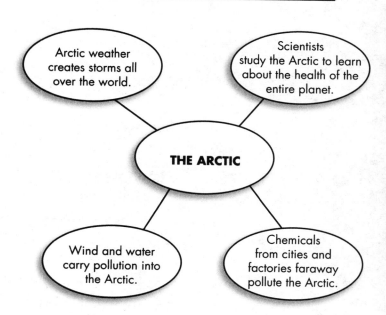

What Do You Call a Cyclone?

by Shannon Murray

Gloria and Bob were really messy. Camille and Opal were just plain out of control. Andrew and Hugo did lots of **damage**. Were these the world's worst children? No, they were some of the world's worst cyclones.

A cyclone is a strong wind and rainstorm. The storm, shaped like a pinwheel, forms over the ocean. As the storm grows, the winds around the center of the storm get stronger. Amazingly, the center of the storm, called the eye, stays **calm** and still. After forming over an ocean, a cyclone sometimes hits land. Some cyclones are so **powerful** they can wipe out a whole town.

In the Atlantic Ocean, a cyclone is called a hurricane. In the Pacific, it is called a typhoon. You may have heard of hurricane Hugo or typhoon Linda—two famous cyclones. But cyclones did not always have names. In the early 1900s, a weathercaster in Australia began to name hurricanes after people he did not like. Then, in 1952, forecasters started naming all tropical storms with women's names. But some women complained. They said that these dangerous storms should not be named only after women. In 1979, the **practice** of naming every other storm with a man's name began. This means that if one storm gets a woman's name, the next will get a man's name.

Today the name of a hurricane might be used once and then again in six years. Some names, though, will never be used twice. That's because these storms were so bad that their names were **retired**. Camille, Hugo, Andrew, and Katrina are storm names that we will never use again.

Think About It

What did you learn about cyclones?

Name _____ Date _____

Check Your **Understanding**

Fill in the letter with the best answer for each question.

1. What conclusion can you draw about cyclones?
  (A) Cyclones never hurt anyone.
  (B) A cyclone is a snowstorm.
  (C) Since 1979, there haven't been any powerful cyclones.
  (D) Some cyclones are stronger than others.

2. What conclusion can you draw about where cyclones form?
  (A) Cyclones form only over the Atlantic Ocean.
  (B) Cyclones form over both the Atlantic Ocean and the Pacific Ocean.
  (C) Cyclones form only over the Pacific Ocean.
  (D) The worst cyclones form over the Pacific Ocean.

3. A bad cyclone can
  (A) blow a house down.
  (B) not blow a house down.
  (C) not be stronger than a rainstorm.
  (D) be too weak to blow anything down.

4. When did people begin naming cyclones?
  (A) 1952   (C) 1979
  (B) the early 1900s   (D) the 18th century

5. What is the difference between a hurricane and a typhoon?
  (A) A hurricane occurs in the Atlantic Ocean, and a typhoon occurs in the Pacific.
  (B) A cyclone is never called a typhoon.
  (C) A hurricane is stronger than a typhoon.
  (D) A typhoon is stronger than a hurricane.

Vocabulary

Find each vocabulary word in the selection. The words and sentences around it will help you figure out its meaning.

Fill in the letter with the best definition of the underlined word.

1. Cyclones can do a lot of <u>damage</u>.
  (A) wind   (C) noise
  (B) rain   (D) harm

2. The eye of the storm stays <u>calm</u> and still.
  (A) having to do with the ocean
  (B) violent and noisy
  (C) quiet and peaceful
  (D) lucky

3. Some cyclones are so <u>powerful</u> they can wipe out a whole town.
  (A) very strong   (C) brief
  (B) hungry   (D) very weak

4. The <u>practice</u> of using a man's name for every other storm began in 1979.
  (A) usual way of doing something
  (B) unusual way of doing something
  (C) mistake
  (D) fear

5. Some storms were so bad that their names were <u>retired</u>.
  (A) written in a book
  (B) no longer used
  (C) thought to be false
  (D) used again and again

Hi-Lo Nonfiction Passages for Struggling Readers Grades 4-5 • Scholastic Inc.

Name_____ Date_____

Word Work

A **suffix** is a word part that comes at the end of a base word. Knowing the meaning of a suffix helps you figure out the meaning of the whole word. The suffix **-ful** means "full of."

color + ful = colorful

Write a word that fits the definition by adding the suffix *-ful*.

1. full of fear   **fear_____**

2. full of respect   **respect_____**

3. full of cheer   **cheer_____**

4. full of harm   **harm_____**

5. full of joy   **joy_____**

Add the suffix *-ful* to the base word in dark type to complete the sentence.

6. The **power_____** storm could bring terrible winds and flooding.

7. I tried to be **help_____** by finding the flashlights and candles.

8. We were **hope_____** that the storm might turn and head back out to sea.

9. The storm finally turned, and I was **joy_____** that our home was safe.

10. Some people lost their homes, and they were **sorrow_____**.

Write Now

In "What Do You Call a Cyclone?" you read about cyclones and how they are named. Answer the questions below. You can find the information in the selection.

> **1.** What is a cyclone?
>
> **2.** Where are cyclones formed?
>
> **3.** What sort of damage can cyclones do?

• Pretend you are a cyclone. Plan to write a poem telling your name and where you are forming. Describe what you look like and what you are doing. Finally, tell what it feels like to be a powerful cyclone. Jot down ideas for your poem. The pictures in the selection and the answers on your chart will help you.

• Write your poem. Remember to write as if you were a cyclone speaking.

AN INTERVIEW WITH
Ed Stivender,
STORYTELLER

by Emily McLaughlin

Set Your Purpose

What is it like to be a storyteller? Read this interview to find out.

Emily McLaughlin found out what it is like to be a storyteller when she interviewed Ed Stivender.

Emily: How did you become a storyteller?

Ed: I started with **acting**. I was in a school play in the third grade. My teacher told me I did an **exemplary** job. After that, I acted in plays in grade school, high school, and college.

Emily: When did you begin telling stories?

Ed: After college, I worked with a group of storytellers. Then I taught high school. I told stories about the lessons to my students. They learned better that way. I have been working on my own since 1976.

Emily: Where do you tell your stories?

Ed: I have been in countries all over the world! I tell stories at schools and at storytelling festivals. I also wrote books of stories and made a few tapes.

Emily: What do you like about storytelling?

Ed: I like telling stories to children in third, fourth, and fifth grades the best. They understand my jokes. Also, I like the **applause** from the audience. It feels good when people clap because they like what I do. It is like a dance between the storyteller and the audience.

Emily: How many stories do you know?

Ed: I have **memorized** about 40 stories. I am always learning new ones.

Emily: What kinds of stories do you tell?

Ed: I like to tell folktales about Br'er Possum and Br'er Rabbit. Another favorite story is "Jack and the Magic Boat." I write my own stories, too.

Emily: Do you have any **hints** for becoming a storyteller?

Ed: Yes. Start now! Plan a storytelling time. Get kids together to listen and tell stories. Help each other. You can all become storytellers!

Think About It

What does Ed Stivender like about being a storyteller?

Name_____ Date_____

Check Your Understanding

Fill in the letter with the best answer for each question.

1. Ed probably acted in grade school, high school, and college because
   - Ⓐ he did not have anything else to do.
   - Ⓑ he was a good actor and enjoyed it.
   - Ⓒ his teacher said he had to.
   - Ⓓ he did not like sports.

2. You can tell that Ed is a successful storyteller because
   - Ⓐ he went to high school and college.
   - Ⓑ he has many favorite stories.
   - Ⓒ he likes to retell folktales.
   - Ⓓ he has been working on his own since 1976.

3. Ed tells his stories all over the world. That means
   - Ⓐ a lot of people know about him.
   - Ⓑ he likes to fly in airplanes.
   - Ⓒ he does not have time to write books.
   - Ⓓ he wants to make a lot of money.

4. Ed thinks that if children want to become storytellers, they should
   - Ⓐ listen only to adult storytellers.
   - Ⓑ go to college to learn to be storytellers.
   - Ⓒ get together with one another and tell stories.
   - Ⓓ go to storytelling festivals.

5. What else does Ed do besides telling stories?
   - Ⓐ He teaches college.
   - Ⓑ He writes stories.
   - Ⓒ He coaches football and baseball.
   - Ⓓ He writes songs for country singers.

Vocabulary

Find each vocabulary word in the selection. The words and sentences around it will help you figure out its meaning.

Fill in the letter with the best definition of the underlined word.

1. Ed started <u>acting</u> in plays back in the third grade.
   - Ⓐ playing the part of someone else
   - Ⓑ writing
   - Ⓒ reading to the teacher
   - Ⓓ singing in a band

2. His teacher told him he did an <u>exemplary</u> job as an actor.
   - Ⓐ bad
   - Ⓒ very good
   - Ⓑ extra
   - Ⓓ playful

3. He loves the <u>applause</u> from the audience.
   - Ⓐ flowers
   - Ⓒ letters
   - Ⓑ clapping
   - Ⓓ laughing

4. Ed has <u>memorized</u> about 40 stories.
   - Ⓐ written down
   - Ⓒ listened to
   - Ⓑ paid money for
   - Ⓓ learned by heart

5. He does have some <u>hints</u> for becoming a storyteller.
   - Ⓐ helpful tips
   - Ⓒ friends
   - Ⓑ books
   - Ⓓ costumes

Name _____ **Date** _____

Word Work

> A **noun** names a person, place, or thing.
> A **plural noun** names more than one person, place, or thing. To make the plural of most nouns, add **-s**.
>
> dog ⟶ dogs
>
> If a noun ends in *y*, we usually change the *y* to *i* and add *-es*.
>
> daisy ⟶ daisies

> Some nouns are made plural by changing the base word.
>
> man ⟶ men
> fungus ⟶ fungi

Write the plural of each word.

1. teacher _____
2. story _____
3. book _____
4. country _____
5. interview _____

Read each sentence. Write the correct plural form of the word in dark type.

6. **child** — Ed loves to tell stories to _____.

7. **mouse** — I heard a funny story about two _____ who always teased a cat.

8. **goose** — Have you heard the story about a group of _____?

9. **foot** — I like the story about the ant with huge shoes on his _____.

10. **woman** — Several _____ and their children showed up to hear the stories.

Write Now

The timeline below shows when Ed Stivender started telling stories. What did he do between then and the present time that helped him become a famous storyteller?

Third-Grade Play		**Present**

storyteller all over the world

- Plan to write a timeline mapping out a plan for you to reach a personal goal. For example, you may want to try out for a school play, be a baseball player, or become a firefighter. First, look back to the story to see what Ed did to become a storyteller. Complete Ed's timeline.

- Write your own timeline. Include the steps you might take to help you reach your goal.

A Born Champion

by Emile LeClair

At home, she tries to be a regular person. She hangs out with friends, goes to the movies, shops at the mall, and dreams about the future.

But she's no regular person, and many of her dreams have already come true.

Her name is Tara Lipinski.

When Tara was only three, she zoomed around on roller skates. Walking and running were not speedy enough for her. At age five, she won a roller-skating championship!

Then, at age six, Tara **realized** she could go faster on ice skates. Her first experience on the ice was a **wobbly** one. Her father said she flopped around. But when Tara left the ice that day, she was skating as if she were on roller skates. In only a few years, she proved she was a natural born ice-skater.

In 1988, Tara went to Nagano, Japan. Amateur athletes from around the world had come to **compete** in the Winter Olympic Games. Two weeks before the Games, Tara talked to a reporter:

Set Your Purpose

What is a champion? How does someone become a champion? Read this article to find out.

312

Reporter: Why do you like figure skating?

Tara: Skating is fun. I love it because I can be myself when I am on the ice.

Reporter: What's the hardest trick you do?

Tara: I do two triple loops in a row. I jump in the air, spin around three times, land, and do it again right away. It's tough!

Reporter: How do you keep up your skills?

Tara: I practice! I'm at the rink by 8 a.m., and I practice until 3 p.m. I also eat **pasta** and other healthy foods to stay strong.

Reporter: Do you have a message for kids?

Tara: Work hard and believe in yourself!

Tara made history in Nagano. She won a gold **medal**! She was only 14 years old, and she was the youngest girl ever to become an Olympic figure-skating champion!

Think About It

What do you think makes Tara a champion? Would you be willing to do what she does to be a champion? Why or why not?

Name_____   Date_____

Check Your Understanding

Fill in the letter with the best answer for each question.

1. When Tara is at home, she likes to
   Ⓐ spend time with her friends and act like a regular person.
   Ⓑ get in extra practice time with her coach.
   Ⓒ spend time by herself.
   Ⓓ watch movies of her championship performances.

2. What does the description of Tara on roller skates tell you about her?
   Ⓐ She was clumsy.
   Ⓑ She was a slow learner.
   Ⓒ She got tired easily.
   Ⓓ She was energetic and daring.

3. How can you tell that Tara tries to take care of herself?
   Ⓐ She won a medal at the Olympic Games.
   Ⓑ She is a regular person.
   Ⓒ She goes to the movies.
   Ⓓ She eats healthy food.

4. Why did Tara start ice-skating?
   Ⓐ She liked the idea of being able to move really fast.
   Ⓑ Her father wanted her to ice-skate.
   Ⓒ All her friends were ice-skaters.
   Ⓓ She didn't like roller skating.

5. What conclusion can you draw from Tara's words?
   Ⓐ Ice-skating is easy.
   Ⓑ She is a dedicated and talented ice-skater.
   Ⓒ An Olympic champion can't be a regular person.
   Ⓓ Tara is afraid of hurting herself.

Vocabulary

Find each vocabulary word in the selection. The words and sentences around it will help you figure out its meaning.

Fill in the letter with the best definition of the underlined word.

1. At six, Tara <u>realized</u> she could go faster on ice skates.
   Ⓐ tried   Ⓒ went faster
   Ⓑ figured out   Ⓓ was born

2. At first, she was <u>wobbly</u> on the ice.
   Ⓐ shaky   Ⓒ steady and straight
   Ⓑ perfect   Ⓓ easy

3. Athletes from around the world <u>compete</u> in the Olympics.
   Ⓐ watch   Ⓒ talk about
   Ⓑ forget about   Ⓓ try to win

4. Tara eats <u>pasta</u> and other healthy foods.
   Ⓐ pastry   Ⓒ lunch
   Ⓑ kind of noodle Ⓓ type of cake

5. Tara won a gold <u>medal</u>.
   Ⓐ something that is not important
   Ⓑ speech
   Ⓒ object given for winning a contest
   Ⓓ message

Hi-Lo Nonfiction Passages for Struggling Readers: Grades 4–5 • Scholastic Inc.

Name _____ Date _____

Word Work

> **Synonyms** are words that have similar meanings. For example, *child* and *kid* are synonyms.

Fill in the letter of the synonym of the word in dark type.

1. The skater **realized** that she would have to practice a lot to win.
Ⓐ lost
Ⓒ practiced
Ⓑ said
Ⓓ understood

2. I wonder if ice skaters get dizzy when they **spin** around.
Ⓐ twirl
Ⓒ stand
Ⓑ sit
Ⓓ rest

3. She's famous, but she acts like a **regular** person.
Ⓐ scary
Ⓒ ordinary
Ⓑ hungry
Ⓓ tired

4. The audience cheered when the **champion** received her gold medal.
Ⓐ loser
Ⓒ reporter
Ⓑ winner
Ⓓ artist

5. She is a **speedy** skater who likes to zoom around the ice.
Ⓐ forgotten
Ⓒ wrong
Ⓑ fast
Ⓓ slow

> A **prefix** comes at the beginning of a word and changes the meaning of the word. Knowing the meaning of a prefix helps you figure out the meaning of the whole word. The prefix **dis-** means "not" or "lack of." The prefix **mis-** means "bad, wrongly, or badly."
>
> **disagree** ⟶ **not to agree**
> **misbehave** ⟶ **to behave badly**

Read the definitions. Add the prefix *dis-* or *mis-* to the base word to make a new word that fits the definition.

6. lead wrongly _____**lead**

7. not approve _____**approve**

8. not continue _____**continue**

9. guided badly _____**guided**

10. lack of belief _____**belief**

Write Now

Look at the web. It tells about Tara Lipinski.

• Plan to write a description of someone you know well. Make a web like the one shown. Add details that tell about the person you will describe.

• Write your description. Use the details in your web. Make the person come alive in the minds of your readers. Give specific details that show how the person talks and acts and feels. If you wish, add a drawing of the person.

Distinguishing Fact & Opinion

❖ When reading a story or an article, it's helpful to look for facts and opinions.

- As you read, ask yourself: "Can this statement be checked or proven?" and "Is this what someone believes or feels?"

- A statement that can be proven is a **fact**.

- A statement of what someone believes or feels is an **opinion**.

- Words such as *think, believe, probably, beautiful,* and *good* are clues that a statement expresses an opinion.

❖ Read this paragraph. Look for **facts** and **opinions**.

Facts
These statements can be checked or proven.

Opinions
The second and last sentences cannot be proven. The words *really funny, I think,* and *strangest* are signals that these are the author's opinions.

Funny Money

People have not always used money in the form of bills and coins. They used some really funny things for money. Some Native Americans used wampum—beads made from shells—for money. In long-ago Mexico, the Aztecs used cacao beans for money. Tea leaves pressed into bricks were used as money in some part of Asia. On the Pacific Island of Yap, money was in the form of wheel-shaped stones that were so big and heavy they couldn't be moved! I think that was the strangest money of all!

❖ You could chart some of the **facts** and **opinions** in this paragraph like this:

Statement	Fact	Opinion	Clue
People used some really funny things for money.		✓	"really funny"
Native Americans used wampum.	✓		can be checked
Aztecs used cacao beans.	✓		can be checked
People from Yap used heavy stones.	✓		can be checked
I think that was the strangest money of all!		✓	"I think" and "strangest"

Your Turn

❖ Read this passage. Look for **facts** and **opinions**. Make a chart like the one above.

Goodbye to George?

I think Andrew Jackson must be our most popular president today. Or at least he's the one we see most often, thanks to ATMs (automated teller machines). ATMs give cash mostly in the form of $20 bills. Jackson's picture is on that bill.

Three presidents aren't seen at all anymore, which is very sad. William McKinley appeared on $500 bills. Grover Cleveland's face was on $1,000 bills. James Madison could be seen on $5,000 bills. However, the government stopped making these bills in 1969.

Will we now have to say goodbye to George Washington? Some members of Congress want to replace the $1 bill with a coin. I feel that getting rid of George is a terrible idea!

Take a Hike

by Clare La Plante

Set Your Purpose

What is the longest hiking trail in the United States? Read this article to find out.

What hiking trail runs through the mountains all the way from Maine to Georgia? It is the Appalachian (AP ah LAY shun) Trail, called AT for short. Each year, many people set out to hike the AT. Marked **footpaths** with small trail **signs** show the way.

The AT is the longest trail—about 2,000 miles long. It goes through 14 states. Along the trail, there are simple shelters for hikers. But some prefer to sleep **under** the stars.

Snakes, rabbits, and birds are common sights along the AT. In Maine, hikers might **spot** moose from the trail. Wildlife is everywhere. Take a hike. Then stop and take a look!

Think About It

Would you like to hike part of the AT or the whole trail? Why?

Name _____ **Date** _____

Check Your Understanding

Fill in the letter with the best answer for each question.

1. Which statement is a fact?
Ⓐ The Appalachian Trail runs through 14 states.
Ⓑ The best part of the trail is in Maine.
Ⓒ It's fun to hike 2,000 miles.

2. Which statement is an opinion?
Ⓐ Trail signs show the way.
Ⓑ Hiking on the Appalachian Trail is very hard.
Ⓒ The AT goes from Maine to Georgia.

3. The Appalachian Trail is about
Ⓐ 20 miles long.
Ⓑ 200 miles long.
Ⓒ 2,000 miles long.

4. People who hike the whole Appalachian Trail probably
Ⓐ do it in one day.
Ⓑ take a few days.
Ⓒ take several weeks or months.

Vocabulary

Find each vocabulary word in the selection. The words and sentences around it will help you figure out its meaning.

Fill in the letter with the best definition of the underlined word.

1. Marked <u>footpaths</u> go through the mountains.
Ⓐ rocks
Ⓑ paths
Ⓒ bridges

2. Small <u>signs</u> show hikers the way.
Ⓐ waters
Ⓑ fences
Ⓒ markers

3. Some hikers like to sleep <u>under</u> the stars.
Ⓐ beneath
Ⓑ beyond
Ⓒ behind

4. In Maine, hikers might <u>spot</u> a moose.
Ⓐ catch
Ⓑ see
Ⓒ call

Hi-Lo Nonfiction Passages for Struggling Readers: Grades 4-5 • Scholastic Inc.

Name _____ Date _____

Word Work

The letters **st** stand for the beginning sounds in *star*.

The letters **sm** stand for the beginning sounds in *smile*.

The letters **sn** stand for the beginning sounds in *snake*.

The letters **sl** stand for the beginning sounds in *slipper*.

Say the name of each picture. Then complete each word by writing the letters *st, sm, sn,* or *sl*.

1. ___airs

2. ___eaker

3. ___oke

4. ___ide

5. ___ail

Read the words below. Write the word that completes each sentence.

stormy   snow   stop   slept   small

6. Did you _____ to eat lunch on the trail?

7. Look for all the _____ trail signs.

8. Winter _____ sometimes covers the trail.

9. Last night we _____ under the stars.

10. One day was cold and _____.

Write Now

In the article "Take a Hike!" you read about the Appalachian Trail. Imagine that you have just spent several days hiking and camping along the trail.

• Plan to write a journal entry. Make a word web like this one. Add more words to the web to tell what you did and saw on your hikes.

• Write your journal entry. Tell about the fun you had on the Appalachian Trail. Use words from the web. Then draw a picture of yourself hiking.

Rube Goldberg's Funny Pictures

by Dave Kochman

Set Your Purpose

Do cartoons make you laugh? Read this article about Rube Goldberg's funny cartoons.

Rube Goldberg wanted to **draw** cartoons. His dad wanted him to be an engineer. Goldberg tried that first. Then he told his dad he just had to draw. So Goldberg worked as an office boy at a newspaper. He drew lots of cartoons for his boss. Finally, he got the job he wanted.

Goldberg knew there were two ways to do things—the **simple** way and the hard way. He **believed** people like doing things the hard way. So Goldberg's cartoons show very hard ways to do easy **tasks**.

Today people still laugh at Goldberg's cartoons. Look at this one. Does it make you laugh?

Think About It

Why is this cartoon funny?

WEEKLY INVENTION

SAFETY DEVICE FOR WALKING ON ICY PAVEMENTS.

WHEN YOU SLIP ON ICE, YOUR FOOT KICKS PADDLE (A), LOWERING FINGER (B), SNAPPING TURTLE (C) EXTENDS NECK TO BITE FINGER, OPENING ICE TONGS (D) AND DROPPING PILLOW (E), THUS ALLOWING YOU TO FALL ON SOMETHING SOFT!

RUBE GOLDBERG (TM) RGI 100

Name _____   Date _____

Check Your **Understanding**

Fill in the letter with the best answer for each question.

1. Which statement is an opinion about Rube Goldberg?

Ⓐ Rube Goldberg drew the funniest cartoons.

Ⓑ Rube Goldberg worked as an office boy.

Ⓒ Rube Goldberg was a cartoonist.

2. Which statement is a fact about Rube Goldberg?

Ⓐ Everyone should laugh at Goldberg's cartoons.

Ⓑ Goldberg's father should not have forced him to be an engineer.

Ⓒ Goldberg's cartoons showed the hard way to do things.

3. How did Rube Goldberg get the job he wanted?

Ⓐ He drew lots of cartoons for his boss.

Ⓑ He became an engineer.

Ⓒ He sold a book of cartoons.

4. Rube Goldberg became a cartoonist because

Ⓐ he did things the hard way.

Ⓑ his father was an engineer.

Ⓒ he never gave up trying.

Vocabulary

Find each vocabulary word in the selection. The words and sentences around it will help you figure out its meaning.

Fill in the letter with the best definition of the underlined word.

1. Rube Goldberg liked to <u>draw</u> cartoons.

Ⓐ make a picture

Ⓑ whistle

Ⓒ laugh hard at

2. You have a <u>simple</u> job to do.

Ⓐ easy

Ⓑ long

Ⓒ hard

3. He <u>believed</u> the Tigers would win.

Ⓐ wished

Ⓑ knew

Ⓒ thought

4. You must finish your <u>tasks</u> before you go play.

Ⓐ worries

Ⓑ cereal

Ⓒ jobs

Name _____ Date _____

Word Work

> The letters **ay** stand for the **long-a** sound in a *tray*.
>
> The letters **ai** stand for the **long-a** sound in *train*.

Look at the pictures. Find the picture whose name has the long-*a* sound. Fill in the letter of that picture.

1. Ⓐ   Ⓑ
2. Ⓐ Ⓑ
3. Ⓐ Ⓑ
4. Ⓐ   Ⓑ
5. Ⓐ Ⓑ

Read the words below. Write the word that completes each sentence.

day   stay   paint   clay   rain

6. A _____ is 24 hours long.

7. The _____ falls from the clouds in the sky.

8. You must _____ home when you are sick.

9. The old barn needs a new coat of _____.

10. The teacher molded a bowl out of _____.

Write Now

In the article "Rube Goldberg's Funny Pictures," you read about how he wanted to be a cartoonist. Look at the web shown. It shows the skills and traits that made him a good cartoonist.

- Think about what you want to be when you grow up. Plan to write a paragraph about your future job. Make a web like the one shown to organize your ideas.

- Write your paragraph. Include ideas from your web. Then draw a picture of yourself in your future career.

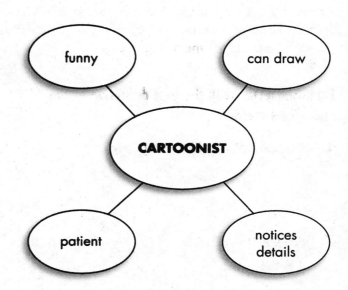

Hi-Lo Nonfiction Passages for Struggling Readers: Grades 4-5 • Scholastic Inc.

325

A Natural Wonder

by Emile LeClaire

Set Your Purpose

The Grand Canyon is one of the world's natural wonders. Read this article to find out why.

Visitors stand on the South Rim of the Grand Canyon in Arizona. As they look across the deep gorge, they **murmur** to one another.

"Wow!" "Cool!" "Awesome!"

The Grand Canyon is awesome. The colors of the canyon's stone walls can take your breath away. The colors can be gray, green, red, orange, and gold.

The colors are beautiful. But it's the size of the Grand Canyon that really makes people **gasp**. It's huge! The **widest** spot of the canyon is 18 miles across!

The canyon is long, too. If visitors look down into the canyon, they see the Colorado River. It flows along the canyon **floor** for 227 miles! From end to end, the state of Massachusetts is only about 190 miles! A raft ride down the length of the river through the Grand Canyon can take two weeks.

The Grand Canyon is also deep—almost 6,000 feet deep! A hike up and down the canyon takes two days. The trails are **steep** and winding. Some people hike on foot. Others ride burros or mules.

The Grand Canyon was made a National Park in 1919. That first year, about 44,000 people came to see it. Today, about 5 million people a year come to view the Grand Canyon. It's truly one of the world's natural wonders.

Think About It

What makes the Grand Canyon a natural wonder?

327

Name _____ Date _____

Check Your Understanding

Fill in the letter with the best answer for each question.

1. Which of these is a fact?
- Ⓐ The Grand Canyon is an awesome sight.
- Ⓑ The colors on the cliffs are beautiful.
- Ⓒ The Grand Canyon is amazing.
- Ⓓ The Grand Canyon is in Arizona.

2. Which of these is an opinion?
- Ⓐ The Grand Canyon is 18 miles across.
- Ⓑ The Colorado River flows through the Grand Canyon.
- Ⓒ Hiking down the Grand Canyon is hard.
- Ⓓ The Grand Canyon is about 6,000 feet deep at its deepest point.

3. The author probably believes that
- Ⓐ the Grand Canyon is a wonderful treasure.
- Ⓑ not enough people visit the Grand Canyon.
- Ⓒ people can't hike up the Grand Canyon.
- Ⓓ everyone should live in Arizona.

4. From the information in the selection, you can guess that
- Ⓐ the Grand Canyon was the first National Park.
- Ⓑ the Grand Canyon is longer than some states.
- Ⓒ people visit the Grand Canyon only in summertime.
- Ⓓ it is impossible to reach the bottom of the Grand Canyon.

5. Which sentence would not be used in a summary of the selection?
- Ⓐ The Grand Canyon walls are a variety of colors.
- Ⓑ The Grand Canyon is extremely wide, long, and deep.
- Ⓒ Massachusetts is only 190 miles long from end to end.
- Ⓓ The Grand Canyon was made a National Park in 1919.

Vocabulary

> Find each vocabulary word in the selection. The words and sentences around it will help you figure out its meaning.

Fill in the letter with the best definition of the underlined word.

1. Visitors <u>murmur</u> words of wonder.
- Ⓐ write
- Ⓑ yell
- Ⓒ whisper
- Ⓓ give

2. The river flows along the canyon <u>floor</u>.
- Ⓐ bottom surface
- Ⓑ wide river
- Ⓒ raft or small boat
- Ⓓ top of something

3. The canyon's <u>widest</u> part is 18 miles.
- Ⓐ farthest distance across
- Ⓑ most wild
- Ⓒ thick all around
- Ⓓ most wonderful

4. The trails are <u>steep</u> and winding.
- Ⓐ flat and straight
- Ⓑ floating in the air
- Ⓒ almost straight up and down
- Ⓓ buried deep beneath the ground

5. The Grand Canyon makes people <u>gasp</u>.
- Ⓐ take something from someone
- Ⓑ be bored with something
- Ⓒ jump out from behind something
- Ⓓ take a short, quick breath

Name _____ Date _____

Word Work

A **noun** names a person, place, or thing. A **plural noun** names more than one person, place, or thing. To make the plural of most nouns, add **-s**.

book ⟶ books

Write the plural of each word.

1. visitor _____

2. week _____

3. color _____

4. trail _____

5. guest _____

Read each sentence. Write the correct plural form of the word in dark type.

6. **mule**   We rode _____ down into the canyon.

7. **day**   It took almost two _____ to get to the bottom.

8. **tent**   Then we set up _____ and camped.

9. **night**   We stayed for three _____.

10. **vacation**   Of all our _____, this one was the best.

Write Now

In "A Natural Wonder," you read about Grand Canyon's history and why so many people go to visit it. The chart below shows some of the information you learned.

The Grand Canyon	
Colors	stone walls are gray, green, red, orange, and gold
Size	18 miles wide 227 miles long, almost 6,000 feet deep
History	became a National Park in 1919

- Plan to write a paragraph that describes a place you have visited or read about. Brainstorm some ideas about the place by making a chart like the one shown. Choose ideas from your chart to include in your description.

- Write your paragraph. Tell what is special about the place you are describing.

WHO CAN MAKE THE BEST SAND CASTLE?

by Emily McLaughlin

Set Your Purpose

What would you see at a sand-castle contest? Read this article to find out.

It is 37 feet high. It weighs 19,000 tons. It is as long as a football field. It has roads so you can walk through it. It's on a beach in Florida. Believe it or not—it's a sand castle!

Cities and towns all over the world have sand-castle contests. People like to build interesting things. Not all of them are castles. People build beautiful sand animals. They build delicious-looking food. They create funny or silly people. Some builders **enter** the contests to win the prizes. They can win money and free gifts. Others enter because **building** with sand is so much fun.

South Padre Island, Texas, has a sand-castle contest every year. Some people work in groups. Others build by themselves. All of the people find their own places to build on the beach. They get sand and water. For two days, the builders are busy **molding** figures of different shapes. Then the judges choose the best sand **statues**.

There is a special contest for kids. They make sand animals. The people who are watching vote on the best animals.

If you are near a beach, there may be a sand-castle contest coming up. Even if there isn't a contest, that's okay. Get your bucket and shovel. Sit down in the **damp** sand, and start building!

Think About It

Why do people enter sand-castle contests? What kinds of things might you like to build in the sand?

Name_____ Date_____

Check Your Understanding

Fill in the letter with the best answer for each question.

1. Which sentence states a fact?

   Ⓐ The sand animals are beautiful.

   Ⓑ The kids make the best sand animals.

   Ⓒ One sand castle was 37 feet high.

   Ⓓ Sand animals are fun to make.

2. Which states an opinion?

   Ⓐ The people find a place to build.

   Ⓑ Building sand castles is fun.

   Ⓒ There are prizes for the winners.

   Ⓓ People build sand food and animals.

3. Which sentence states a fact?

   Ⓐ Some sand animals look silly.

   Ⓑ Some of the builders probably get bored after a while.

   Ⓒ Sand-castle contests must be really interesting.

   Ⓓ The judges choose the best sand animals.

4. Which materials are used for building a sand castle?

   Ⓐ sand and water

   Ⓑ wood, brick, and sand

   Ⓒ mud, sand, and sticks

   Ⓓ wood and water

5. Which sentence best describes people who enter sand-castle contests?

   Ⓐ They like to create things.

   Ⓑ They like to eat delicious food.

   Ⓒ They like to relax on the beach.

   Ⓓ They like to swim in the ocean.

Vocabulary

> Find each vocabulary word in the selection. The words and sentences around it will help you figure out its meaning.

Fill in the letter with the best definition of the underlined word.

1. Some builders <u>enter</u> the contest to win prizes.

   Ⓐ finish   Ⓒ sign up for

   Ⓑ enjoy   Ⓓ read about

2. People enjoy the contest because <u>building</u> with sand is so much fun.

   Ⓐ making something

   Ⓑ playing something

   Ⓒ destroying something

   Ⓓ cooking something

3. For two days, builders are busy <u>molding</u> figures made of sand.

   Ⓐ moving   Ⓒ cooking

   Ⓑ shaping   Ⓓ breaking

4. The judges choose the best sand <u>statues</u>.

   Ⓐ builders   Ⓒ cities

   Ⓑ figures   Ⓓ contests

5. <u>Damp</u> sand is needed for building sand castles.

   Ⓐ very dry   Ⓒ somewhat wet

   Ⓑ very cold   Ⓓ somewhat rocky

Name_____   Date_____

Word Work

A **noun** names a person, place, or thing. A **plural noun** names more than one person, place, or thing. To make the plural of most nouns, add **-s**.

book ⟶ books

Write the plural of each word.

1. ton _____

2. field _____

3. castle _____

4. town _____

5. animal _____

Read each sentence. Write the correct plural form of the word in dark type.

6. prize   Some people enter to win _____.

7. builder   Other _____ enter because it is fun.

8. place   All of the people get their own _____ on the beach.

9. judge   Then the _____ view their work.

10. statue   They choose the best sand _____.

Write Now

Here are some facts and opinions about sand-castle contests.

Facts	Opinions
Contests are held all over the world.	The contests are fun.
The winners get prizes.	Money is the best prize.

- Plan to create a poster advertising a sand-castle contest. Make a list of more facts and opinions about sand-castle contests using information from the article.

- Create your poster. Use some of the facts and opinions from your list. Draw a picture for your poster.

The Surprising Story of Jeans

by Carole Osterink

Set Your Purpose

What could be surprising about jeans? They're the ultimate everyday clothes. Read the article to find out about these everyday clothes.

Do you know about the California Gold Rush? It happened in 1849. Gold was discovered and 40,000 people called prospectors went to look for it.

Levi Strauss heard about them. He went to California in 1853. But he didn't go to find lumps of gold. He went to sell **materials** needed for everyday life. He thought prospectors would need canvas for tents. It turned out they needed pants. So he made pants out of his canvas. This marked the **birth** of Levi's® jeans.

Soon Levi had used up all his canvas. So he switched to another material—denim. The pants he made were strong. They **wore** well. They had sturdy pockets to hold gold nuggets. Word spread. Soon everybody wanted "Levi's pants." They started calling them just "Levi's." In time Levi's became another name for jeans.

150 Years of Blue-Jean History

1853–1949

Cowhands and workers wear Levi's jeans.

1950s

Teens start wearing Levi's. Boys wear them to school. Girls can't because of dress codes. But they wear them after school.

1960s

The whole world wants Levi's. College students go to Europe carrying suitcases loaded with jeans. They sell the jeans there to make travel money.

1970s

A pair of Levi's goes on display at the Smithsonian. It's part of the American history collection.

1990s

Jeans with buttons continue their comeback. They're like the first pants for the gold rush prospectors Levi made in 1853.

Think About It

What was the most surprising thing you learned about jeans?

Name _____ **Date** _____

Check Your **Understanding**

Fill in the letter with the best answer for each question.

1. Which of these statements is an opinion?
   - Ⓐ Levi Strauss went to California in 1853.
   - Ⓑ Levi Straus must be a very clever man.
   - Ⓒ Levi Strauss made pants out of canvas.
   - Ⓓ Levi's became another word for jeans.

2. Which of these statements is a fact?
   - Ⓐ In 1976, Levi's went on display at the Smithsonian.
   - Ⓑ Jeans are the best kind of clothes.
   - Ⓒ Jeans are the most important clothes in American history.
   - Ⓓ Everyone needs a pair of jeans.

3. Which detail supports the idea that the whole world wanted Levi's in the 1960s?
   - Ⓐ Levi's is another name for jeans.
   - Ⓑ The first Jeans were worn by prospectors.
   - Ⓒ There were too many tourists in Europe.
   - Ⓓ Students brought suitcases of Levi's to Europe and sold them there.

4. Why is a pair of Levi's on display at the Smithsonian?
   - Ⓐ The jeans were worn by a famous person.
   - Ⓑ It's the first pair Levi Strauss ever made.
   - Ⓒ The jeans were worn by a character in a movie.
   - Ⓓ Levi's jeans are part of American history.

5. Levi Strauss started out
   - Ⓐ making pants for cowhands.
   - Ⓑ making pants from canvas.
   - Ⓒ putting buttons on jeans.
   - Ⓓ prospecting for gold.

Vocabulary

Find each vocabulary word in the selection. The words and sentences around it will help you figure out its meaning.

Fill in the letter with the best definition of the underlined word.

1. The <u>birth</u> of Levi's jeans occurred in California.
   - Ⓐ having to do with an invention
   - Ⓑ improvement
   - Ⓒ the beginning of something new
   - Ⓓ the popularity of

2. Denim is one of the strongest <u>materials</u> used for pants.
   - Ⓐ fabrics   Ⓒ tents
   - Ⓑ words   Ⓓ ropes

3. Because the pants were made of denim, they <u>wore</u> well.
   - Ⓐ appeared   Ⓒ were colored
   - Ⓑ tore apart   Ⓓ lasted in use

4. College students went to Europe carrying suitcases <u>loaded</u> with jeans.
   - Ⓐ open   Ⓒ filled
   - Ⓑ in addition to Ⓓ left

5. Jeans with buttons make a <u>comeback</u>.
   - Ⓐ return   Ⓒ brief appearance on TV
   - Ⓑ commercial   Ⓓ first appearance

Name _____   Date _____

Word Work

> **Synonyms** are words that have similar meanings. For example, *little* and *small* are synonyms.

> A **compound word** is made of two shorter words. Combining the meanings of the two shorter words often explains the meaning of the compound word.
>
> **weekend** = **end** of the **week**

Fill in the letter of the word that means the same or about the same as the underlined word.

1. Something that is <u>sturdy</u> is
   - Ⓐ old.
   - Ⓑ soft.
   - Ⓒ strong.
   - Ⓓ difficult.

2. To <u>switch</u> is to
   - Ⓐ sweep.
   - Ⓑ sew.
   - Ⓒ promise.
   - Ⓓ change.

3. Another word for <u>discover</u> is
   - Ⓐ find.
   - Ⓑ melt.
   - Ⓒ reappear.
   - Ⓓ hide.

4. Something that is <u>surprising</u> is
   - Ⓐ frightening.
   - Ⓑ new.
   - Ⓒ unexpected.
   - Ⓓ scary.

5. Another word for <u>nuggets</u> is
   - Ⓐ coins.
   - Ⓑ lumps.
   - Ⓒ candies.
   - Ⓓ seeds.

Look at the compound words below. Write the word that best completes each sentence.

everybody   comeback   cowhand
suitcases   everyday

6. Jeans are our favorite _____ wear.

7. Does _____ own a pair of jeans?

8. You don't have to be a _____ to wear jeans.

9. How many _____ at the airport have jeans in them?

10. Jeans with buttons made a _____ in the 1990s.

Write Now

In "The Surprising History of Jeans," you learned about a useful and popular piece of clothing.

- Plan to write a paragraph describing your favorite everyday wear. How does it look and feel? Think about why you like this particular piece of clothing. Put your ideas in a web like the one shown.

- Write your paragraph. Remember to use a lot of adjectives to describe your favorite piece of clothing.

A Hospital for Dolphins & Whales

by Laura Alavosus

Set Your Purpose

Who takes care of whales and dolphins when they get sick? Read this article to find out.

Dolphins and whales swim in the sea. Some people think they are fish, but they're not. They are **mammals**. They swim underwater and come up to breathe air like you and me.

People sometimes find dolphins and whales **stranded** on the beach. No one knows why. One guess is that waves push them there during a storm. Another **guess** is that sick dolphins and whales come out of the water to die.

If you saw a dolphin or whale on a beach, what would you do? You could call the Dolphin and Whale Hospital.

In 1999, a sick dolphin was found on a beach in Florida. They named him Peanut. Doctors at the Dolphin and Whale Hospital found sea sponges and shells in his **stomach**. These things may have made Peanut sick. The doctors helped him get better. Then they put him back into the sea.

Think About It

What other people or places help animals?

Name _____ Date _____

Check Your Understanding

Fill in the letter with the best answer for each question.

1. It is a fact that dolphins and whales
- Ⓐ are fish.
- Ⓑ like to sun on the beach.
- Ⓒ are mammals.
- Ⓓ belong in the hospital.

2. Which sentence states an opinion about the dolphin named Peanut?
- Ⓐ Peanut had a lot of things in his stomach.
- Ⓑ Peanut went to the Dolphin and Whale Hospital.
- Ⓒ Peanut is a good name for a dolphin.
- Ⓓ Peanut was found on a beach in Florida.

3. Which of the following is <u>not</u> a fact from the story?
- Ⓐ Dolphins and whales sometimes wash up on beaches.
- Ⓑ Peanut became famous and starred in a movie.
- Ⓒ Whales and dolphins breathe air.
- Ⓓ Peanut got better at the Dolphin and Whale Hospital.

4. Why do we see dolphins and whales on beaches?
- Ⓐ They want to dry off in the sun.
- Ⓑ No one knows for sure.
- Ⓒ They like to roll in the sand.
- Ⓓ They don't know how to swim.

Vocabulary

> Find each vocabulary word in the selection. The words and sentences around it will help you figure out its meaning.

Fill in the letter with the best definition of the underlined word.

1. Whales and dolphins are <u>mammals</u>.
- Ⓐ animals that can talk
- Ⓑ animals that breathe water
- Ⓒ animals that breathe air
- Ⓓ animals that can't breathe

2. People sometimes find dolphins <u>stranded</u> on the beach.
- Ⓐ walking
- Ⓑ happy
- Ⓒ playing
- Ⓓ run up

3. Another <u>guess</u> is that sick dolphins come out of the water to die.
- Ⓐ belief
- Ⓑ question
- Ⓒ picture
- Ⓓ example

4. The things in Peanut's <u>stomach</u> may have made him sick.
- Ⓐ arms and legs
- Ⓑ head and neck
- Ⓒ fins and flippers
- Ⓓ belly

Hi-Lo Nonfiction Passages for Struggling Readers Grades 4-5 • Scholastic Inc.

Name _____ Date _____

Word Work

> A **contraction** is a short way of writing two words as one. In a contraction, one or more letters are left out. An apostrophe (') takes the place of the missing letters.
>
> **who is = who's**

Read the words in dark type. Circle the contraction they make.

1. they are	they'll	they're	they'd
2. you have	you're	you'll	you've
3. we will	we'd	we've	we'll
4. I am	I'm	I've	I'll
5. do not	didn't	don't	doesn't

Read each sentence. Write the contraction for the underlined words.

6. <u>She is</u> taking us to the beach.

_____

7. <u>I am</u> going with my friends.

_____

8. <u>They are</u> all good swimmers.

_____

9. He <u>does not</u> see any whales or dolphins.

_____

10. <u>She will</u> take a picture of that seagull.

_____

Write Now

In the article "A Hospital for Dolphins & Whales," you read about a sick dolphin named Peanut.

- Pretend you are part of Peanut's family. Peanut is missing and you are looking for him. Plan to create a Missing Mammal Poster. Make a chart like the one shown here. Be sure to offer a reward.

- Make a poster. Use information from your chart. Don't forget to draw a picture of Peanut, the missing mammal.

Missing Mammal	
Who is missing?	Peanut
What is Peanut?	
Where was he last seen?	Off a Florida beach
What is the reward?	

Hi-Lo Nonfiction Passages for Struggling Readers: Grades 4–5 • Scholastic Inc.

America's Lady Liberty

adapted by William Smith

Set Your Purpose

Who is America's Lady Liberty? Why is she important to our nation? Read this article to find out.

She stands in New York Harbor, proud and tall. She is a breathtaking **sight** with her majestic crown and her blazing torch held high.

For more than 100 years, day and night, this wonderful lady has **greeted** visitors to our shores. She has never tired of her job. Nor has she ever **failed** to thrill those who see her for the first time. To all Americans and to all who come to America from afar, she stands as a **symbol** of freedom.

Who is this great lady? Some people call her Lady Liberty. You may know her as the Statue of Liberty. She was a gift from France for America's 100th birthday. She was shipped here in 350 pieces! Putting the statue together took four months!

Now read the labels to learn more about America's Lady Liberty.

TORCH

At night, hundreds of light bulbs light the torch. Her torch is said to guide the way for people **seeking** freedom in America.

COPPER SKIN

For the statue's 100th birthday, people worked hard to make her look like new. Her shiny copper skin was still rich and green. Only the torch, which was rebuilt, needed new copper.

CROWN

There are seven spikes in her crown. They stand for the world's seven continents. Visitors can climb 354 steps inside the statue to peek out of the crown.

TABLET

The date July 4, 1776, is carved here in Roman numerals. That's the day we declared our freedom from England.

BASE

The statue's base is 154 feet high. From the bottom of her base to the tip of her torch, the statue is 305 feet tall.

Think About It

Who is Lady Liberty? What does she symbolize, or stand for?

Name _____   Date _____

Check Your **Understanding**

Fill in the letter with the best answer for each question.

1. Which of these is a fact?

ⓐ The Statue of Liberty is breathtaking to look at.

ⓑ Putting the statue together took four months.

ⓒ Nothing stands for freedom as much as Lady Liberty.

ⓓ The spikes on her crown look very sharp.

2. Which of these is an opinion?

ⓐ The Statue of Liberty was a gift from France for our 100th birthday.

ⓑ It was shipped to America in 350 pieces.

ⓒ America celebrates its independence on July 4.

ⓓ Lady Liberty looks grand with her crown and torch.

3. Where is the Statue of Liberty located?

ⓐ a French harbor

ⓑ New York Harbor

ⓒ Rome, Italy

ⓓ Liberty, France

4. What problem was solved by shipping the statue in pieces to America?

ⓐ how to light the torch

ⓑ how to make her skin shiny

ⓒ how to get the huge statue to America

ⓓ how to build stairs inside a statue

5. What purpose does Lady Liberty's torch serve?

ⓐ to light up New York Harbor

ⓑ to guide those looking for freedom

ⓒ to hold those who climb to the top of the statue

ⓓ to stand for the world's seven continents

Vocabulary

Find each vocabulary word in the selection. The words and sentences around it will help you figure out its meaning.

Fill in the letter with the best definition of the underlined word.

1. The Statue of Liberty is a breathtaking <u>sight</u>.

ⓐ large crown

ⓑ something plain and boring

ⓒ something that is seen

ⓓ harbor

2. She stands as a <u>symbol</u> of freedom.

ⓐ synonym   ⓒ sign

ⓑ tower   ⓓ building

3. Lady Liberty has <u>greeted</u> visitors to our shores.

ⓐ become tired   ⓒ stood on

ⓑ frightened   ⓓ welcomed

4. She has never <u>failed</u> to thrill those who see her for the first time.

ⓐ been excited

ⓑ did not succeed

ⓒ traveled a great distance

ⓓ wanted

5. Her torch guides the way for people <u>seeking</u> freedom in America.

ⓐ looking for   ⓒ escaping from

ⓑ setting on fire   ⓓ lifting

Hi-Lo Nonfiction Passages for Struggling Readers Grades 4-5 • Scholastic Inc.

Name_____   Date_____

Word Work

Synonyms are words that have similar meanings. For example, *symbol* and *sign* are synonyms.

The **long-a** sound can be spelled several different ways. Look at these examples:

break   **f<u>ai</u>led**   **pl<u>ay</u>**

Read the words below. Then write the word that has almost the same meaning as the underlined word.

welcomed   guests   lead
look   usually

1. Long ago, many <u>visitors</u> came to America by boat. _____

2. They crowded the decks to take a <u>peek</u> at their new home. _____

3. Their first sight was <u>often</u> the Statue of Liberty. _____

4. Sometimes they were <u>greeted</u> at the docks by relatives. _____

5. Many had no family to <u>guide</u> them around their new country. _____

Fill in the letter of the word in each group that has the long-a vowel sound.

6. Ⓐ dance   Ⓒ hand
      Ⓑ large   Ⓓ birthday

7. Ⓐ mail   Ⓒ spread
      Ⓑ liar   Ⓓ please

8. Ⓐ barn   Ⓒ strap
      Ⓑ steak   Ⓓ facts

9. Ⓐ stray   Ⓒ hard
      Ⓑ France   Ⓓ stands

10. Ⓐ handle   Ⓒ drain
       Ⓑ quarter   Ⓓ stall

Write Now

Look at the labels around the picture of the Statue of Liberty in the article. They give facts and details about America's Lady Liberty.

• Plan to make a poster of a special place. Think of a place that has meaning to you. It may be a place you like to go to play or to sit and think. Make a list of facts and details that you can use for labels.

• Make your poster. Draw a picture of the place. Add labels and facts that tell about this place. Write one sentence at the bottom that tells what this place means to you.

Living Flashlights

by Anna Nunes

Set Your Purpose

You may have seen a firefly flash its light on and off. What other living things light up? Read this article to find out!

Imagine that you are in the darkest part of the forest. Suddenly a small flashing light darts in front of you. What could it be?

Have you ever tried to find your way in the dark? You could use a mushroom as a flashlight! That's not as strange as it sounds. Some plants and animals are their own flashlights!

Many creatures on the land can make light. You've probably seen fireflies as they flash their lights on a warm summer night. But have you ever seen a glow-in-the-dark mushroom? There is such a mushroom. It grows on rotting trees in **tropical** forests where the air is very warm and wet. This mushroom makes its own light. Scientists think that it does this to **entice** bugs. The bugs then take mushroom spores, or seeds, to other trees to grow.

346

A flashlight fish

How Do Animals and Plants Make Light?

How do these living things light up? Do they have tiny lightbulbs and batteries inside them? No, of course not. In most cases, light comes from chemicals that break apart inside the plant or the animal. The separated chemicals mix with oxygen or other substances. Light is released, and the plant or animal glows.

Most of the plants and animals on Earth that give off light live in the ocean. Scientists think that more than half of the animals in the sea can **generate** light. Many kinds of fish, shrimp, and squid in the upper layers of the sea have this amazing **capability**.

One example is the flashlight fish. These unusual sea creatures send out light that can be seen from 100 feet away. They do this to confuse their **predators**, or animals that want to eat them. Tiny plant-like creatures called algae are another example. They live in jellyfish. They give off a yellowish glow that shines out through the jellyfish. The light attracts food for both the jellyfish and the algae.

Think About It

What facts did you learn about plants and animals that give off light? What else would you like to know?

Name _____ Date _____

Check Your Understanding

Fill in the letter with the best answer for each question.

1. Which of the following is a fact?
- Ⓐ Tiny algae live inside some jellyfish.
- Ⓑ A glow-in-the-dark mushroom is an amazing sight.
- Ⓒ Having a built-in flashlight is a cool idea.
- Ⓓ Fireflies are wonderful to see.

2. Which of the following is an opinion?
- Ⓐ Many creatures on land can make light.
- Ⓑ Flashlight fish have a good name.
- Ⓒ More than half of sea creatures glow.
- Ⓓ Some plants can make their own light.

3. Which of the following is <u>not</u> a fact?
- Ⓐ Bugs help mushrooms spread from tree to tree.
- Ⓑ Some shrimp and squid produce light.
- Ⓒ Some plants glow.
- Ⓓ You shouldn't eat things that glow.

4. How are the flashlight fish and glowing algae alike?
- Ⓐ They are both tiny plant-like creatures.
- Ⓑ They both live in the ocean and give off light.
- Ⓒ They both make light in their bellies.
- Ⓓ They both glow to attract food.

5. What is the main idea of this selection?
- Ⓐ Bugs are attracted to glowing mushrooms.
- Ⓑ Plants and animals have tiny flashlights and batteries inside them.
- Ⓒ Many plants and animals can make their own light.
- Ⓓ It is hard to see in the dark.

Vocabulary

> Find each vocabulary word in the selection. The words and sentences around it will help you figure out its meaning.

Fill in the letter with the best definition of the underlined word.

1. Mushrooms grow on rotting trees in <u>tropical</u> forests.
- Ⓐ any
- Ⓑ hot, moist
- Ⓒ ice-covered
- Ⓓ treeless

2. The mushroom glows to <u>entice</u> bugs.
- Ⓐ attack or invade
- Ⓑ insult
- Ⓒ show pleasure
- Ⓓ attract

3. Many animals in the sea can <u>generate</u> light.
- Ⓐ sell a product
- Ⓑ breathe
- Ⓒ make
- Ⓓ watch carefully

4. Some fish have this amazing <u>capability</u>.
- Ⓐ power
- Ⓑ opportunity
- Ⓒ wish
- Ⓓ brightness

5. Flashlight fish confuse their <u>predators</u>.
- Ⓐ animals that no longer exist
- Ⓑ plants that animals eat
- Ⓒ chemical products
- Ⓓ animals that eat other animals

Hi-Lo Nonfiction Passages for Struggling Readers: Grades 4–5 • Scholastic Inc.

Name_____ Date_____

Word Work

> **Synonyms** are words that have similar meanings. For example, *large* and *big* are synonyms.

Read the sentences and the words below. Write the word that means almost the same as the word in dark type.

small   shines   animals   draw   create

1. I got a book about lions, zebras, and other **creatures** of Africa. _____

2. The magnet will **attract** those paper clips to it. _____

3. This campfire will **produce** enough heat to warm us. _____

4. Compared to a huge elephant, a mouse is **tiny**. _____

5. The North Star **glows** brighter than any other star in the sky. _____

> The **long-*i*** sound can be spelled in several different ways. Look at these examples.
>
> tr**ie**d   l**igh**t   ins**i**d**e**

Circle all the words in each sentence that have the long-*i* sound. Then underline the letters that spell the long-*i* sound in each word.

6. We saw a film about a team that tries to take pictures of sea life.

7. It was as dark as night far under the water.

8. We spied a very bright blinking light on one side of the screen.

9. It was a treat to see a flashlight fish because they usually hide when a camera comes near.

10. The sight of the glowing jellyfish was a nice surprise.

Write Now

Look at the chart. It starts at the top with a very wide topic of interest: Unusual Plants and Animals. Then it narrows the topic to make it more specific. In this chart, "mushrooms that glow" has been circled. This is one of the narrow topics that the writer of "Living Flashlights" chose to write about.

- Plan to make a chart for another topic. Use the chart shown as your model. For example, your topic idea might be "sneakers." That topic would fit in a larger category of "footwear" inside of an even larger category of "fashion."

- Write your chart. Add some notes about what you might want to say about your topic.

Unusual Plants and Animals

Plants	Animals
mushrooms that glow	

Hi-Lo Nonfiction Passages for Struggling Readers: Grades 4–5 • Scholastic Inc.

349

Answer Key

Swimming in Stingray City (pp. 14–15)
Check Your Understanding
1. B 2. B 3. A 4. C
Vocabulary
1. C 2. C 3. A 4. A
Word Work
1. gentle 2. gym 3. giant 4. germ
5. ginger 6. George 7. (game) 8. (grab)
9. gentleman 10. (girl)
Write Now: Answers will vary.

The Mystery of the Great Stones
(pp. 18–19)
Check Your Understanding
1. A 2. B 3. C 4. A
Vocabulary
1. B 2. B 3. C 4. A
Word Work
1. pig 2. swim 3. sock 4. chin 5. mop
6. A 7. C 8. B 9. D 10. A
Write Now: Answers will vary.

Here Comes the Parade (pp. 22–23)
Check Your Understanding
1. B 2. B 3. C 4. C 5. D
Vocabulary
1. A 2. D 3. C 4. A 5. B
Word Work
1. B 2. A 3. A 4. B 5. A 6. B 7. B
8. B 9. A 10. B
Write Now: Answers will vary.

Monopoly on Atlantic City (pp. 26–27)
Check Your Understanding
1. A 2. D 3. B 4. A 5. A
Vocabulary
1. C 2. A 3. C 4. A 5. D
Word Work
1. A 2. B 3. B 4. A 5. A 6. brainchild
7. salesman 8. seashore 9. boardwalk
10. flashlight
Write Now: Answers will vary.

Amelia Did! (pp. 30–31)
Check Your Understanding
1. B 2. D 3. A 4. B 5. C
Vocabulary
1. C 2. B 3. D 4. C 5. A
Word Work
1. searched 2. chirp 3. house 4. crowd
5. early 6. how 7. girl 8. mouth 9. allow
10. own
Write Now: Answers will vary.

Welcome to the Grand Ole Opry
(pp. 34–35)
Check Your Understanding
1. A 2. D 3. C 4. A 5. B
Vocabulary
1. A 2. B 3. A 4. C 5. B
Word Work
1. artist 2. careful 3. colorful 4. shameful
5. guitarist 6. violin 7. use 8. fear 9. organ
10. wonder
Write Now: Answers will vary.

Join the Roller Coaster Club!
(pp. 38–39)
Check Your Understanding
1. D 2. A 3. B 4. A 5. D
Vocabulary
1. D 2. D 3. D 4. C 5. A
Word Work
1. terrifying 2. destroyed 3. old 4. like

5. give 6. low 7. B 8. D 9. C 10. B
Write Now: Answers will vary.

Snakes: They Are Everywhere!
(pp. 44–45)
Check Your Understanding
1. B 2. B 3. A 4. C
Vocabulary
1. B 2. A 3. C 4. A
Word Work
1. A 2. B 3. B 4. B 5. B 6. note 7. cute
8. kite 9. time 10. cane
Write Now: Answers will vary.

Desert Life (pp. 48–49)
Check Your Understanding
1. D 2. C 3. A 4. A 5. D
Vocabulary
1. A 2. A 3. B 4. B 5. C
Word Work
1. thunderstorm 2. sunrise 3. nightfall
4. sailboat 5. teacup 6. rattlesnakes
7. wildlife 8. underground 9. sunlight
10. sandstorms
Write Now: Answers will vary.

The Sneaker Story (pp. 52–53)
Check Your Understanding
1. C 2. D 3. D 4. B 5. D
Vocabulary
1. A 2. D 3. B 4. B 5. C
Word Work
1. shoes 2. spies 3. lights 4. pumps
5. athletes 6. companies 7. classmates
8. cities 9. families 10. schools
Write Now: Answers will vary.

Leonardo Da Vinci (pp. 56–57)
Check Your Understanding
1. D 2. B 3. C 4. D 5. C
Vocabulary
1. B 2. C 3. D 4. B 5. C
Word Work
1. countless 2. first 3. famous 4. smiling
5. strange 6. Leonardo's 7. woman's
8. questions' 9. waves' 10. moon's
Write Now: Answers will vary.

You Can't Throw a Boomerang Away
(pp. 60–61)
Check Your Understanding
1. C 2. A 3. C 4. D
Vocabulary
1. A 2. B 3. D 4. B
Word Work
1. clock 2. plug 3. flower 4. plant 5. clam
6. play 7. plane 8. flat 9. climb 10. fly
Write Now: Answers will vary.

Meet a Fine Feathered Dino!
(pp. 64–65)
Check Your Understanding
1. B 2. C 3. B 4. B 5. D
Vocabulary
1. C 2. D 3. C 4. B 5. D
Word Work
1. named 2. lived 3. saving 4. related
5. hoping 6. birdhouse 7. bluebird
8. snowstorm 9. birdlike 10. toenail
Write Now: Answers will vary.

Mystery on the Beach (pp. 68–69)
Check Your Understanding
1. A 2. C 3. A 4. D 5. B

Vocabulary
1. C 2. A 3. D 4. A 5. B
Word Work
1. return 2. unbelievable 3. underground
4. unexplained 5. renew 6. A 7. C 8. B
9. D 10. C
Write Now: Answers will vary.

People Take to the Skies (pp. 72–73)
Check Your Understanding
1. A 2. C 3. B 4. D 5. C
Vocabulary
1. A 2. A 3. D 4. B 5. C
Word Work
1. noting 2. declaring 3. smiling 4. liking
5. hoping 6. float 7. gentle 8. watched
9. capture 10. flame
Write Now: Answers will vary.

Sky Dancers (pp. 76–77)
Check Your Understanding
1. A 2. D 3. C 4. A 5. B
Vocabulary
1. B 2. C 3. A 4. C 5. D
Word Work
1. B 2. A 3. C 4. D 5. A 6. stop for a
while 7. kidding you 8. clumsy 9. be good
at 10. become
Write Now: Answers will vary.

From Boy to President (pp. 80–81)
Check Your Understanding
1. A 2. D 3. B 4. B 5. C
Vocabulary
1. A 2. A 3. B 4. C 5. D
Word Work
1. placed 2. baked 3. urged 4. worked
5. stayed 6. played 7. walking 8. hunting
9. moved 10. looked
Write Now: Answers will vary.

It Came From Mars! (pp. 84–85)
Check Your Understanding
1. C 2. B 3. D 4. A 5. C
Vocabulary
1. B 2. A 3. C 4. D 5. A
Word Work
1. guided 2. surprising 3. found 4. piece
5. crashed 6. Mars 7. smaller 8. far
9. water 10. born
Write Now: Answers will vary.

Meet M.C. Escher (pp. 88–89)
Check Your Understanding
1. A 2. C 3. D 4. B 5. C
Vocabulary
1. C 2. A 3. D 4. C 5. B
Word Work
1. carved 2. talked 3. liked 4. stated
5. smiled 6. drawing 7. worked 8. making
9. wanted 10. standing
Write Now: Answers will vary.

Wild, Wild Snowstorm (pp. 94–95)
Check Your Understanding
1. B 2. C 3. A 4. C
Vocabulary
1. B 2. C 3. A 4. B
Word Work
1. grapes 2. frog 3. dress 4. frown
5. dragon 6. ground 7. fresh 8. friend
9. group 10. drift
Write Now: Answers will vary.

Shark: Friend or Enemy? (pp. 98–99)
Check Your Understanding
1. C 2. D 3. A 4. B 5. D
Vocabulary
1. C 2. D 3. C 4. D 5. C
Word Work
1. protect 2. truths 3. often 4. easy 5. slow
6. waters 7. hammers 8. eyes 9. stripes
10. tigers
Write Now: Answers will vary.

Titanic! (pp. 102–103)
Check Your Understanding
1. B 2. A 3. B 4. C 5. D
Vocabulary
1. B 2. D 3. C 4. D 5. C
Word Work
1. discontinue 2. repaint 3. disfavor
4. reheat 5. dishonest 6. B 7. C 8. B
9. C 10. A
Write Now: Answers will vary.

Balloons Galore! (pp. 106–107)
Check Your Understanding
1. B 2. C 3. A 4. C 5. D
Vocabulary
1. B 2. C 3. A 4. C 5. D
Word Work
1. A 2. B 3. A 4. A 5. B 6. A 7. B
8. B 9. A 10. B
Write Now: Answers will vary.

**Why Are the Fish Swimming in the
Forest?** (pp. 110–111)
Check Your Understanding
1. C 2. A 3. D 4. A 5. B
Vocabulary
1. A 2. C 3. A 4. A 5. B
Word Work
1. B 2. A 3. A 4. B 5. beach 6. crash
7. ships 8. shells 9. think 10. check
Write Now: Answers will vary.

Into the Caves (pp. 114–115)
Check Your Understanding
1. A 2. D 3. A 4. B 5. B
Vocabulary
1. D 2. A 3. C 4. D 5. A
Word Work
1. C 2. A 3. D 4. B 5. A 6. I've
7. book's 8. didn't 9. don't 10. doesn't
Write Now: Answers will vary.

Those Shoes Are a Crime! (pp. 118–119)
Check Your Understanding
1. B 2. D 3. A 4. A 5. D
Vocabulary
1. A 2. C 3. A 4. D 5. C
Word Work
1. incomplete 2. redo 3. invisible
4. rearrange 5. inaccurate 6. C 7. B
8. A 9. D 10. C
Write Now: Answers will vary.

A Frog Mystery (pp. 122–123)
Check Your Understanding
1. C 2. D 3. C 4. D 5. A
Vocabulary
1. C 2. A 3. D 4. B 5. A
Word Work
1. C 2. D 3. A 4. C 5. B 6. teacher
7. quickly 8. farmer 9. painter 10. quietly
Write Now: Answers will vary.

A 7,000-Mile Shortcut! (pp. 128–129)
Check Your Understanding
1. C 2. A 3. B 4. A
Vocabulary
1. A 2. B 3. B 4. C
Word Work
1. B 2. C 3. A 4. C 5. B 6. ships 7. trip
8. fill 9. insects 10. sick
Write Now: Answers will vary.

Thank You, Benjamin Banneker!
(pp. 132–133)
Check Your Understanding
1. B 2. C 3. D 4. A 5. D
Vocabulary
1. B 2. C 3. D 4. A 5. A
Word Work
1. leads 2. cheer 3. builds 4. writes
5. care 6. painter 7. cleaner 8. respectful
9. hopeful 10. singer
Write Now: Answers will vary.

Where Is London Bridge? (pp. 136–137)
Check Your Understanding
1. B 2. A 3. B 4. D 5. C
Vocabulary
1. C 2. D 3. A 4. C 5. A
Word Work
1. C 2. D 3. B 4. C 5. A 6. new
7. heavy 8. lively 9. down 10. dry
Write Now: Answers will vary.

Replanting the Past (pp. 140–141)
Check Your Understanding
1. B 2. D 3. A 4. D 5. C
Vocabulary
1. B 2. C 3. B 4. D 5. A
Word Work
1. B 2. A 3. A 4. B 5. ranches 6. horses
7. patches 8. dresses 9. boxes 10. wagons
Write Now: Answers will vary.

Save Our Wetlands (pp. 146–147)
Check Your Understanding
1. A 2. D 3. B 4. A
Vocabulary
1. C 2. A 3. C 4. B
Word Work
1. harmful 2. joyless 3. powerless
4. hopeful 5. colorless 6. colorful
7. homeless 8. forgetful 9. respectful
10. fearless
Write Now: Answers will vary.

Video Games—Past and Present
(pp. 150–151)
Check Your Understanding
1. C 2. B 3. D 4. C
Vocabulary
1. D 2. A 3. B 4. C
Word Work
1. A 2. B 3. C 4. B 5. C 6. was not
7. I have 8. you would 9. It is 10. we will
Write Now: Answers will vary.

What's Inside a Robot? (pp. 154–155)
Check Your Understanding
1. C 2. A 3. A 4. D 5. C
Vocabulary
1. D 2. A 3. A 4. C 5. B
Word Work
1. B 2. D 3. C 4. A 5. D 6. living
7. invited 8. stapled 9. making 10. raised

Animals of Australia (pp. 158–159)
Check Your Understanding
1. D 2. C 3. B 4. B
Vocabulary
1. C 2. C 3. D 4. B
Word Work
1. B 2. A 3. B 4. B 5. A 6. down
7. brown 8. pouches 9. loud 10. ground
Write Now: Answers will vary.

What's Funny About the Funny Bone?
(pp. 162–163)
Check Your Understanding
1. C 2. B 3. A 4. C 5. D
Vocabulary
1. A 2. A 3. D 4. C 5. B
Word Work
1. eyelid 2. kneecap 3. eardrum
4. backbone 5. fingernail 6. eyeglasses
7. newspaper 8. overtime 9. hamstring
10. weekend

Planting a Vegetable Garden
(pp. 168–169)
Check Your Understanding
1. B 2. B 3. A 4. C
Vocabulary
1. B 2. C 3. A 4. B
Word Work
1. monkey 2. zebra 3. moon 4. vase
5. pizza 6. May 7. vegetable 8. potatoes
9. zoo 10. visit
Write Now: Answers will vary.

Carving a Cameo (pp. 172–173)
Check Your Understanding
1. C 2. B 3. B 4. C
Vocabulary
1. C 2. A 3. B 4. C
Word Work
1. A 2. C 3. B 4. B 5. A 6. fix 7. drips
8. sits 9. stick 10. flips
Write Now: Answers will vary.

Sledding: Not Just for Kids
(pp. 176–177)
Check Your Understanding
1. B 2. B 3. A 4. D 5. C
Vocabulary
1. A 2. A 3. A 4. A 5. B
Word Work
1. wrongly 2. snowy 3. sandy 4. quickly
5. brightly 6. correctly 7. rainy 8. safely
9. hilly 10. windy
Write Now: Answers will vary.

An Actor's Day (pp. 180–181)
Check Your Understanding
1. C 2. C 3. A 4. D 5. D
Vocabulary
1. C 2. A 3. B 4. A 5. C
Word Work
1. quickly 2. sailor 3. inventor 4. loudly
5. director 6. instructs 7. quiet 8. conducts
9. proud 10. collects
Write Now: Answers will vary.

Unknown! (pp. 184–185)
Check Your Understanding
1. C 2. B 3. D 4. B
Vocabulary
1. B 2. A 3. A 4. C
Word Work
1. unhappy 2. rewrite 3. redo 4. unexplored

5. untrue 6. rethink 7. A 8. B 9. C 10. D
Write Now: Answers will vary.

Jackie Robinson: American Hero
(pp. 188–189)
Check Your Understanding
1. B 2. A 3. B 4. D 5. A
Vocabulary
1. B 2. A 3. B 4. D 5. C
Word Work
1. D 2. A 3. B 4. E 5. C 6. sad
7. teased 8. brag 9. give up
10. in a joyful mood
Write Now: Answers will vary.

What a Catch! (pp. 192–193)
Check Your Understanding
1. C 2. A 3. C 4. C 5. B
Vocabulary
1. A 2. A 3. C 4. A 5. B
Word Work
1. B 2. A 3. A 4. B 5. B 6. A 7. A
8. B 9. A 10. A
Write Now: Answers will vary.

Something Fishy (pp. 196–197)
Check Your Understanding
1. B 2. B 3. A 4. B 5. C
Vocabulary
1. B 2. C 3. B 4. D 5. C
Word Work
1. seemed 2. learned 3. liked 4. joined
5. danced 6. visited 7. refused 8. surprising
9. learning 10. discovering
Write Now: Answers will vary.

Keep the Great Lakes Great!
(pp. 200–201)
Check Your Understanding
1. A 2. D 3. A 4. B 5. B
Vocabulary
1. D 2. C 3. A 4. D 5. B
Word Work
1. C 2. C 3. A 4. D 5. B 6. city's
7. farmers' 8. country's 9. scientists'
10. workers'
Write Now: Answers will vary.

Waves for You (pp. 206–207)
Check Your Understanding
1. C 2. A 3. B 4. A
Vocabulary
1. B 2. A 3. C 4. A
Word Work
1. A 2. B 3. A 4. C 5. A 6. wave
7. lake 8. face 9. shade 10. take
Write Now: Answers will vary.

Kid Inventors (pp. 210–211)
Check Your Understanding
1. A 2. D 3. D 4. B 5. A
Vocabulary
1. B 2. A 3. C 4. D 5. B
Word Work
1. invented; inventing 2. locked; locking
3. happened; happening 4. played; playing
5. worked; working 6. inventing 7. starting
8. enjoyed 9. needed 10. jumping
Write Now: Answers will vary.

Home, Sweet Home! (pp. 214–215)
Check Your Understanding
1. C 2. B 3. D 4. A 5. B
Vocabulary
1. C 2. B 3. D 4. A 5. C

Word Work
1. skyscraper 2. hardworking 3. underground
4. sometimes 5. themselves 6. snowball
7. storybook 8. starlight 9. flagpole
10. firefighter
Write Now: Answers will vary.

Pet Pals (pp. 218–219)
Check Your Understanding
1. C 2. B 3. B 4. D
Vocabulary
1. C 2. B 3. D 4. A
Word Work
1. you will 2. he is 3. we are 4. you have
5. I am 6. Aren't; Are not 7. They're; They are
8. Don't; they'll; Do not; they will 9. won't; will
not 10. I'd; I would
Write Now: Answers will vary.

Insects That Go for the Gold!
(pp. 222–223)
Check Your Understanding
1. D 2. C 3. C 4. A
Vocabulary
1. B 2. A 3. D 4. A
Word Work
1. smarter 2. hardest 3. lowest 4. darker
5. quietest 6. slowest 7. smaller 8. louder
9. tallest 10. warmest
Write Now: Answers will vary.

What a Good Dad! (pp. 226–227)
Check Your Understanding
1. B 2. D 3. B 4. A 5. B
Vocabulary
1. D 2. C 3. A 4. D 5. B
Word Work
1. harms 2. alone 3. thin 4. upper
5. wrong 6. visited 7. guided 8. living
9. floating 10. liked
Write Now: Answers will vary.

Globe Hopping (pp. 230–231)
Check Your Understanding
1. D 2. B 3. C 4. A 5. A
Vocabulary
1. B 2. C 3. A 4. D 5. A
Word Work
1. different 2. catch 3. last 4. lose 5. out
6. initials 7. houses 8. players 9. games
10. candies
Write Now: Answers will vary.

Mr. Naismith's Game (pp. 234–235)
Check Your Understanding
1. D 2. A 3. C 4. D 5. A
Vocabulary
1. C 2. A 3. D 4. C 5. B
Word Work
1. teachers 2. students 3. balconies
4. objects 5. factories 6. exercises
7. players 8. communities 9. baskets
10. trophies
Write Now: Answers will vary.

The Great Wall of China (pp. 240–241)
Check Your Understanding
1. C 2. B 3. A 4. A
Vocabulary
1. A 2. B 3. C 4. B
Word Work
1. B 2. B 3. A 4. B 5. A 6. A 7. miles
8. safe 9. gates 10. stones
Write Now: Answers will vary.

Saguaros of the Southwest
(pp. 244–245)
Check Your Understanding
1. A 2. B 3. C 4. C 5. B
Vocabulary
1. C 2. A 3. D 4. C 5. D
Word Work
1. E 2. A 3. D 4. C 5. B 6. mouse's
7. saguaros' 8. desert's 9. bats'
10. Arizona's
Write Now: Answers will vary.

Go, Dog, Go! (pp. 248–249)
Check Your Understanding
1. B 2. B 3. C 4. A 5. B
Vocabulary
1. B 2. A 3. C 4. D 5. D
Word Work
1. football 2. touchdown 3. ballpark
4. everyone 5. doghouse 6. scored
7. exciting 8. liked 9. imagined 10. weaving
Write Now: Answers will vary.

Surprise! 10,000 for Dinner
(pp. 252–253)
Check Your Understanding
1. C 2. A 3. B 4. C 5. B
Vocabulary
1. A 2. A 3. C 4. D 5. C
Word Work
1. pods 2. creatures 3. dishes 4. classes
5. watches 6. dolphins 7. whistles 8. foxes
9. blowholes 10. ears
Write Now: Answers will vary.

A Tasty Time (pp. 256–257)
Check Your Understanding
1. A 2. C 3. C 4. D 5. B
Vocabulary
1. C 2. D 3. C 4. A 5. B
Word Work
1. A 2. B 3. B 4. A 5. A 6. A 7. C
8. B 9. D 10. D
Write Now: Answers will vary.

Oceans in Motion (pp. 260–261)
Check Your Understanding
1. A 2. B 3. A 4. A 5. B
Vocabulary
1. A 2. D 3. B 4. D 5. C
Word Work
1. smallest 2. cool 3. hotter 4. falling
5. tiny 6. hardest 7. lightest 8. colder
9. deepest 10. nearer
Write Now: Answers will vary.

A Sticky, Sweet Disaster (pp. 264–265)
Check Your Understanding
1. B 2. C 3. C 4. C 5. D
Vocabulary
1. B 2. C 3. B 4. C 5. A
Word Work
1. cookies 2. gallons 3. cities 4. waves
5. ponies 6. smell 7. sign 8. discovered
9. took 10. dunked
Write Now: Answers will vary.

What's a Chunnel? (pp. 268–269)
Check Your Understanding
1. B 2. D 3. A 4. C 5. A
Vocabulary
1. C 2. B 3. D 4. C 5. A
Word Work
1. crunch 2. English 3. thousand 4. shiver
5. another 6. Chunnel 7. ship 8. through

9. bunch 10. other
Write Now: Answers will vary.

Champions of the Games (pp. 272–273)
Check Your Understanding
1. B 2. D 3. C 4. B 5. A
Vocabulary
1. A 2. C 3. A 4. A 5. D
Word Work
1. likes 2. education 3. talks 4. started
5. defeat 6. C 7. B 8. A 9. E 10. D
Write Now: Answers will vary.

Her Name Was Sacajawea
(pp. 278–279)
Check Your Understanding
1. A 2. C 3. B 4. A
Vocabulary
1. A 2. A 3. C 4. B
Word Work
1. meat 2. dream 3. sweet 4. heat
5. teeth 6. reach 7. seen 8. lead
9. streams 10. deep
Write Now: Answers will vary.

Who Invented Arthur? (pp. 282–283)
Check Your Understanding
1. A 2. D 3. A 4. B 5. B
Vocabulary
1. B 2. D 3. C 4. C 5. A
Word Work
1. enjoyed 2. fast 3. usually 4. hard
5. terrific 6. on 7. same 8. bright 9. started
10. right
Write Now: Answers will vary.

The Yak (pp. 286–287)
Check Your Understanding
1. D 2. C 3. B 4. C 5. C
Vocabulary
1. B 2. A 3. D 4. D 5. D
Word Work
1. large 2. powerful 3. drag 4. grip
5. difficult 6. tall 7. thick 8. shaggy
9. strong 10. cold
Write Now: Answers will vary.

A Story in Stone (pp. 290–291)
Check Your Understanding
1. B 2. A 3. C 4. B 5. D
Vocabulary
1. D 2. C 3. A 4. B 5. C
Word Work
1. B 2. D 3. B 4. A 5. C 6. aren't
7. haven't 8. isn't 9. weren't 10. couldn't
Write Now: Answers will vary.

A Gorilla Saves the Day (pp. 294–295)
Check Your Understanding
1. D 2. C 3. B 4. B 5. B
Vocabulary
1. C 2. D 3. C 4. B 5. C
Word Work
1. A 2. C 3. A 4. B 5. D 6. reopen
7. unusual 8. disappear 9. rethink
10. uncertain
Write Now: Answers will vary.

Bunnicula (pp. 298–299)
Check Your Understanding
1. C 2. B 3. A 4. D 5. C
Vocabulary
1. A 2. A 3. D 4. C 5. B
Word Work
1. A 2. C 3. E 4. B 5. D 6. watch

7. frighten 8. cute 9. enjoyable 10. desire
Write Now: Answers will vary.

The Arctic: Closer Than You Think
(pp. 302–303)
Check Your Understanding
1. A 2. D 3. B 4. C 5. B
Vocabulary
1. B 2. D 3. B 4. C 5. A
Word Work
1. D 2. A 3. B 4. A 5. C 6. pair
7. Arctic 8. part 9. stairs 10. chair
Write Now: Answers will vary.

What Do You Call a Cyclone?
(pp. 306–307)
Check Your Understanding
1. D 2. B 3. A 4. B 5. A
Vocabulary
1. D 2. C 3. A 4. A 5. B
Word Work
1. fearful 2. respectful 3. cheerful 4. harmful
5. joyful 6. powerful 7. helpful 8. hopeful
9. joyful 10. sorrowful
Write Now: Answers will vary.

An Interview with Ed Stivender,
Storyteller (pp. 310–311)
Check Your Understanding
1. B 2. D 3. A 4. C 5. B
Vocabulary
1. A 2. C 3. B 4. D 5. A
Word Work
1. teachers 2. stories 3. books 4. countries
5. interviews 6. children 7. mice 8. geese
9. feet 10. women
Write Now: Answers will vary.

A Born Champion (pp. 314–315)
Check Your Understanding
1. A 2. D 3. D 4. A 5. B
Vocabulary
1. B 2. A 3. D 4. B 5. C
Word Work
1. D 2. A 3. C 4. B 5. B 6. mislead
7. disapprove 8. discontinue 9. misguided
10. disbelief
Write Now: Answers will vary.

Take a Hike (pp. 320–321)
Check Your Understanding
1. A 2. B 3. C 4. C
Vocabulary
1. B 2. C 3. A 4. B
Word Work
1. stairs 2. sneaker 3. smoke 4. slide
5. snail 6. stop 7. small 8. snow 9. slept
10. stormy
Write Now: Answers will vary.

Rube Goldberg's Funny Pictures
(pp. 324–325)
Check Your Understanding
1. A 2. C 3. A 4. C
Vocabulary
1. A 2. A 3. C 4. C
Word Work
1. B 2. A 3. A 4. B 5. A 6. day 7. rain
8. stay 9. paint 10. clay
Write Now: Answers will vary.

A Natural Wonder (pp. 328–329)
Check Your Understanding
1. D 2. C 3. A 4. B 5. C

Vocabulary
1. C 2. A 3. A 4. C 5. D
Word Work
1. visitors 2. weeks 3. colors 4. trails
5. guests 6. mules 7. days 8. tents 9. nights
10. vacations
Write Now: Answers will vary.

Who Can Make the Best Sand Castle?
(pp. 332–333)
Check Your Understanding
1. C 2. B 3. D 4. A 5. A
Vocabulary
1. C 2. A 3. B 4. B 5. C
Word Work
1. tons 2. fields 3. castles 4. towns
5. animals 6. prizes 7. builders 8. places
9. judges 10. statues
Write Now: Answers will vary.

The Surprising Story of Jeans
(pp. 336–337)
Check Your Understanding
1. B 2. A 3. D 4. D 5. B
Vocabulary
1. C 2. A 3. D 4. C 5. A
Word Work
1. C 2. D 3. A 4. C 5. B 6. everyday
7. everybody 8. cowhand 9. suitcases
10. comeback
Write Now: Answers will vary.

A Hospital for Dolphins & Whales
(pp. 340–341)
Check Your Understanding
1. C 2. C 3. B 4. B
Vocabulary
1. C 2. D 3. A 4. D
Word Work
1. they're 2. you've 3. we'll 4. I'm 5. don't
6. She's 7. I'm 8. They're 9. doesn't
10. She'll
Write Now: Answers will vary.

America's Lady Liberty (pp. 344–345)
Check Your Understanding
1. B 2. D 3. B 4. C 5. B
Vocabulary
1. C 2. C 3. D 4. B 5. A
Word Work
1. guests 2. look 3. usually 4. welcomed
5. lead 6. D 7. A 8. B 9. A 10. C
Write Now: Answers will vary.

Living Flashlights (pp. 348–349)
Check Your Understanding
1. A 2. B 3. D 4. B 5. C
Vocabulary
1. B 2. D 3. C 4. A 5. D
Word Work
1. animals 2. draw 3. create 4. small
5. shines 6. tries, life 7. night 8. spied,
bright, light, side 9. flashlight, hide 10. sight,
nice, surprise
Write Now: Answers will vary.